Conference of the North American Chapter of the Association for Computational Linguistics: Human Language Technologies (NAACL HLT 2022)

Demonstrations

Online
10 - 15 July 2022

ISBN: 978-1-7138-5620-7

Printed from e-media with permission by:

Curran Associates, Inc.
57 Morehouse Lane
Red Hook, NY 12571

Some format issues inherent in the e-media version may also appear in this print version.

Association for Computational Linguistics
209 N. Eighth Street
Stroudsburg, Pennsylvania 18360

Phone: 1-570-476-8006
Fax: 1-570-476-0860

acl@aclweb.org

Additional copies of this publication are available from:

Curran Associates, Inc.
57 Morehouse Lane
Red Hook, NY 12571 USA
Phone: 845-758-0400
Fax: 845-758-2633
Email: curran@proceedings.com
Web: www.proceedings.com

NAACL 2022

The 2022 Conference of the North American Chapter of the Association for Computational Linguistics: Human Language Technologies

Proceedings of the Demonstrations Session

July 10-15, 2022

The NAACL organizers gratefully acknowledge the support from the following sponsors.

Diamond

Platinum

Gold

Silver

Bronze

D&I Champions

D&I Contributors

D&I Allies

DeepMind

Order copies of this and other ACL proceedings from:

Association for Computational Linguistics (ACL)
209 N. Eighth Street
Stroudsburg, PA 18360
USA
Tel: +1-570-476-8006
Fax: +1-570-476-0860
acl@aclweb.org

Introduction

Welcome to the proceedings of the system demonstration track of NAACL-HLT 2022 on Jul 10–15. NAACL-HLT 2022 will be a hybrid conference.

The system demonstration track invites submissions ranging from early prototypes to mature production-ready systems. This year we received 35 submissions, of which 14 were selected for inclusion in the program (acceptance rate 40%) after being reviewed by at least three members of the program committee.

This is the second year NAACL-HLT incorporated ethical considerations in the review process. In the standard review stage, members of the program committee are given the option to flag a paper as needing separate ethics reviews. Papers flagged as needing separate ethics reviews by at least one member from the program committee are subsequently reviewed by two members from the NAACL-HLT 2022 ethics committee. This year, compared to last year, had none that raised an ethics flag.

This year was the first year that the demo track at NAACL-HLT had different types of reproducibility badge(s). There were 6 papers that decided to participate and all of them successfully earned at least one badge.

We would like to thank the members of the program committee for their timely help in reviewing the submissions. We also thank the many authors who submitted their work to the demonstration track. The demonstration papers will be presented through pre-recorded talks and one live online Q&A session.

Best,
Qiang Ning, Hannaneh Hajishirzi and Avi Sil NAACL-HLT 2022 Demonstration Track Chairs

Program Committee

Demonstration Chairs

Qiang Ning, Amazon
Hannaneh Hajishirzi
Avi Sil, IBM Research

Program Committee

Akari Asai, University of Washington
Ameet Deshpande, Princeton University
David Wadden, Department of Computer Science, University of Washington
Jaydeep Sen, International Business Machines
Tiancheng Zhao, Carnegie Mellon University
Ahmed Abdelali, Hamad Bin Khalifa University
Aldrian Obaja Muis, Carnegie Mellon University
Ales Horak, Masaryk University
Alexandros Papangelis, Amazon
Ali Hürriyetoğlu, Koc University
Aljoscha Burchardt, German Research Center for AI
Alok Debnath, Trinity College, Dublin
Andrea Varga, Theta Lake Ltd
Chengzhi Zhang, Nanjing University of Science and Technology
Carl Edwards, Allen Institute for Artificial Intelligence
Changhan Wang, Meta AI
Chenchen Ding, National Institute of Information and Communications Technology (NICT)
Chenkai Sun, University of Illinois, Urbana Champaign
Chi Han, University of Illinois, Urbana Champaign
Chien-Sheng Wu, Salesforce AI
Christos Christodoulopoulos, Amazon
Chung-Chi Chen, National Tsing Hua University
Constantine Lignos, Brandeis University
Daniel F Campos, University of Illinois, Urbana Champaign
Daniel Hershcovich, University of Copenhagen
Daniel Cer, Google
Danilo Croce, University of Roma Tor Vergata
David Wadden, Department of Computer Science, University of Washington
Denis Newman-Griffis, University of Sheffield
Dian Yu, Google
Diane Napolitano, The Associated Press
Diego Antognini, International Business Machines
Dimitris Galanis, Institute for Language and Speech Processing
Djamé Seddah, Inria Paris
Dong-Ho Lee, University of Southern California
Eleftherios Avramidis, German Research Center for AI
Erion Çano, University of Vienna
Eugene Kharitonov, Meta
Federico Fancellu, Samsung AI Toronto
Feifei Pan, Rensselaer Polytechnic Institute

Guangyou Zhou, Institute of Automation, Chinese Academy of Sciences
Guanyi Chen, Utrecht University
Gábor Berend, University of Szeged
Hamada M Zahera, Paderborn University
Hamdy Mubarak, Qatar Computing Research Institute
Harshit Kumar, International Business Machines
Hen-Hsen Huang, Institute of Information Science, Academia Sinica
Hongshen Chen, JD.com
Imed Zitouni, Google
James Fan, University of Texas, Austin
Jeff Jacobs, Columbia University
Jhih-Jie , National Tsing Hua University
Jian SUN, Alibaba Group, DAMO Academy
Jiarun Cao, University of Manchester
Jingjing Wang, Soochow University
John Heyer, Massachusetts Institute of Technology
John Sie Yuen Lee, City University of Hong Kong
Joo-Kyung Kim, Amazon Alexa AI
Khalid Al Khatib, University of Groningen
Lei Shu, Google
Leonhard Hennig, German Research Center for AI
Liang-Chih Yu, Yuan Ze University
Mamoru Komachi, Tokyo Metropolitan University, Japan
Manling Li, University of Illinois, Urbana Champaign
Margot Mieskes, University of Applied Sciences Darmstadt
Marina Danilevsky, International Business Machines
Marina Litvak, Ben-Gurion University of the Negev
Mark Last, Ben-Gurion University of the Negev
Michael Desmond, International Business Machines
Michal Shmueli-Scheuer, University of California, Irvine
Miguel A. Alonso, Universidade da Coruña
Miruna Clinciu, Heriot-Watt University
Mohaddeseh Bastan, State University of New York at Stony Brook
Mozhdeh Gheini, USC/ISI
Natalia Vanetik, SCE
Nikola Ljubešić, Jožef Stefan Institute
Omri Abend, Hebrew University of Jerusalem, Technion
Oren Pereg, Intel
Pablo Ruiz, Université de Strasbourg
Paulo Fernandes, Roberts Wesleyan College
Pengfei Yu, University of Illinois at Urbana-Champaign
Philipp Koehn, Meta
Philippe Laban, SalesForce.com
Philippe Muller, IRIT, University of Toulouse
Pierre Nugues, Lund University
Prokopis Prokopidis, Institute for Language and Speech Processing, Athena Research Center
Qi Zeng, University of Illinois, Urbana Champaign
Qi Zhang, Fudan University
Qian Liu, Beihang University
Qingyun Wang, University of Illinois, Urbana Champaign
Rafael Anchiêta, Federal Institute of Piauí

Rahul Aralikatte, University of Copenhagen
Ridong Jiang, National University of Singapore
Rodrigo Agerri, University of the Basque Country
Roee Aharoni, Google
Rui Wang, Vipshop (China) Co., Ltd.
Saarthak Khanna, Amazon
Saurav Sahay, Intel
Sebastin Santy, University of Washington
Seid Muhie Yimam, Universität Hamburg
Sha Li, University of Illinois, Urbana Champaign
Shaobo Cui, EPFL - EPF Lausanne
Stella Markantonatou, ATHENA RIC
Sudeep Gandhe, Google
Sudipta Kar, Amazon
Sumit Bhatia, Adobe Systems
Sven Schmeier, German Research Center for AI
Thierry Declerck, German Research Center for AI
Tsuyoshi Okita, Kyushu Institute of Technology
Tuan Lai, University of Illinois, Urbana Champaign
Wenlin Yao, Tencent AI Lab
Wolfgang Maier, Mercedes Benz Research & Development
Xianchao Wu, NVIDIA
Xianpei Han, Institute of Software, CAS
Xiaodan Hu, University of Illinois, Urbana-Champaign
Xintong Li, Baidu
Xuan Wang, University of Illinois, Urbana Champaign
Xutan Peng, University of Sheffield
Yada Pruksachatkun, New York University Center for Data Science
Yanran Li, The Hong Kong Polytechnic University
Yixin Cao, Singapore Management University
Youngsoo Jang, Korea Advanced Institute of Science and Technology
Yujiu Yang, Graduate School at Shenzhen,Tsinghua University
Yun He, Texas A&M University
Yuntian Deng, Harvard University
Yusuke Miyao, The University of Tokyo
Yusuke Oda, LegalForce
Zeljko Agic, Unity Technologies
Zeynep Akkalyoncu, University of Waterloo
Zhen Xu, PCG Tencent
Zhenhailong Wang, University of Illinois at Urbana-Champaign
Zhongqing Wang, Soochow University, China
Zhuoxuan Jiang, Tencent Inc.
Zixuan Zhang, University of Illinois at Urbana-Champaign
Carl Strathearn, Napier University

Table of Contents

textless-lib: a Library for Textless Spoken Language Processing

Eugene Kharitonov★, Jade Copet★, Kushal Lakhotia▲, Tu Anh Nguyen★, Paden Tomasello★
Ann Lee★, Ali Elkahky★, Wei-Ning Hsu★, Abdelrahman Mohamed★, Emmanuel Dupoux★†, Yossi Adi★
★ Meta AI Research, † EHESS
▲ Outreach
{kharitonov, jadecopet, adiyoss}@fb.com

Abstract

Textless spoken language processing research aims to extend the applicability of standard NLP toolset onto spoken language and languages with few or no textual resources. In this paper, we introduce `textless-lib`, a PyTorch-based library aimed to facilitate research in this research area. We describe the building blocks that the library provides and demonstrate its usability by discuss three different use-case examples: (i) speaker probing, (ii) speech resynthesis and compression, and (iii) speech continuation. We believe that `textless-lib` substantially simplifies research the textless setting and will be handful not only for speech researchers but also for the NLP community at large. The code, documentation, and pre-trained models are available at `https://github.com/facebookresearch/textlesslib/`.

1 Introduction

Textless spoken language modeling (Lakhotia et al., 2021) consists in jointly learning the acoustic and linguistic characteristics of a natural language from raw audio samples without access to textual supervision (e.g. lexicon or transcriptions). This area of research has been made possible by converging progress in self-supervised speech representation learning (Schneider et al., 2019; Baevski et al., 2020; Oord et al., 2018; Hsu et al., 2021; Chorowski et al., 2021; Chen et al., 2021; Chung et al., 2021; Wang et al., 2021; Ao et al., 2021), language modeling (Peters et al., 2018; Devlin et al., 2019; Liu et al., 2019; Brown et al., 2020; Lewis et al., 2020), and speech synthesis (Ren et al., 2019; Kumar et al., 2019; Yamamoto et al., 2020; Ren et al., 2020; Kong et al., 2020; Morrison et al., 2021).

Lakhotia et al. (2021) presented a Generative Spoken Language Modeling (GSLM) pipeline trained from raw audio, consisting in a speech en-

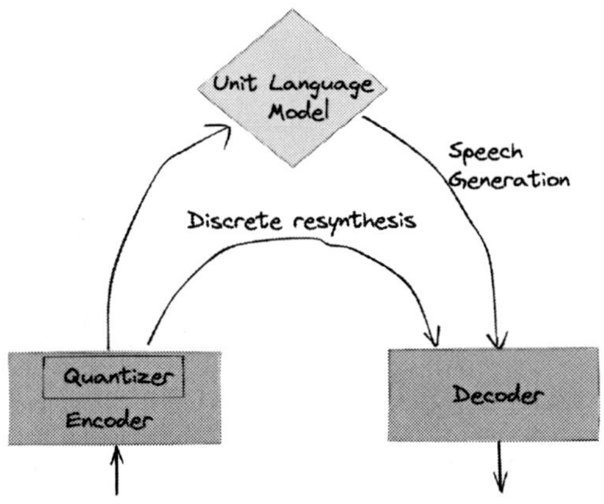

Figure 1: A visual description for textless modeling of spoken language. One can perform language modeling for speech continuations (Lakhotia et al., 2021) or a direct speech resynthesis (Polyak et al., 2021).

coder (converting speech to discrete units), a language model (based on units) and a decoder (converting units back to speech). These components enabled the generation of new speech by sampling units from the language model. Polyak et al. (2021) proposed an improved encoder/decoder working from disentangled quantized content and F0 units and showed how such a system could be used for efficient audio compression. Kharitonov et al. (2021a) proposed a modified language model system capable of jointly modelling content units and F0 yielding expressive generations. Lastly, Kreuk et al. (2021) demonstrated that the language model can be replaced by a sequence to sequence model achieving the first high quality speech emotion conversion system (including laughter and yawning).

The textless approach has several advantages. First, it would be beneficial for the majority of the world's languages that do not have large textual resources or even a widely used standardized orthography (Swiss German, dialectal Arabic, Igbo, etc.). Despite being used by millions of people, these languages have little chance of being served by current

Proceedings of the 2022 Conference of the North American Chapter of the Association for Computational Linguistics: Human Language Technologies: System Demonstrations, pages 1 - 9
July 10-15, 2022 ©2022 Association for Computational Linguistics

text-based technology. Moreover, "high-resource" languages can benefit from such modeling where the oral and written forms are mismatched in terms of lexicon and syntax. Second, directly modeling spoken language from raw audio allows us to go beyond lexical content and also model linguistically relevant signals such as prosodic features, intonation, non-verbal vocalizations (e.g., laughter, yawning, etc.), speaker identity, etc. All of these are virtually absent in text.

Although great progress has been made in modeling spoken language, it still requires domain expertise and involves a complicated setting. For instance, the official implementation of the GSLM pipeline (Lakhotia et al., 2021) consists of roughly four different launching scripts with a few dozens of checkpoints. Similarly, running the official implementation of Polyak et al. (2021), requires using four scripts from two different repositories.

We present `textless-lib`, a PyTorch library for textless spoken language processing. It makes processing, encoding, modeling, and generating of speech as simple as possible. With a few lines of code, one can perform speech continuation, audiobook compression, representation analysis by probing, speech-to-speech translation, etc. We provide all the necessary building blocks, example pipelines, and example tasks. We believe such a simple to use API will encourage both speech and NLP communities to deepen and extend the research work on modeling spoken language without text and unlock potential future research directions.

2 Background

Below we provide an overview of the common textless spoken language modeling pipeline. In a nutshell, such pipeline is usually comprised of: i) Speech-to-Units (S2U) encoders that automatically discover discrete representations or units which can be used to encode speech into "pseudo-text"; ii) Units-to-Units (U2U) models that are used for units modeling. This can take a form as Unit-Language-Model (uLM) for speech continuation (Lakhotia et al., 2021; Kharitonov et al., 2021a), sequence-to-sequence models for speech emotion conversion (Kreuk et al., 2021) or translation tasks (Lee et al., 2021a,b); iii) Units-to-Speech (U2S) models to reconstruct back the speech signals.

Alternatively, one could drop the U2U component and perform a direct speech resynthesis (Polyak et al., 2021). This can be used for speech compression, voice conversion, or developing a better understanding of the learned representation using probing methods. See Figure 1 for a visual description of the full system. We provide a detailed description for each of the above-mentioned components in the following subsections.

Type	Model	Dataset
Encoders	HuBERT	LS-960
	CPC	LL-6k
Quantizers	k-means	LS-960 w. 50 units
		LS-960 w. 100 units
		LS-960 w. 200 units
		LS-960 w. 500 units
F0 extract.	YAAPT	-
Decoders	Tacotron2	LJ Speech
	WaveGlow	LJ Speech

Table 1: Summary of the pre-trained models provided in `textless-lib`. We denote LibriSpeech and Libri-Light as LS-960 and LL-6k accordingly. All quantizers were trained on "dev-clean" partition of LibriSpeech.

2.1 Speech to Units

Consider the domain of audio samples as $\mathcal{X} \subset \mathbb{R}$. The representation for an audio waveform is therefore a sequence of samples $\boldsymbol{x} = (x^1, \dots, x^T)$, where each $x^i \in \mathcal{X}$ for all $1 \leq t \leq T$. We denote the S2U encoder as, $E(\boldsymbol{x}) = \mathbf{z}$, where $\mathbf{z} = (\boldsymbol{z}^1, \dots, \boldsymbol{z}^L)$ is a spectral representation of $\boldsymbol{x}$ sampled at a lower frequency, each $\boldsymbol{z}^i$ for $1 \leq i \leq L$ is a d-dimensional vector, and $L < T$.

Next, as the representations obtained by E are continuous, an additional quantization step is needed. We define a quantization function Q, which gets as input dense representations and outputs a sequence of discrete tokens corresponding to the inputs' quantized version. Formally, $Q(\mathbf{z}) = \boldsymbol{z}_q$, where $\boldsymbol{z}_q = (z_q^1, \dots, z_q^L)$ such that $z_q^i \in \{1, \dots, K\}$ and K is the size of the vocabulary. After quantization one can either operate on the original discrete sequences (duped) or collapse repeated units (e.g., $0, 0, 1, 1, 2 \rightarrow 0, 1, 2$), we refer to such sequences as "deduped". Working with the deduped sequences simplifies modeling long sequences, however, the tempo information is lost.

2.2 Units to Speech

Converting a sequence of units to audio is akin to the Text-to-Speech (TTS) problem, where we consider the discrete units as "pseudo-text". This can be solved by adopting a standard TTS architecture. For instance, Lakhotia et al. (2021) trained a Tacotron2 model (Shen et al., 2018) to perform units to mel-spectrogram conversion followed by

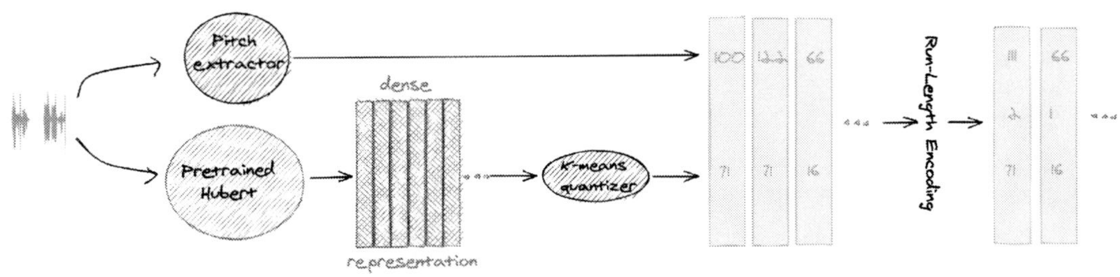

Figure 2: We represent speech as three aligned, synchronised streams: discrete pseudo-units, duration, and pitch.

a WaveGlow (Prenger et al., 2019) neural vocoder for time-domain reconstruction.

Formally, to reconstruct a time-domain speech signal from a sequence of discrete units, z_q we define the composition as, $V(G(z_q)) = \hat{x}$, where G is a mel-spectrogram estimation module (e.g., Tacotron2), and V is a phase vocoder module responsible for time-domain synthesis (e.g., WaveGlow). The input sequence z_q can be either the original sequence or its deduped version.

Interestingly, one can simplify the synthesis process when working with the duped unit sequences. As we have a direct mapping between the duped discrete unit sequence to the time domain signal (e.g., each unit corresponds to a 20ms window) one can remove G, and directly feed z_q to V. This was successfully done in (Polyak et al., 2021) for speech resynthesis using the HiFi-GAN neural vocoder (Kong et al., 2020). Alternatively, as suggested by (Kreuk et al., 2021; Lee et al., 2021b) one can train a unit duration prediction model and use the predicted durations to inflate the sequence and feed the discrete sequence directly to V.

2.3 Unit to Units

Equipped with the models to encode spoken language into discrete unit sequences and convert them back to speech samples, one can conveniently use common NLP architectures to model spoken language. Consider M to be a sequence modeling function that gets as input a discrete unit sequence z_q and outputs another discrete units sequence, denoted as $\hat{z}_q$. Generally, $\hat{z}_q$ can represent different generations, depending on the modeling task. For instance, Lakhotia et al. (2021) and Kharitonov et al. (2021a) set M to be a Transformer and trained a generative spoken language model. Similarly, Kreuk et al. (2021) set M to be a sequence-to-sequence model, hence can cast the emotion conversion problem as a translation task.[1]

[1]Examples are provided at `speechbot.github.io/`.

3 Library Overview

In this section, we present the `textless-lib` library, intending to simplify future research on textless spoken language modeling. Additionally, the proposed package will remove the main barrier of processing and synthesizing speech, which requires domain expertise, for other language researchers (e.g., NLP researchers) who are interested in modeling spoken language, analyzing the learned representations, etc.

To support the above, it is essential to provide the main building blocks described in Section 2, together with pre-trained models, with minimal coupling between them (a list of the supported pretrained models can be seen on Table 1). This will allow researchers to flexibly use the provided pretrained building blocks or develop new building blocks and use them anywhere in their pipeline. We decided to exclude both U2U models as well as evaluation metrics from the core functionality of the library as we believe these models should be an example usage. There are plenty of ways to evaluate the overall pipeline (Lakhotia et al., 2021; Dunbar et al., 2019, 2020; Nguyen et al., 2020) and different ways to model the "pseudo-text" units (Shi et al., 2021; Kharitonov et al., 2021a; Polyak et al., 2021; Kreuk et al., 2021; Lee et al., 2021a), hence including them as an integral part of the library will make it overcomplicated.

3.1 Interfaces

The pipeline presented in Figure 1 hints a straightforward way to decouple elements of the library into two principal blocks: (i) encoding speech; and (ii) decoding speech, with the only interdependence being the format of the data in-between (e.g., vocabulary size). Such interfaces enable interesting mix-and-match combinations as well as conducting research on each component independently. We firstly present those two interfaces, then we discuss helpers for dataloading.

```
1  url = "dev-clean"
2  existing_root = "./data"
3  dense_model_name = "hubert-base-ls960"
4  quantizer_name = "kmeans"
5  vocab_size = 100
6
7  encoder = SpeechEncoder.by_name(
8    dense_model_name=dense_model_name,
9    quantizer_model_name=quantizer_name,
10   vocab_size=vocab_size,
11   deduplicate=True,
12 ).cuda()
13
14 quantized_dataset = QuantizedLibriSpeech(
15   root=existing_root, speech_encoder=encoder, url=url)
16
17 datum = quantized_dataset[0]
18 # datum['units'] = tensor([71, 12, 63, ...])
```

Figure 3: `textless-lib` provides an "encoded" view for standard datasets, such as LibriSpeech.

Encoders and Vocoders. We denote the encoders as `SpeechEncoder`. These modules encompass all steps required to represent raw audio as discrete unit sequences (i.e., pseudo-text units and, optionally duration and pitch streams).

`SpeechEncoder` obtains a dense vector representation from a given self-supervised model, discretizes the dense representation into units, extracts pitch, aligns it with the unit streams, and potentially, applies run-length encoding with per-frame pitch averaging. See Fig. 2 for a visual description.

For each sub-model, a user might choose to use a pre-trained model or provide a custom `torch.nn.Module` module instead. An example of the former is demonstrated in lines 7-12 in Figure 3, in which a HuBERT model and a corresponding k-means codebook with a pre-defined K (i.e., vocabulary size) are automatically retrieved.

Conversely, vocoders take as input a discretized sequence and convert it back to the audio domain. As with `SpeechEncoder`, we can retrieve a pretrained model by setting the expected input specification (model, quantizer, and the size of the codebook), see Figure 4 lines 17-21.

Datasets, Dataloaders, and Preprocessing. Apart from encoders and vocoders, in the `textless-lib` we provide several components aimed to simplify frequent data loading use-cases. First, we provide a set of standard datasets (e.g., LibriSpeech) wrapped to produce quantized representations (see Fig. 3 lines 14-15). Those datasets are implemented via a `QuantizeDataset` wrapper which can be used to wrap any map-style PyTorch dataset, containing raw waveform data.

```
1  dense_model_name = "hubert-base-ls960"
2  quantizer_name, vocab_size = "kmeans", 100
3  input_file, output_file = "input.wav", "output.wav"
4
5  encoder = SpeechEncoder.by_name(
6    dense_model_name=dense_model_name,
7    quantizer_model_name=quantizer_name,
8    vocab_size=vocab_size,
9    deduplicate=True,
10 ).cuda()
11
12 waveform, sample_rate = torchaudio.load(input_file)
13
14 encoded = encoder(waveform.cuda())
15 units = encoded["units"]  # tensor([71, ...], ...)
16
17 vocoder = TacotronVocoder.by_name(
18   dense_model_name,
19   quantizer_name,
20   vocab_size,
21 ).cuda()
22
23 audio = vocoder(units)
24
25 torchaudio.save(output_file,
26                 audio.cpu().float().unsqueeze(0),
27                 22_050)
```

Figure 4: Fully functioning code for discrete audio resynthesis. An audio file is loaded, coverted into a sequence of pseudo-units and transformed back into audio with Tacotron2. The model setup code will download required checkpoints and cache them locally.

The `QuantizeDataset` runs an instance of a dense representation model, which can be computationally heavy (e.g., the HuBERT-base model has 7 convolutional layers and 12 Transformer layers). Unfortunately, such heavy preprocessing can starve the training loop. Hence, we provide two possible solutions: (i) as part of the `textless-lib` we provide a way to spread `QuantizeDataset` and `DataLoader` preprocessing workers (each with its copy of a dense model) across multiple GPUs, hence potentially balancing training and preprocessing across different devices; (ii) in cases where on-the-fly preprocessing is not required (e.g., there is no randomized data augmentation (Kharitonov et al., 2021b)), an alternative is to preprocess the entire dataset in advance. `textless-lib` provides a tool for preprocessing arbitrary sets of audio files into a stream of pseudo-unit tokens and, optionally, streams of per-frame tempo and F0 values, aligned to the token stream. The tool uses multi-GPU and multi-node parallelism to speed up the process.

Model	Quantized?	Vocab. size	Accuracy
HuBERT	-	-	0.99
HuBERT	✓	50	0.11
HuBERT	✓	100	0.19
HuBERT	✓	200	0.29
HuBERT	✓	500	0.48
CPC	-	-	0.99
CPC	✓	50	0.19
CPC	✓	100	0.32
CPC	✓	200	0.34
CPC	✓	500	0.40

Table 2: Speaker probing. Test accuracy on predicting speaker based on HuBERT & CPC representations.

Model	Vocab. size	Bitrate, bit/s	WER
Topline	-	$512 \cdot 10^3$	2.2
HuBERT	50	125.5	24.2
HuBERT	100	167.4	13.5
HuBERT	200	210.6	7.9

Table 3: Bitrate/ASR WER trade-off. Topline corresponds to the original data encoded with 32-bit PCM.

3.2 Pre-trained Models

As part of `textless-lib` we provide several pre-trained models that proved to work best in prior work (Lakhotia et al., 2021; Polyak et al., 2021). In future, we will maintain the list of the models to be aligned with state-of-the-art.

Dense representations. We support two dense representation models: (i) HuBERT base-960h model (Hsu et al., 2021) trained on LibriSpeech 960h dataset, with a framerate of 50 Hz; (ii) Contrastive Predictive Coding (CPC) model (Rivière and Dupoux, 2020; Oord et al., 2018) trained on the 6K hours subset from LibriLight (Kahn et al., 2020) with a framerate of 100 Hz. Both models provided the best overall performance according to (Lakhotia et al., 2021; Polyak et al., 2021).

Pitch extraction. Following Polyak et al. (2021) we support F0 extraction using the YAAPT pitch extraction algorithm (Kasi and Zahorian, 2002). We plan to include other F0 extraction models, e.g. CREPE (Kim et al., 2018).

Quantizers. With the `textless-lib` we provide several pre-trained quantization functions for both HuBERT and CPC dense models using a vocabulary sizes $K \in \{50, 100, 200, 500\}$. For the quantization function, we trained a k-means algorithm using the "dev-clean" part in the LibriSpeech dataset (Panayotov et al., 2015).

Pitch normalization. Following Kharitonov et al. (2021a), we applied per-speaker pitch normalization to reduce inter-speaker variability. For single speaker datasets, we do not perform F0 normalization and the span of pitch values is preserved. Under the `textless-lib` we provide two pitch-normalization methods: per-speaker and prefix-based. In the per-speaker normalization, we assume the mean F0 value per speaker is known in advance. While in the prefix-based normalization method a part of the audio is used to calculate the mean pitch. Those two options provide useful trade-offs. In the first case, we need to have a closed set of speakers but have a better precision while in the second we sacrifice quality but gain flexibility.

Vocoder. In the initial release of the library, we provide Tacotron2 as a mel-spectrogram estimation module (i.e., the G function) followed by WaveGlow (Prenger et al., 2019) neural vocoder (i.e., the V function) as used by Lakhotia et al. (2021).[2] These operate on deduplicated pseudo-unit streams with vocabulary sizes of 50, 100, and 200. In a follow-up release, we aim to include HiFi-GAN-based vocoders similarly to Polyak et al. (2021); Kharitonov et al. (2021a). We found those to generate better audio quality with higher computational performance. However, as described in Section 2, the main drawback of dropping G and directly feeding the discrete units to V is the need for a unit duration prediction model. We plan to include such models as well in the next release.

4 Examples

Alongside the core functionality of the library, we provide a set of illustrative examples. The goal of these examples is two-fold: (a) to illustrate the usage of particular components of the library, and (b) to serve as a starter code for a particular type of application. For instance, a probing example (Section 4.1) can be adapted for better studying used representations, while discrete resynthesis (Section 4.2) could provide a starter code for an application operating on units (e.g., language modeling or a high-compression speech codec).

4.1 Speaker Probing

A vibrant area of research studies properties of "universal" pre-trained representations, such as GLoVE (Pennington et al., 2014) and BERT (Devlin et al., 2018). Examples span from probing for linguistic properties (Adi et al., 2017b; Ettinger

[2]WaveGlow is used as a part of `TacotronVocoder`. Both Tacotron2 and WaveGlow were trained on LJ speech (Ito and Johnson, 2017).

HE PASSES ABRUPTLY FROM PERSONS	OF ABRUPT ACID FROM WHICH HE PROCEEDS ARIGHT BY ...
HE PASSES ABRUPTLY FROM PERSONS	AND CHARCOAL EACH ONE OF THE CHARCOAL ...
HE PASSES ABRUPTLY FROM PERSONS	FEET AND TRAY TO A CONTENTION OF ASSOCIATION THAT ...

Table 4: Three continuations of the same prompt (in pink), generated by the speech continuation example under different random seeds. Sampled from a language model trained trained on HuBERT-100 units.

et al., 2016; Adi et al., 2017a; Conneau et al., 2018; Hewitt and Manning, 2019) to discovering biases (Bolukbasi et al., 2016; Caliskan et al., 2017).

In contrast, widely used pre-trained representations produced by HuBERT (Hsu et al., 2021) and wav2vec 2.0 (Baevski et al., 2020) are relatively understudied. Few existing works include (van Niekerk et al., 2021; Higy et al., 2021).

We believe our library can provide a convenient tool for research in this area. Hence, as the first example, we include a probing experiment similar to the one proposed in (van Niekerk et al., 2021; Adi et al., 2019). We study whether the extracted representations contain speaker-specific information. In this example, we experiment with quantized and continuous representations provided by CPC and HuBERT. We randomly split LibriSpeech dev-clean utterances into train/test (90%/10%) sets[3] and train a two-layer Transformer for 5 epochs to predict a speaker's anonymized identifier, based on an utterance they produced. From the results reported in Table 2 we see that the continuous representations allow identifying speaker on hold-out utterances. In contrast, the quantization adds some speaker-invariance, justifying its use.

4.2 Speech Resynthesis

The next example is the discrete speech resynthesis, i.e., the speech audio $\rightarrow$ deduplicated units $\rightarrow$ speech audio pipeline. Fig. 4 illustrates how simple its implementation is with `textless-lib`.

The discrete resynthesis operation can be seen as a lossy compression of the speech. Indeed, if a sequence of n units (from a vocabulary $\mathcal{U}$) encodes a speech segment of length l, we straightforwardly obtain a lossy codec with bitrate $\frac{n}{l}\lceil\log_2|\mathcal{U}|\rceil$ bits per second. Further, the token stream itself can be compressed using entropy encoding and, assuming a unigram token model, the compression rate becomes: $-\frac{n}{l}\cdot\sum_{u\in\mathcal{U}}\mathbb{P}(u)\log_2\mathbb{P}(u)$. In Table 3 we report compression rate/word error rate (WER) trade-off achievable with the HuBERT-derived unit systems, as a function of the vocabulary size. WER is calculated using the wav2vec 2.0-based Automatic Speech Recognition (ASR) w.r.t. and uses the ground-truth transcripts. To calculate the compression rate, the unigram token distribution was fitted on the transcript of LibriLight 6K dataset (Rivière and Dupoux, 2020). From Table 3 we observe that discretized HuBERT representations have a strong potential for extreme speech compression (Polyak et al., 2021).[4] Our provided implementation reports the bitrate.

4.3 Speech Continuation

Finally, we include a `textless-lib` re-implementation of the full GSLM speech continuation pipeline (Lakhotia et al., 2021), as depicted in Figure 1. Table 4 presents ASR transcripts of three different continuations of the same prompt, generated using different random seeds. We use a LARGE wav2vec 2.0 model, trained on LibriSpeech-960h with CTC loss. Its decoder uses the standard KenLM 4-gram language model.

5 Discussion and Future Work

We introduced `textless-lib`, a Pytorch library aimed to advance research in textless modeling of spoken language, by simplifying textless processing and synthesizing spoken language. We described the main building blocks used to preprocess, quantize, and synthesize speech. To demonstrate the usability of the library, we provided three usage examples related to (i) representation probing, (ii) speech compression, and (iii) speech continuation. The proposed library greatly simplifies research in the textless spoken language processing, hence we believe it will be a handful not only for speech researchers but to the entire NLP community.

As a future work for `textless-lib` we envision improving performance of the existing building blocks, adding new example tasks (e.g., translation (Lee et al., 2021b) or dialog (Nguyen et al., 2022)), extending the set of provided pre-trained models, and introducing the possibility of training the different components.

[3]We have to create a new split as the standard one has disjoint sets of speakers, making this experiment impossible.

[4]In contrast to our setup, Polyak et al. (2021) worked with non-deduplicated streams, hence obtained different bitrates.

References

Yossi Adi, Einat Kermany, Yonatan Belinkov, Ofer Lavi, and Yoav Goldberg. 2017a. Analysis of sentence embedding models using prediction tasks in natural language processing. *IBM Journal of Research and Development*, 61(4/5):3–1.

Yossi Adi, Einat Kermany, Yonatan Belinkov, Ofer Lavi, and Yoav Goldberg. 2017b. Fine-grained analysis of sentence embeddings using auxiliary prediction tasks.

Yossi Adi, Neil Zeghidour, Ronan Collobert, Nicolas Usunier, Vitaliy Liptchinsky, and Gabriel Synnaeve. 2019. To reverse the gradient or not: An empirical comparison of adversarial and multi-task learning in speech recognition. In *ICASSP 2019-2019 IEEE International Conference on Acoustics, Speech and Signal Processing (ICASSP)*, pages 3742–3746. IEEE.

Junyi Ao, Rui Wang, Long Zhou, Shujie Liu, Shuo Ren, Yu Wu, Tom Ko, Qing Li, Yu Zhang, Zhihua Wei, et al. 2021. Speecht5: Unified-modal encoder-decoder pre-training for spoken language processing. *arXiv preprint arXiv:2110.07205*.

Alexei Baevski, Henry Zhou, Abdelrahman Mohamed, and Michael Auli. 2020. wav2vec 2.0: A framework for self-supervised learning of speech representations. *arXiv preprint arXiv:2006.11477*.

Tolga Bolukbasi, Kai-Wei Chang, James Y Zou, Venkatesh Saligrama, and Adam T Kalai. 2016. Man is to computer programmer as woman is to homemaker? debiasing word embeddings. *Advances in neural information processing systems*, 29:4349–4357.

Tom B. Brown et al. 2020. Language models are few-shot learners. In *Proc. of NeurIPS*.

Aylin Caliskan, Joanna J Bryson, and Arvind Narayanan. 2017. Semantics derived automatically from language corpora contain human-like biases. *Science*, 356(6334):183–186.

Sanyuan Chen, Chengyi Wang, Zhengyang Chen, Yu Wu, Shujie Liu, Zhuo Chen, Jinyu Li, Naoyuki Kanda, Takuya Yoshioka, Xiong Xiao, et al. 2021. Wavlm: Large-scale self-supervised pre-training for full stack speech processing. *arXiv preprint arXiv:2110.13900*.

Jan Chorowski, Grzegorz Ciesielski, Jarosław Dzikowski, Adrian Lancucki, Ricard Marxer, Mateusz Opala, Piotr Pusz, Paweł Rychlikowski, and Michał Stypułkowski. 2021. Aligned contrastive predictive coding. *arXiv preprint arXiv:2104.11946*.

Yu-An Chung, Yu Zhang, Wei Han, Chung-Cheng Chiu, James Qin, Ruoming Pang, and Yonghui Wu. 2021. W2v-bert: Combining contrastive learning and masked language modeling for self-supervised speech pre-training. *arXiv preprint arXiv:2108.06209*.

Alexis Conneau, German Kruszewski, Guillaume Lample, Loïc Barrault, and Marco Baroni. 2018. What you can cram into a single vector: Probing sentence embeddings for linguistic properties. *arXiv preprint arXiv:1805.01070*.

Jacob Devlin, Ming-Wei Chang, Kenton Lee, and Kristina Toutanova. 2018. Bert: Pre-training of deep bidirectional transformers for language understanding. *arXiv preprint arXiv:1810.04805*.

Jacob Devlin et al. 2019. BERT: Pre-training of deep bidirectional transformers for language understanding. In *Proc. of NAACL*.

Ewan Dunbar, Robin Algayres, Julien Karadayi, Mathieu Bernard, Juan Benjumea, Xuan-Nga Cao, Lucie Miskic, Charlotte Dugrain, Lucas Ondel, Alan W. Black, Laurent Besacier, Sakriani Sakti, and Emmanuel Dupoux. 2019. The Zero Resource Speech Challenge 2019: TTS without T. In *Proc. INTERSPEECH*, pages 1088–1092.

Ewan Dunbar, Julien Karadayi, Mathieu Bernard, Xuan-Nga Cao, Robin Algayres, Lucas Ondel, Laurent Besacier, Sakriani Sakti, and Emmanuel Dupoux. 2020. The Zero Resource Speech Challenge 2020: Discovering discrete subword and word units. In *Proc. INTERSPEECH*, pages 4831–4835.

Allyson Ettinger, Ahmed Elgohary, and Philip Resnik. 2016. Probing for semantic evidence of composition by means of simple classification tasks. In *Proceedings of the 1st Workshop on Evaluating Vector-Space Representations for NLP*, pages 134–139.

John Hewitt and Christopher D Manning. 2019. A structural probe for finding syntax in word representations. In *Proceedings of the 2019 Conference of the North American Chapter of the Association for Computational Linguistics: Human Language Technologies, Volume 1 (Long and Short Papers)*, pages 4129–4138.

Bertrand Higy, Lieke Gelderloos, Afra Alishahi, and Grzegorz Chrupała. 2021. Discrete representations in neural models of spoken language. *arXiv preprint arXiv:2105.05582*.

Wei-Ning Hsu, Benjamin Bolte, Yao-Hung Hubert Tsai, Kushal Lakhotia, Ruslan Salakhutdinov, and Abdelrahman Mohamed. 2021. Hubert: Self-supervised speech representation learning by masked prediction of hidden units. *arXiv preprint arXiv:2106.07447*.

Keith Ito and Linda Johnson. 2017. The lj speech dataset. `https://keithito.com/LJ-Speech-Dataset/`.

J. Kahn, M. Rivière, W. Zheng, E. Kharitonov, Q. Xu, P. E. Mazaré, J. Karadayi, V. Liptchinsky, R. Collobert, C. Fuegen, T. Likhomanenko, G. Synnaeve, A. Joulin, A. Mohamed, and E. Dupoux. 2020. Libri-light: A benchmark for ASR with limited or no supervision. In *IEEE International Conference on Acoustics, Speech and Signal Processing (ICASSP)*, pages 7669–7673.

Kavita Kasi and Stephen A Zahorian. 2002. Yet another algorithm for pitch tracking. In *2002 ieee international conference on acoustics, speech, and signal processing*, volume 1, pages I–361. IEEE.

Eugene Kharitonov, Ann Lee, Adam Polyak, Yossi Adi, Jade Copet, Kushal Lakhotia, Tu-Anh Nguyen, Morgane Rivière, Abdelrahman Mohamed, Emmanuel Dupoux, et al. 2021a. Text-free prosody-aware generative spoken language modeling. *arXiv preprint arXiv:2109.03264*.

Eugene Kharitonov, Morgane Rivière, Gabriel Synnaeve, Lior Wolf, Pierre-Emmanuel Mazaré, Matthijs Douze, and Emmanuel Dupoux. 2021b. Data augmenting contrastive learning of speech representations in the time domain. In *2021 IEEE Spoken Language Technology Workshop (SLT)*, pages 215–222. IEEE.

Jong Wook Kim, Justin Salamon, Peter Li, and Juan Pablo Bello. 2018. Crepe: A convolutional representation for pitch estimation. In *ICASSP*.

Jungil Kong, Jaehyeon Kim, and Jaekyoung Bae. 2020. HiFi-GAN: Generative adversarial networks for efficient and high fidelity speech synthesis. In *Proc. of NeurIPS*.

Felix Kreuk, Adam Polyak, Jade Copet, Eugene Kharitonov, Tu-Anh Nguyen, Morgane Rivière, Wei-Ning Hsu, Abdelrahman Mohamed, Emmanuel Dupoux, and Yossi Adi. 2021. Textless speech emotion conversion using decomposed and discrete representations. *arXiv preprint arXiv:2111.07402*.

Kundan Kumar, Rithesh Kumar, Thibault de Boissiere, Lucas Gestin, Wei Zhen Teoh, Jose Sotelo, Alexandre de Brébisson, Yoshua Bengio, and Aaron Courville. 2019. Melgan: Generative adversarial networks for conditional waveform synthesis. *arXiv preprint arXiv:1910.06711*.

Kushal Lakhotia, Evgeny Kharitonov, Wei-Ning Hsu, Yossi Adi, Adam Polyak, Benjamin Bolte, Tu-Anh Nguyen, Jade Copet, Alexei Baevski, Adelrahman Mohamed, et al. 2021. Generative spoken language modeling from raw audio. *arXiv preprint arXiv:2102.01192*.

Ann Lee, Peng-Jen Chen, Changhan Wang, Jiatao Gu, Xutai Ma, Adam Polyak, Yossi Adi, Qing He, Yun Tang, Juan Pino, and Wei-Ning Hsu. 2021a. Direct speech-to-speech translation with discrete units. *arXiv preprint arXiv:2107.05604*.

Ann Lee, Hongyu Gong, Paul-Ambroise Duquenne, Holger Schwenk, Peng-Jen Chen, Changhan Wang, Sravya Popuri, Juan Pino, Jiatao Gu, and Wei-Ning Hsu. 2021b. Textless speech-to-speech translation on real data. *arXiv preprint arXiv:2112.08352*.

Mike Lewis et al. 2020. BART: Denoising sequence-to-sequence pre-training for natural language generation, translation, and comprehension. In *Proc. of ACL*.

Yinhan Liu et al. 2019. RoBERTa: A robustly optimized BERT pretraining approach. *arXiv preprint arXiv:1907.11692*.

Max Morrison, Rithesh Kumar, Kundan Kumar, Prem Seetharaman, Aaron Courville, and Yoshua Bengio. 2021. Chunked autoregressive gan for conditional waveform synthesis. *arXiv preprint arXiv:2110.10139*.

Tu Anh Nguyen, Maureen de Seyssel, Patricia Rozé, Morgane Rivière, Evgeny Kharitonov, Alexei Baevski, Ewan Dunbar, and Emmanuel Dupoux. 2020. The Zero Resource Speech Benchmark 2021: Metrics and baselines for unsupervised spoken language modeling. In *Advances in Neural Information Processing Systems (NeurIPS) – Self-Supervised Learning for Speech and Audio Processing Workshop*.

Tu Anh Nguyen, Eugene Kharitonov, Jade Copet, Yossi Adi, Wei-Ning Hsu, Ali Elkahky, Paden Tomasello, Robin Algayres, Benoit Sagot, Abdelrahman Mohamed, and Dupoux Emmanuel. 2022. Generative spoken dialogue language modeling. *arXiv preprint arXiv:2203.16502*.

Aaron van den Oord, Yazhe Li, and Oriol Vinyals. 2018. Representation learning with contrastive predictive coding. *arXiv preprint arXiv:1807.03748*.

Vassil Panayotov, Guoguo Chen, Daniel Povey, and Sanjeev Khudanpur. 2015. Librispeech: an asr corpus based on public domain audio books. In *2015 IEEE international conference on acoustics, speech and signal processing (ICASSP)*, pages 5206–5210. IEEE.

Jeffrey Pennington, Richard Socher, and Christopher D Manning. 2014. Glove: Global vectors for word representation. In *Proceedings of the 2014 conference on empirical methods in natural language processing (EMNLP)*, pages 1532–1543.

Matthew Peters et al. 2018. Deep contextualized word representations. In *Proc. of NAACL*.

Adam Polyak, Yossi Adi, Jade Copet, Eugene Kharitonov, Kushal Lakhotia, Wei-Ning Hsu, Abdelrahman Mohamed, and Emmanuel Dupoux. 2021. Speech resynthesis from discrete disentangled self-supervised representations. *arXiv preprint arXiv:2104.00355*.

Ryan Prenger, Rafael Valle, and Bryan Catanzaro. 2019. Waveglow: A flow-based generative network for speech synthesis. In *ICASSP 2019-2019 IEEE International Conference on Acoustics, Speech and Signal Processing (ICASSP)*, pages 3617–3621. IEEE.

Yi Ren, Chenxu Hu, Xu Tan, Tao Qin, Sheng Zhao, Zhou Zhao, and Tie-Yan Liu. 2020. Fastspeech 2: Fast and high-quality end-to-end text to speech. *arXiv preprint arXiv:2006.04558*.

Yi Ren, Yangjun Ruan, Xu Tan, Tao Qin, Sheng Zhao, Zhou Zhao, and Tie-Yan Liu. 2019. Fastspeech: Fast, robust and controllable text to speech. *arXiv preprint arXiv:1905.09263*.

Morgane Rivière and Emmanuel Dupoux. 2020. Towards unsupervised learning of speech features in the wild. In *IEEE Spoken Language Technology Workshop (SLT)*, pages 156–163.

Steffen Schneider, Alexei Baevski, Ronan Collobert, and Michael Auli. 2019. wav2vec: Unsupervised pre-training for speech recognition. *arXiv preprint arXiv:1904.05862*.

Jonathan Shen, Ruoming Pang, Ron J Weiss, Mike Schuster, Navdeep Jaitly, Zongheng Yang, Zhifeng Chen, Yu Zhang, Yuxuan Wang, Rj Skerrv-Ryan, et al. 2018. Natural tts synthesis by conditioning wavenet on mel spectrogram predictions. In *2018 IEEE International Conference on Acoustics, Speech and Signal Processing (ICASSP)*, pages 4779–4783. IEEE.

Jing Shi, Xuankai Chang, Tomoki Hayashi, Yen-Ju Lu, Shinji Watanabe, and Bo Xu. 2021. Discretization and re-synthesis: an alternative method to solve the cocktail party problem. *arXiv preprint arXiv:2112.09382*.

Benjamin van Niekerk, Leanne Nortje, Matthew Baas, and Herman Kamper. 2021. Analyzing speaker information in self-supervised models to improve zero-resource speech processing. *arXiv preprint arXiv:2108.00917*.

Chengyi Wang, Yu Wu, Yao Qian, Kenichi Kumatani, Shujie Liu, Furu Wei, Michael Zeng, and Xuedong Huang. 2021. Unispeech: Unified speech representation learning with labeled and unlabeled data. *arXiv preprint arXiv:2101.07597*.

Ryuichi Yamamoto, Eunwoo Song, and Jae-Min Kim. 2020. Parallel wavegan: A fast waveform generation model based on generative adversarial networks with multi-resolution spectrogram. In *ICASSP 2020-2020 IEEE International Conference on Acoustics, Speech and Signal Processing (ICASSP)*, pages 6199–6203. IEEE.

Web-based Annotation Interface for Derivational Morphology

Lukáš Kyjánek
Charles University, Faculty of Mathematics and Physics
Institute of Formal and Applied Linguistics
Prague, Czechia
kyjanek@ufal.mff.cuni.cz

Abstract

The paper presents a visual interface for manual annotation of language resources for derivational morphology. The interface is web-based and created using relatively simple programming techniques, and yet it rapidly facilitates and speeds up the annotation process, especially in languages with rich derivational morphology. As such, it can reduce the cost of the process. After introducing manual annotation tasks in derivational morphology, the paper describes the new visual interface and a case study that compares the current annotation method to the annotation using the interface. In addition, it also demonstrates the opportunity to use the interface for manual annotation of syntactic trees. The source codes are freely available under the MIT License on GitHub.

1 Introduction

Making manual annotations is a common task when a high-quality language resource is created. The more complex the annotation task, the more time consuming it is for an annotator, an expert in a linguistic field captured by the resource. Consequently, the cost of creating such resource can be high. The simplest approach is to simplify the task; however, it is not possible in many cases.

This paper presents such task and how to approach it in the field of annotating language resources of derivational morphology. When annotating derivational data, annotators must make many decisions at once. This complexity leads not only to the prolongation of the annotation process but also to mistakes that must be additionally re-annotated. As the simplification of these decisions is out of the question, a freely available web-based visual interface has been created to make the annotation process easier for annotators. The fact that annotating derivational morphology using the interface is faster than the currently used annotation method is also validated by real annotators.

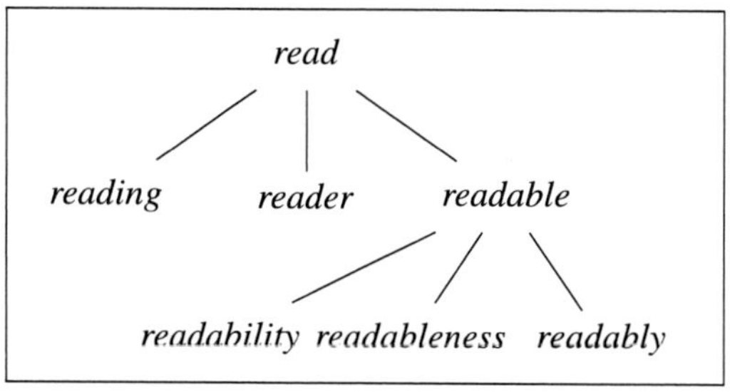

Figure 1: A derivational family of the verb *read*.

The paper is structured as follows. Section 2 describes the current state of annotating derivational morphology. Section 3 focuses on the new interface as well as its applicability to other annotation tasks. Section 4 provide a comparison of the current annotation method *versus* the utilisation of the interface. Section 5 concludes the paper.

2 Related Work

2.1 Linguistic Background

Morphological derivation is a process of forming new lexemes by modifying the already existing ones. For instance, the noun *reader* is derived by attaching the lexical affix *-er* to the morphological base of the verb *read*. Štekauer et al. (2012) document this process across many world languages.

One of the widely known approaches to derivational morphology (cf. Dokulil 1962; Buzássyová 1974; Horecký et al. 1989; Furdík 2004; Štekauer 2005) models all derivationally related lexemes (DERIVATIONAL FAMILY) on the basis of:

(i) a system of directly derivationally related lexemes grouped around a single base lexeme, e.g., *read* > *read-ing*, *read-er*, and *read-able*;
(ii) a sequence of consecutive derivatives, e.g., *read* > *read-able* > *read-abil-ity*.

If these parts are applied recursively to a single underived lexeme, it results in derivational families structured in rooted trees, see Figure 1.

Proceedings of the 2022 Conference of the North American Chapter of the Association for Computational Linguistics: Human Language Technologies: System Demonstrations, pages 10 - 16
July 10-15, 2022

2.2 Data Resources

There is a lot of lexical resources of derivational morphology (cf. Kyjánek 2018),[1] many of which model derivational families in rooted trees, concurring with the above-mentioned theory.[2] Most of the other existing resources that capture derivational families in non-tree-shaped data structures have been harmonised into the rooted trees and are available in the Universal Derivations collection (Kyjánek et al., 2020; Kyjánek et al., 2021).[3]

The reasons why some resources do not model derivational families in rooted trees cover a whole range from technical to theoretical reasons.[4] For example, DErivBase for German (Zeller et al., 2013) has been created by exploiting so-called *derivational rules* extracted from grammars in a form of sophisticated regular expressions which the authors have utilised to search derivationally related lexemes in a given lexeme set. Consequently, the resulting resource violates the main constraint of the rooted tree structure that each lexeme can have at most one base lexeme, e.g., the adjective *glatt* (*smooth*) and the verb *glätten* (*to smooth*) are captured as bases for the noun *Glätte* (*smoothness*). The manual annotation is thus necessary not only before the creation of a high-quality resource but also after that for its harmonisation, for example.

2.3 Manual Annotation Process

Annotators in the field of derivational morphology have to make many small decisions at once, even if they are only supposed to annotate Boolean decision like whether a given derivational relation is acceptable, e.g., *glatt* (*smooth*) > *Glätte* (*smoothness*) vs. *glätten* (*to smooth*) > *Glätte* (*smoothness*). To fulfil the conditions of the linguistic approach described in Section 2.1, they must decide (i) whether a given derived lexeme is really a derivative; if yes, then (ii) from which base lexeme it is derived; and (iii) whether the final decision does not violate constraints of the rooted tree structure with other derivationally related lexemes; and (iv) whether they decide consistently across derivational families. As these questions are interrelated, their simplification seems to be out of the question.

```
+   glatt_A     Glätte_Nf
+   glatt_A     glätten_V
+   glätten_V   glättend_A
-   glätten_V   Glätte_Nf
```

Figure 2: Example of a common .tsv file format for manual annotation. The data is stored in columns (annotator's mark, base lexeme, and derivative; lexemes are equipped with part-of-speech tags: `A` for adjectives, `V` for verbs, `Nf` for feminine nouns).

One of the common ways of making manual annotation of derivational relations is to list them in a file and assign each of them with a mark representing the presence/absence of the relation in the resulting rooted tree, see Figure 2. The annotation task seems easy if the data for annotation is small; however, the data is relatively large in practice. For instance, you can see manual annotations of one thousand relations from Wiktionary annotated before their addition into DeriNet for Czech.[5] Moreover, individual derivational families can be relatively large, especially in languages with rich derivational morphology, which even complicates the annotation process.

2.4 Tools for Linguistic Annotation

To the best of our knowledge, there is no available tool for making manual annotation of derivational morphology. The previous cases have relied on either non-public software developed solely for the annotation project or on simple text-based methods. There are few visualisation tools that at least display the data, e.g., WFL explorer[6] (Passarotti and Mambrini, 2012), DeriNet viewer[7] (Žabokrtský et al., 2016), DeriSearch v1[8] and v2[9] (Vidra and Žabokrtský, 2017, 2020), and Canoonet.[10] However, none of them allows editing the data.

There are also no case studies for annotation of derivational morphology neither in the ACL Anthology nor in the recent Handbook of Linguistic Annotation (Ide and Pustejovsky, 2017). However, the handbook and other similar cases from

[1] Perhaps the earliest modern case of a large-scale resource is CELEX2 (Baayen et al., 1995) with its annotations of derivational morphology of Dutch, English, and German.

[2] For example: DeriNet for Czech (Vidra et al., 2021), Spanish (Faryad, 2021), Persian (Haghdoost et al., 2019), and Russian (Kyjánek et al., 2021), Polish and Spanish Word-Formation Networks (Mateusz et al., 2018a,b), and Word Formation Latin (Litta et al., 2016).

[3] https://ufal.mff.cuni.cz/universal-derivations

[4] They are described in the text on the harmonisation.

[5] https://github.com/vidraj/derinet/blob/master/data/annotations/cs/2018_04_wiktionary/hand-annotated/der0001-1000.tsv

[6] http://wfl.marginalia.it/

[7] https://ufal.mff.cuni.cz/derinet/derinet-viewer

[8] https://ufal.mff.cuni.cz/derinet/derinet-search

[9] https://quest.ms.mff.cuni.cz/derisearch2/v2/databases/

[10] https://www.lehrerfreund.de/schule/1s/online-grammatik-canoo/2319

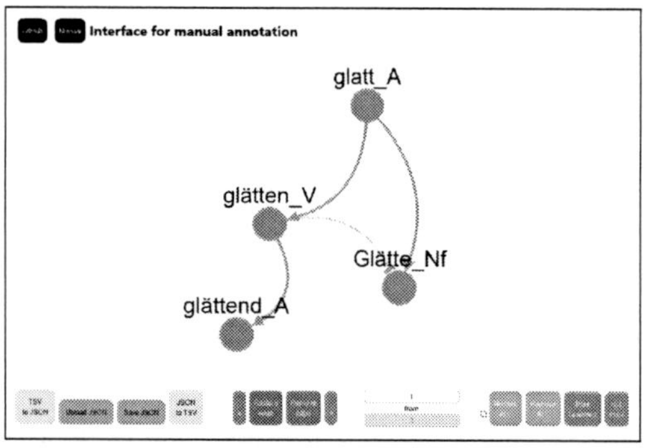

Figure 3: Screenshot of the freely available online Interface for manual annotation of derivational morphology. It captures the same derivational family as Figure 2.

the fields of annotating data resources of syntax (cf. Tyers et al. (2017)) and inflectional morphology (cf. Obeid et al. (2018); Alosaimy and Atwell (2018)) suggest that visualisation of the derivational data and a possibility to edit it in the visualisation interface is one of the best options to facilitate the annotation process.

3 Interface for Manual Annotations

The new interface should visualise the annotated data (cf. Figure 2) and allow annotators to edit it, leading to the facilitation of the annotation process. In this case, the process should lead to the data of derivational morphology annotated into the tree-shaped structure presented in Section 2.1. The functionality and design of the interface have already been tested by real annotators. They provided feedback for re-designing the interface to the current state, see Figure 3. Validation of the interface is presented in Section 4.

The development of such tools however never ends, as many things can be still improved. Therefore, the interface is distributed as open-source (on GitHub)[11] with a detailed manual that includes also example data. It is possible to run the interface both locally and online.[12]

3.1 Technical Properties

The interface is made as a web application thanks to which annotators can run it in any web browser, e.g., Microsoft Edge, Google Chrome, Mozilla Firefox, and Safari. It prevents problems with

[11] `https://github.com/lukyjanek/uder-annotation-interface`

[12] `https://lukyjanek.github.io/subpages/uder-annotation-interface/UDerAnnotation.html`

```
[
 {
  "nodes":
   [
    {"data":
      {"name":"glättend_A","id":"glättend_A"}
    },
    {"data":
      {"name":"Glätte_Nf","id":"Glätte_Nf"}
    },
    {"data":
      {"name":"glatt_A","id":"glatt_A"}
    },
    {"data":
      {"name":"glätten_V","id":"glätten_V"}
    }
   ],
  "edges":
   [
    {"data":
      {"target":"glatt_A","source":"Glätte_Nf",
       "intoTree":"solid"}
    },
    {"data":
      {"target":"glatt_A","source":"glätten_V",
       "intoTree":"solid"}
    },
    {"data":
      {"target":"glätten_V","source":"Glätte_Nf",
       "intoTree":"dotted"}
    },
    {"data":
      {"target":"glätten_V","source":"glättend_A",
       "intoTree":"solid"}
    }
   ]
 }
]
```

Figure 4: Input and output .json format of the annotation data for the interface from Figure 3.

users' installation of any programming environments. The interface is responsive by default (without implementing the interface separately for individual types of devices), so the annotators can annotate not only on their computers but also on touchscreens of their mobile devices. The interface is programmed using HTML5, CCS3, and JavaScript with the libraries jQuery, CytoScape.js, and Notify.js. These technologies runs the interface on the client's side/user's device that brings the mention benefit, but, on the other hand, the interface suffers from the limits of web browsers.[13]

As for the input/output file formats, the interface is ready to process derivational families stored in the .json format; see Figure 4. There is also a function implemented to convert the .tsv file into the .json file and *vice versa* (the `TSV_to_JSON` and `JSON_to_TSV` buttons).

3.2 Design and Functionality

The interface screen consists of top and bottom button bars and a central canvas for data visualisation

[13] For instance, Google Chrome has a memory limit of 512MB for 32-bit and 1.4GB for 64-bit systems. However, it is still enough memory for common manual annotation.

and annotation. While the top bar includes support buttons, such as a link to the source codes stored on GitHub and manual, the bottom bar contains buttons for manual annotation.

The data is loaded using the `Upload_JSON` button. The annotator can zoom in/out the screen and move the displayed nodes and their relations. Positions of nodes on canvas are stored in the .json file. Annotators can thus return quickly to already annotated derivational families. During the annotation process, they select relations to be annotated and change their state by one of the following buttons: `Restore_edge` (draws the relation by a solid line representing that it should be present in the resulting family) or `Remove_edge` (dotted line, should be absent). The annotators can switch between families using the green arrow buttons or the text box. At the end of the annotation, the work is saved with the `Save_JSON` button.

Several functionalities have been added based on the annotators' feedback. If the annotator writes a word or its substring to the text box, the interface searches for the family containing the word/substring and visualises it. To facilitate the annotation of families with many relations, there are two buttons that remove and restore all derivational relations in the displayed derivational family. For annotators, it is sometimes easier to remove all edges and build such a large tree from scratch by restoring individual edges. Some buttons list all lexemes from the visualised family and check whether the solid lines in the annotated family are organised in a rooted tree. In addition, keyboard shortcuts have been introduced for all the functions. After all these changes, the annotators confirmed that the interface makes their work easier and faster.

3.3 Applicability to Different Tasks

To show the robustness of the new interface for annotation of data in tree-shaped structures, a brief experiment with annotating syntactic data has been performed. The harmonised syntactic data from the Universal Dependencies collection (Zeman et al., 2021) was selected for this experiment. The only thing in need was to create a script that would convert the input .conllu format into the .json format required by the annotation interface. Figure 5 displays the German sentence '*Absolut empfehlenswert ist auch der Service.*' (*The service is also highly recommended.*) from the corpus GSD (McDonald et al., 2013) in the annotation interface.

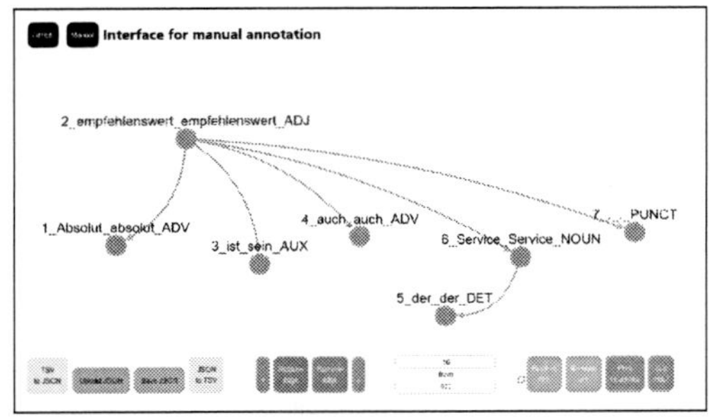

Figure 5: Screenshot of the freely available online Interface for manual annotation of derivational morphology applied to the data from syntactic treebank from Universal Dependencies. The underscores separate id, token, lemma, part-of-speech category.

4 Human Validation

To validate the usefulness of the newly created interface for manual annotation of derivational morphology, as described in the Section 2.3, a simple annotation experiment has been done with human annotators. Two methods of manual annotation are compared: (a) the currently used method when annotators work in the traditional text processor with the .tsv format, and (b) the annotation by using the newly created visual interface with the .json format. The main expectation is that annotating the same data by using the interface should be faster. The individual parts of this experiment, such as the input sample as well as the annotated ones, are stored on the GitHub repository with the source codes.

4.1 Annotation Experiment

The experiment involved 12 human annotators (university students of other than linguistic studies). They all annotated the same sample of derivational families; however, six of the annotators did it in the text processor with the .tsv file format, i.e., the currently used method of annotation such data, while the other six annotators used the newly created visual interface with the .json file format.

The annotators were instructed to annotate the given data in a such way that it concurs with the approach to model derivational families in rooted trees (Section 2.1), i.e., that each lexeme can have at most one base lexeme and that the morphological complexity should grow from the root to the leaves. They also got the instructions related to the individual annotation methods, e.g., all functionalities and buttons of the interface were explained to the annotators who would use the interface.

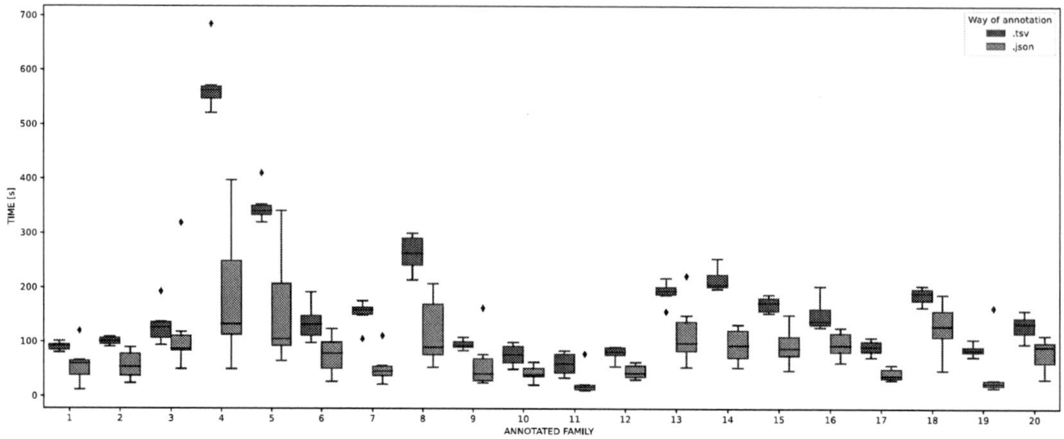

Figure 6: Time spent by annotators on annotating individual 20 derivational families in the .tsv file format and using the new visual interface with the .json file format.

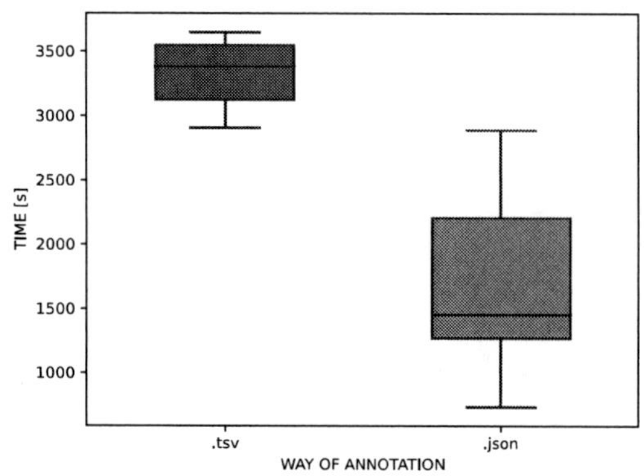

Figure 7: Total time spent by annotators on annotating 20 derivational families in the .tsv file format and using the new visual interface with the .json file format.

4.2 Annotation Sample

The annotation sample consisted of two similar sets of ten different derivational (sub-)families selected from Czech DeriNet with respect to their numbers of lexemes, derivational relations, depths (morphological complexity) of the original trees, and the part-of-speech categories of the tree roots. Each set of the sample thus includes four families with the noun and verbal tree roots and two families with the adjective tree roots; it has the following ranges: for the number of lexemes from 6 to 20, for relations from 6 to 24, for depth from 2 to 5.

A few random incorrect connections (from 2 to 5 relations) were made in all families in the sample. The annotators were supposed to annotate these errors and let the other correct relations.

The division of the sample into two sets of ten families can provide an overview of how the annotators' experience with the annotation using the assigned method influence the time spent on the annotation of individual families. The assumption associated with this is that the time spent over the second set should be less than for the first set because the annotators learn the annotation process with each annotated family. On the other hand, if the visual interface is useful, then the time spent on annotating the .json file format by using the interface should be still lower than on the annotation of the .tsv file format.

As for the specific properties of the individual families in the sample, the smallest families in terms of the number of lexemes are numbered as 1, 2, 9, 10, 11, 12, 19, 20; and the families 9 and 19 includes a complete graph which the annotators have to annotate into the rooted tree structure.

4.3 Results

The main hypothesis that the annotation process is faster if the newly created visual interface is used (with .json format) instead of the current annotation method (with .tsv format) was proved, at least for Czech, a language that has rich derivational morphology. Annotators with the visual interface annotated faster in the case of all annotated derivational families; see Figure 6. However, the difference in time was small for smaller families, which indicates that the current .tsv annotation method is comparably good as the annotation using the interface in the case of derivational families with few tens of relations. If the family is bigger, then the annotators were much faster when using the visual interface. In total, Figure 7 illustrates that the annotation process with visual interface takes noticeably fewer seconds than the currently used annotation method.

The secondary hypothesis that the annotators are faster in the second half of the sample, especially when this half shares the same parameters in terms of numbers of lexemes and relations, was not proved so conclusively as the main hypothesis. There is such trend in the second half of the sample, but the differences are not so radical.

5 Conclusion

When developing high-quality data, especially data that contains more complicated structures, developers often ask for manual annotations. They need the annotations when they create, extend, test, or evaluate the data. Annotation of complex phenomena is time-consuming and increases data production costs. Therefore, it seems worth spending time to simplify the annotation process.

In this paper, a case study about manual annotation of complex phenomena from derivational morphology has been presented. As a way of simplifying the annotation process, a web-based visual annotation interface in which annotators can edit the displayed data has been created. The interface is freely available (cf. Footnote 11). It was created in direct collaboration with several annotators who tested the interface on data of real derivational families and provided useful feedback. The annotators have also rated the annotation process with the created interface as more attractive, easier, and faster, which led to greater savings of time (and potentially money spent on the development of the resulting resource while still achieving high quality). Their feedback has led to the addition of several new functionalities, such as keyboard shortcuts and the button for checking treeness, that significantly speed up the annotation process. In addition, the desired benefits of the interface have been validated by annotators, and the paper describes this validation. It confirms that usage of the new interface rapidly speeds up the annotation process compared to the current method of annotating data for derivational morphology.

In general, this paper underlines that a tool/interface can be created by relatively basic techniques but can still save a lot of annotators' time and effort. One of the crucial points is, however, to be open-minded and to communicate with annotators. Since the annotators know how they must think during the annotating, they can specify their needs and provide informed feedback. There is still (and always will be) a lot of ways in which such interface can be improved or extended; they remain for future work. The important message is that even a simple interface can greatly facilitate the manual annotation process. While a programmer creates such interface in a few hours, annotators can save days of work.

Acknowledgements

This work was supported by the Grant No. GA19-14534S of the Czech Science Foundation, and the Grant No. START/HUM/010 of Grant schemes at Charles University (reg. No. CZ.02.2.69/0.0/0.0/19_073/0016935). It was using language resources developed, stored, and distributed by the LINDAT/CLARIAH-CZ project.

References

Abdulrahman Alosaimy and Eric Atwell. 2018. Web-based Annotation Tool for Inflectional Language Resources. In *Proceedings of the 11th International Conference on Language Resources and Evaluation (LREC 2018)*, pages 3933–3939.

Harald R. Baayen, Richard Piepenbrock, and Leon Gulikers. 1995. CELEX2. Linguistic Data Consortium, Catalogue No. LDC96L14.

Klára Buzássyová. 1974. *Sémantická štruktúra slovenských deverbatív*. Veda, Bratislava.

Miloš Dokulil. 1962. *Tvoření slov v češtině 1: Teorie odvozování slov*. Academia, Prague.

Ján Faryad. 2021. DeriNet.ES 0.6. Institute of Formal and Applied Linguistics (ÚFAL), Faculty of Mathematics and Physics, Charles University; included in the UDer collection.

Juraj Furdík. 2004. *Slovenská slovotvorba*. NÁUKA, Prešov.

Hamid Haghdoost, Ebrahim Ansari, Zdeněk Žabokrtský, and Mahshid Nikravesh. 2019. DeriNet.FA 0.5. Institute of Formal and Applied Linguistics (ÚFAL), Faculty of Mathematics and Physics, Charles University; included in the UDer collection.

Ján Horecký, Klára Buzássyová, Ján Bosák, et al. 1989. *Dynamika slovnej zásoby súčasnej slovenčiny*. Veda, Bratislava.

Nancy Ide and James Pustejovsky. 2017. *Handbook of Linguistic Annotation*, 1st edition. Springer Publishing Company, Incorporated.

Lukáš Kyjánek, Zdeněk Žabokrtský, Jonáš Vidra, and Magda Ševčíková. 2021. Universal Derivations v1.1. LINDAT/CLARIAH-CZ digital library at the Institute of Formal and Applied Linguistics (ÚFAL), Faculty of Mathematics and Physics, Charles University.

Lukáš Kyjánek, Zdeněk Žabokrtský, Magda Ševčíková, and Jonáš Vidra. 2020. Universal Derivations 1.0, A Growing Collection of Harmonised Word-Formation Resources. *The Prague Bulletin of Mathematical Linguistics*, 115:5–30.

Lukáš Kyjánek. 2018. Morphological Resources of Derivational Word-Formation Relations. Technical Report TR-2018-61, Faculty of Mathematics and Physics, Charles University.

Lukáš Kyjánek, Olga Lyashevskaya, Anna Nedoluzhko, Daniil Vodolazsky, and Zdeněk Žabokrtský. 2021. DeriNet.RU 0.5. Institute of Formal and Applied Linguistics (ÚFAL), Faculty of Mathematics and Physics, Charles University; included in the UDer collection.

Eleonora Litta, Marco Passarotti, and Chris Culy. 2016. Formatio Formosa est. Building a Word Formation Lexicon for Latin. In *Proceedings of the 3rd Italian Conference on Computational Linguistics*, pages 185–189.

Lango Mateusz, Magda Ševčíková, and Zdeněk Žabokrtský. 2018a. Polish Word-Formation Network 0.5. Institute of Formal and Applied Linguistics (ÚFAL), Faculty of Mathematics and Physics, Charles University; included in the UDer collection.

Lango Mateusz, Magda Ševčíková, and Zdeněk Žabokrtský. 2018b. Spanish Word-Formation Network 0.5. Institute of Formal and Applied Linguistics (ÚFAL), Faculty of Mathematics and Physics, Charles University; included in the UDer collection.

Ryan McDonald, Joakim Nivre, Yvonne Quirmbach-Brundage, Yoav Goldberg, Dipanjan Das, Kuzman Ganchev, Keith Hall, Slav Petrov, Hao Zhang, Oscar Täckström, Claudia Bedini, Núria Bertomeu Castelló, and Jungmee Lee. 2013. Universal Dependency Annotation for Multilingual Parsing. In *Proceedings of the 51st Annual Meeting of the Association for Computational Linguistics (Volume 2: Short Papers)*, pages 92–97, Sofia, Bulgaria. Association for Computational Linguistics.

Ossama Obeid, Salam Khalifa, Nizar Habash, Houda Bouamor, Wajdi Zaghouani, and Kemal Oflazer. 2018. MADARi: A web interface for joint Arabic morphological annotation and spelling correction. In *Proceedings of the 11th International Conference on Language Resources and Evaluation (LREC 2018)*.

Marco Passarotti and Francesco Mambrini. 2012. First Steps towards the Semi-automatic Development of a Wordformation-based Lexicon of Latin. In *Proceedings of the 8th International Conference on Language Resources and Evaluation (LREC 2012)*, pages 852–859.

Pavol Štekauer. 2005. Onomasiological Approach to Word-Formation. In Pavol Štekauer and Rochelle Lieber, editors, *Handbook of Word-Formation*, pages 207–232. Springer, Dordrecht.

Pavol Štekauer, Salvador Valera, and Lívia Körtvélyessy. 2012. *Word-Formation in the World's Languages: A Typological Survey*. Cambridge University Press, New York.

Francis Tyers, Mariya Sheyanova, and Jonathan Washington. 2017. UD Annotatrix: An annotation tool for Universal Dependencies. In *Proceedings of the 16th International Workshop on Treebanks and Linguistic Theories*, pages 10–17.

Jonáš Vidra, Zdeněk Žabokrtský, Lukáš Kyjánek, Magda Ševčíková, Šárka Dohnalová, Emil Svoboda, and Jan Bodnár. 2021. DeriNet 2.1. LINDAT/CLARIAH-CZ digital library at the Institute of Formal and Applied Linguistics (ÚFAL), Faculty of Mathematics and Physics, Charles University; included in the UDer collection.

Jonáš Vidra and Zdeněk Žabokrtský. 2017. Online Software Components for Accessing Derivational Networks. In *Proceedings of the Workshop on Resources and Tools for Derivational Morphology (DeriMo 2017)*, pages 129–139. EDUCatt.

Jonáš Vidra and Zdeněk Žabokrtský. 2020. Next Step in Online Querying and Visualization of Word-Formation Networks. In *Proceedings of the 23rd International Conference on Text, Speech and Dialogue (TSD 2020)*, pages 144–152. Springer.

Britta Zeller, Jan Šnajder, and Sebastian Padó. 2013. DErivBase: Inducing and Evaluating a Derivational Morphology Resource for German. In *ACL*, volume 1, pages 1201–1211. Proceedings of the 51st Annual Meeting of the Association for Computational Linguistics (Volume 1: Long Papers).

Daniel Zeman, Joakim Nivre, Mitchell Abrams, et al. 2021. Universal Dependencies 2.9. LINDAT/CLARIAH-CZ digital library at the Institute of Formal and Applied Linguistics (ÚFAL), Faculty of Mathematics and Physics, Charles University.

Zdeněk Žabokrtský, Magda Ševčíková, Milan Straka, Jonáš Vidra, and Adéla Limburská. 2016. Merging Data Resources for Inflectional and Derivational Morphology in Czech. In *Proceedings of the 10th International Conference on Language Resources and Evaluation (LREC 2016)*, pages 1307–1314.

TurkishDelightNLP: A Neural Turkish NLP Toolkit

Hüseyin Aleçakır
Afiniti
Istanbul
huseyinalecakir@gmail.com

Necva Bölücü
Computer Engineering
Hacettepe University
Ankara
necvaa@gmail.com

Burcu Can
RGCL
University of Wolverhampton
Wolverhampton
b.can@wlv.ac.uk

Abstract

We introduce a neural Turkish NLP toolkit called TurkishDelightNLP that performs computational linguistic analyses from morphological level to semantic level that involves tasks such as stemming, morphological segmentation, morphological tagging, part-of-speech tagging, dependency parsing, and semantic parsing, as well as high-level NLP tasks such as named entity recognition. We publicly share the open-source Turkish NLP toolkit through a web interface that allows an input text to be analysed in real-time, as well as the open source implementation of the components provided in the toolkit, an API, and several annotated datasets such as word similarity test set to evaluate word embeddings and UCCA-based semantic annotation in Turkish. This will be the first open-source Turkish NLP toolkit that involves a range of NLP tasks in all levels. We believe that it will be useful for other researchers in Turkish NLP and will be also beneficial for other high-level NLP tasks in Turkish.

1 Introduction

Turkish is one of the low-resource languages with a rich morphology. Although still limited, there has been an increasing interest in Turkish NLP in the last decade. Being a morphologically productive language is the main drawback of the Turkish NLP research. Current deep learning models are notoriously data-hungry. When it comes to morphologically productive languages, the data requirement substantially increases compared to other morphologically poor languages. This is due to the number of different word forms that can be generated via inflection and/or derivation. Although current word embedding models such as BERT (Devlin et al., 2019) rely on tokenization that considers sub-word tokens rather than word tokens, the recent research (Haley, 2020) still shows that the performance of such models degrades with novel words.

We introduce a new neural Turkish NLP toolkit that involves the following linguistic and NLP tasks in Turkish: Stemming, morphological segmentation, morphological tagging, part-of-speech tagging, dependency parsing, semantic parsing, and named entity recognition. Morphological segmentation, morphological tagging, part-of-speech tagging, and dependency parsing are learned jointly using a multi-task learning approach. Most of the previous work on Turkish morphology and syntax considers morphological and syntactic tasks as independent problems. However, syntax is strongly defined by morphology and vice versa, especially in agglutinative languages. Therefore, in this study, we benefit from the mutual interaction between morphological and syntactic layers in the language.

All components apart from semantic parsing model are built on LSTMs that are capable of learning especially long distance relations. The models also utilise a Bahdanau (Bahdanau et al., 2015) attention mechanism in various layers for an efficient learning of the valuable contextual information within the sentence/word. Moreover, we investigate cross-level information flow between the layers by incorporating information between words in different time steps. As distinct from the other components, semantic parsing model adopts an encoder-decoder model where the encoder is based on self-attention mechanism (Vaswani et al., 2017).

TurkishDelightNLP is available at `http://rgcl.wlv.ac.uk/TurkishNLP/` and the source codes of all components are also publicly available, which are specified in each section below. We also provide API to allow users to process their data using HTTP requests[1]. In addition to the NLP toolkit, we provide few datasets; that are an UCCA-based semantic annotation for Turkish,

[1]The REST API for the TurkishDelightNLP toolkit is available at `https://github.com/halecakir/turkish-delight-nlp-api`.

Proceedings of the 2022 Conference of the North American Chapter of the Association for Computational Linguistics: Human Language Technologies: System Demonstrations, pages 17 - 26

a Turkish stemming training set based on METU-Sabanci Turkish Treebank (Oflazer et al., 2003b), and a word similarity test set along with the human judgements for assessing morphologically rich Turkish word embeddings.

2 Related Work and Tools on Turkish NLP

Despite being a low-resource language, Turkish has been one of the actively studied languages among other low-resource languages especially in the last decade. Numerous models have been recently released for Turkish. However, most of them were not released publicly available, and they were not shared as tools that facilitate generating a result in real time. The earlier studies on Turkish morphology include **morphological analyzers** such as the two-level description of Turkish morphology (Oflazer, 1993), the stochastic morphological analyzer based on finite state transducers (Sak et al., 2009), paradigmatic approaches (Can and Manandhar, 2009, 2012, 2018), and few other open source analyzers such as Zemberek (Akın and Akın, 2007), TRmorph (Çöltekin, 2010), and the syntactically expressive morphological analyzer by Ozturel et al. (2019). The earlier studies also involve **dependency parsers** such as the probabilistic and deterministic dependency parser by Eryiğit et al. (2008), the two-phase statistical parser based on Conditional Random Fields (CRFs) by Durgar El-Kahlout et al. (2014), and the recent neural parser by Tuç and Can (2020). There are a couple of Turkish **stemmers** introduced such as the probabilistic stemmer by Dincer and Karaoğlan (2003), and the finite state machine-based Govde-Turk by Yücebas and Tintin (2017); a few **part-of-speech taggers** were also proposed such as the Hidden Markov Model-based PoS tagger by Dinçer et al. (2008), the deterministic tagger using the two-level morphological description by Oflazer and Kuruoz (1994), and unsupervised Bayesian approaches (Bölücü and Can, 2019, 2021). The first **semantic parsing** annotation for Turkish (Azin and Eryiğit, 2019) has been presented for Abstract Meaning Representation (AMR) (Flanigan et al., 2014) and there is not any other semantic parser introduced for Turkish yet, to our knowledge.

As seen, most of the linguistic analysis tasks on Turkish are based on either statistical or deterministic approaches. Currently, the Turkish NLP research focuses more on NLP applications such as **named entity recognition** (Güneş and Tantuğ, 2018; Güngör et al., 2019; Eşref and Can, 2019), text classification (Tokgoz et al., 2021), sentiment analysis (Gezici et al., 2019; Demirci et al., 2019), offensive language identification (Ozdemir and Yeniterzi, 2020), text summarisation (Ertam and Aydin, 2021), text normalisation (Göker and Can, 2018) with especially the availability of the large pretrained neural word embeddings in almost any language.

Most of the NLP tools in Turkish were released before the deep learning era and they still have not been replaced by the neural network approaches and the researchers in the field still use the old-fashioned statistical and deterministic models for morphological or syntactic processing. We aim to fill this gap with our Turkish NLP toolkit by introducing better performing neural-based methods for Turkish linguistic analysis and NLP. The most similar one to our toolkit is ITU NLP Toolkit (Eryiğit, 2014) that also involves a wide range of NLP tools such as normalization, spell correction, morphological analysis, dependency parsing, and named entity recognition. However, all of their models are independent from each other and they are built on either deterministic or statistical machine learning algorithms. Our toolkit deviates from theirs by adopting neural models and analysing morphology and syntax jointly by considering the interaction between them. Moreover, their toolkit does not involve any semantic parsing as ours.

3 About Turkish

Turkish is an agglutinating language with a rich morphology. The morphological rules are quite regular in Turkish that define the order of the morphemes in a word, as well as the morphophonemic processes such as consonant mutation and vowel harmony, which lead the suffix and the final consonant and vowel in a word to be harmonised with each other mutually. Therefore, a morpheme can have tens of different surface forms in Turkish, which are allomorphs of the same morpheme. In Turkish, syntactic information is encoded in inflectional morphemes. For example, the word ' *yapabileceğim'* (in English, ' I will be able to do') involves the following inflectional morphemes that each correspond to a syntactic role: ' *-abil'* ('be able'), ' *-eceğ'* (' will'), and ' *-im'* (' I').

In this paper, we propose to process every word considering its left and right context through a cross-level information from morphological segments up to dependencies in a moving window, so that morphological information of the contextual words help to analyse the PoS tags, and the PoS information of the contextual words help to analyse the dependency relations in a sentence.

4 A Neural Turkish NLP Toolkit

The introduced toolkit involves different components that are all described thoroughly below.

4.1 Stemmer

The stemmer is built on an encoder-decoder model that employs a bidirectional LSTM (Can, 2019). The model has two versions, one without an attention mechanism considering all characters with equal probability and another version with Bahdanau attention (Bahdanau et al., 2015) over characters of a given word in both directions to learn character-based contextual information. The model is trained on a dataset with 17025 word types along with their stems obtained from Metu-Sabanci Treebank (Oflazer et al., 2003b). Both the model that is implemented in DyNet (Neubig et al., 2017) and the dataset are publicly available[2]. The accuracy of the stemmer is 85% and comparable to that of Zemberek (Akın and Akın, 2007), and outperforms the other open-source Turkish stemmers (Zafer, 2015).

4.2 Joint Morphology and Syntax Model

A multi-task learning model is proposed for joint learning of morphology and syntax (Can et al., 2022). The model is built upon a multi-layer LSTM structure where each layer contributes to the overall loss in a joint learning framework and the errors from all layers backpropagate from top layer to the bottom. LSTM structure has been preferred both due its low size data requirement compared to transformers and the flexibility of processing sequential information by controlling the vertical information flow between the layers. The model is trained on IMST Turkish Treebank (Sulubacak et al., 2016). The model involves 4 layers where each of them adopts a bidirectional LSTM that is specialised in either morphology or syntax. The layers are dedicated for morphological segmentation, morphological tagging, part-of-speech tagging, and dependency parsing. The order of the layers has been designed based on the direction of the information flow and the size of the units (from smaller to bigger). A separate component for morph2vec (Üstün et al., 2018) that is used to pretrain the morpheme embeddings is also involved.

The joint model is trained and evaluated on UD Turkish Treebank, which is called IMST Treebank (Sulubacak and It, 2018) and it is a re-annotated version of the METU-Sabanci Treebank (Oflazer et al., 2003a). For the pre-trained word embeddings, we use pre-trained 200-dimensional word embeddings trained on Boun Web Corpus (Sak et al., 2008) provided by CoNLL 2018 Shared Task. The overall architecture of the joint model is given in Figure 1, where each coloured component belongs to a different level of processing that starts from morphological segmentation till dependency parsing. Each level is built on LSTMs that sequentially process every unit (i.e. character, morpheme, word, or syntactic information) in a given sentence by utilising the contextual information as well (see Section 4.2.6 for the details of the cross-level information flow). An example analysis is also provided in Figure 2 and Figure 3. All layers are described in detail below. The open-source implementation in DyNet (Neubig et al., 2017) is publicly available[3].

4.2.1 Morpheme-based Word Embeddings: morph2vec

Morph2vec (Üstün et al., 2018) is a morpheme-based word embedding model that learns word embeddings as a weighted sum of word embeddings each of which are obtained from a particular morphological segmentation of a word. It is assumed that the correct morphological segmentation of a word is not known apriori; therefore, each potential morphological segmentation of a word is predicted before training the model. Each morphological segmentation is fed into a bidirectional LSTM with each LSTM unit being fed with a morpheme embedding that is randomly initialised. So each LSTM generates a word embedding for that particular morphological segmentation. Finally, Bahdanau attention mechanism (Bahdanau et al., 2015) is employed to learn the weight of each segmentation-specific word embedding. The morpheme-based embeddings give a better Spearman correlation with the human judgements in word similarity tasks compared to both char2vec (Cao and Rei, 2016) and fasttext (Bojanowski et al.,

[2]https://github.com/burcu-can/Stemmer

[3]https://github.com/halecakir/JointParser

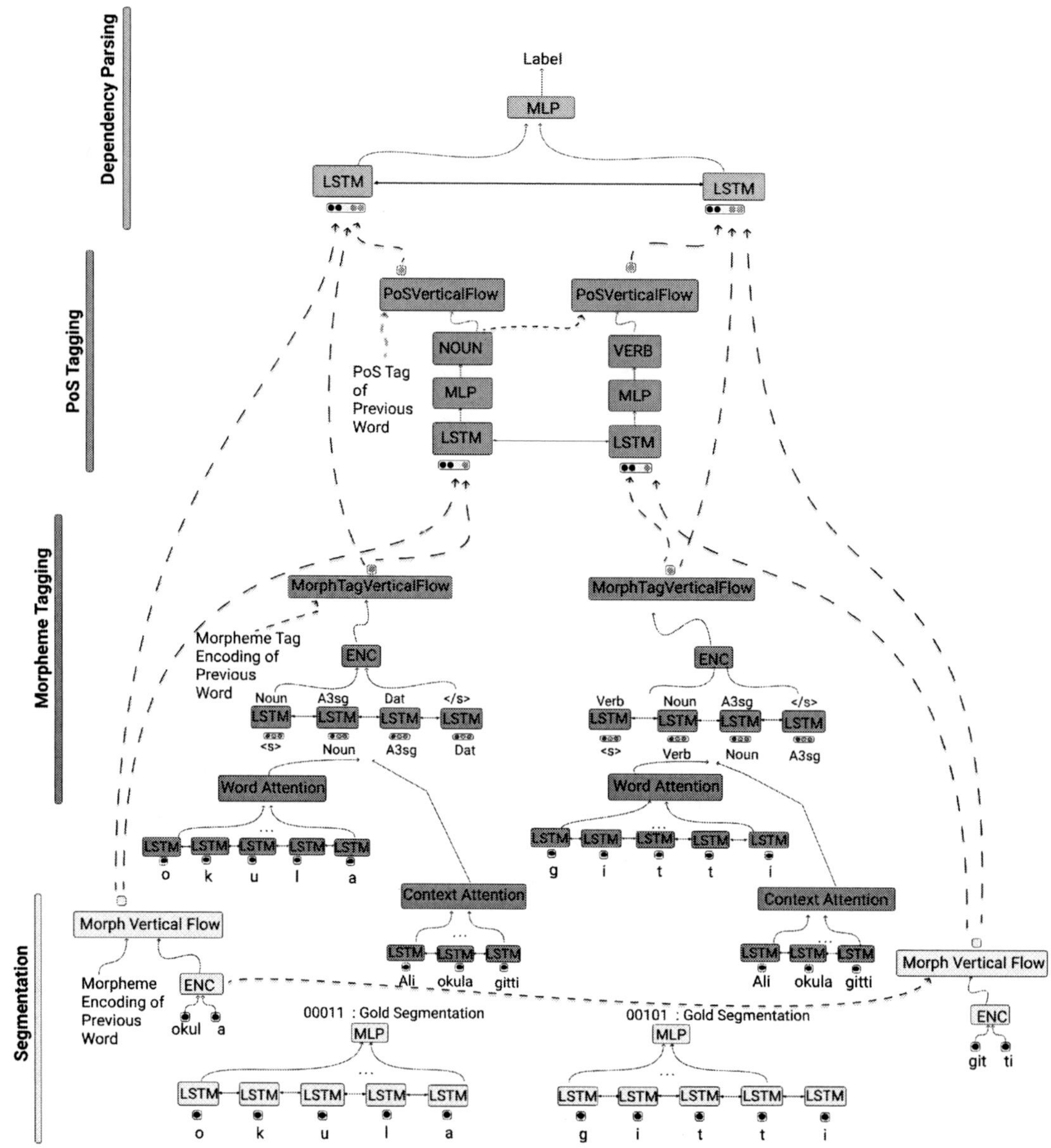

Figure 1: The layers of the proposed joint learning framework. The sentence "Ali okula gitti." ("Ali went to school") is processed from morphology up to dependencies (Can et al., 2022).

2017). The source code in DyNet is publicly available[4], and the datasets for syntactic analogy and word similarity along with the human judgement scores are also publicly available[5].

Morph2vec is pre-trained on METU-Sabanci Turkish Treebank (Oflazer et al., 2003b) before training the joint morphology and syntax model. Therefore, pretrained morpheme embeddings are used during joint learning.

4.2.2 Morphological Segmentation

The lowest layer of the joint model performs morphological segmentation through a bidirectional

[4]https://github.com/burcu-can/morph2vec_dynet

[5]https://nlp.cs.hacettepe.edu.tr/projects/morph2vec/

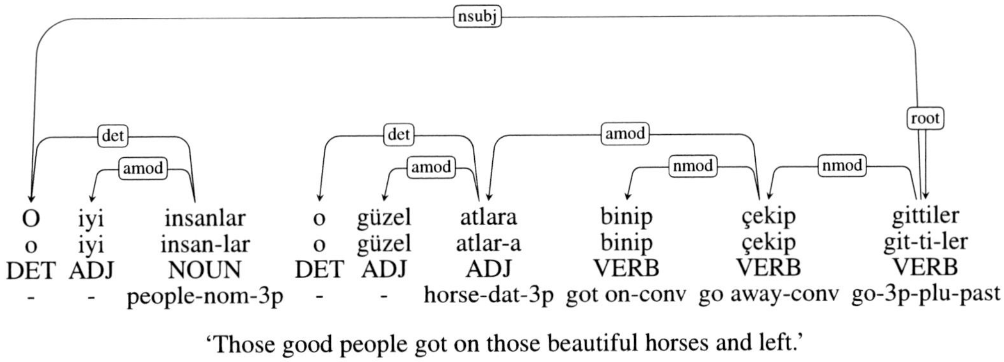

Figure 2: An example analysis of the toolkit for a sentence in Turkish. First line: The orthographic form. Second line: morphological segments. Third line: PoS tags. Fourth line: morphological features ('-' is for null). Dependencies in the article are arrowed (head to dependent) and labeled UD dependencies (de Marneffe et al., 2021).

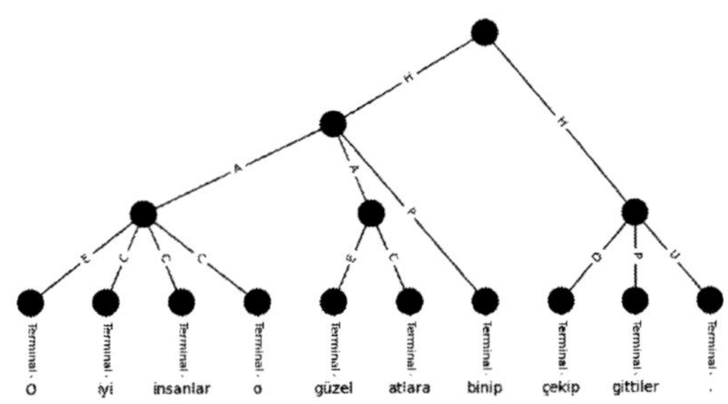

Figure 3: The UCCA-based semantic parse tree of the sentence, *O iyi insanlar o güzel atlara binip çekip gittiler.* (in English, *"Those good people got on those beautiful horses and left")*

LSTM that encodes each character of a given word with one hot encoding. The output at each time step is reduced to a single dimension using a multilayer perceptron (MLP) with sigmoid function to predict whether there is a morpheme boundary after that character or not. Each value above 0.6 refers to a morpheme boundary, and below means that there is not a morpheme boundary at that time step after the current character. Binary cross entropy is used for this layer that contributes to the overall loss of the joint model.

We obtain the gold segments from the rule-based morphological analyser Zemberek (Akın and Akın, 2007) to train the segmentation component since the IMST Treebank does not involve morphological segmentations but only morphological tags. Our joint model performs 98.97% of accuracy on morphological segmentation task[6].

4.2.3 Morphological Tagging

We adopt an encoder-decoder model for the morphological tagging layer. To encode the relevant contextual information both within the word and within the sentence, we use a character encoder and word encoder respectively. The character encoder processes the characters within the given word that will be analysed and the word encoder processes the contextual words in that sentence to better predict the morphological tagging of the given word in a particular context, which can also help to disambiguate the word in a particular context. Both of the encoders are built on bidirectional LSTMs and both of them adopt a Bahdanau attention (Bahdanau et al., 2015) to learn the weights over characters and words. The input to the decoder is the concatenation of the weighted outputs obtained from both character and context encoders. The decoder is also built on a bidirectional LSTM that generates morpheme tags using a softmax function at each time step. Our joint model performs 87.59% FEATS score on morphological tagging, and comparable to a recently introduced neural Turkish morphological tagger that performs 89.54% FEATS score (Dayanık et al., 2018).

[6]It should be noted that the test set is also obtained from Zemberek.

4.2.4 Part-of-Speech Tagging

The PoS tagging layer is built upon a bidirectional LSTM that is fed with the concatenation of word-level (i.e. word2vec embeddings), character-level (learned through a character BiLSTM for each word), morpheme-level (i.e. morph2vec), and morpheme tag encodings of each particular word in a sentence. Morpheme-level word embeddings are obtained from pretrained morph2vec as mentioned before. However, the other embeddings are all randomly initialised and learned during training. The output at each time step is passed through an MLP with softmax activation function to predict the PoS tag of the word at that time step. Our joint model performs exactly the same with the state-of-art PoS tagger by Che et al. (2018) with an accuracy of 94.78%.

4.2.5 Dependency Parsing

The dependency parsing is also built on BiLSTM that is fed with the same embeddings used in PoS tagging layer, and in addition, we concatenate the PoS encodings of the words that are obtained from the previous layer. PoS encodings are randomly initialised and learned during training. The arcs are scored by an MLP that involves a pointer network that predicts whether there is an arc between the given two words or not. Once the scores are predicted by the MLP, the projective trees are generated using Eisner's decoding algorithm (Eisner, 1996). Labels are analogously predicted using another MLP with a softmax function. Our joint model gives comparable results with the state-of-art dependency parsing results of Straka (2018) with 71% UAS and 63.92% LAS (whereas Straka (2018) achieves 72.25% UAS and 66.44% LAS).

4.2.6 Cross-Level Information Flow

The custom in such a multi-layered and multi-task models is to feed the obtained information regarding the current word from the previous layers to pass it over to the upper layers for the same word (Nguyen and Nguyen, 2021). However, to our knowledge, we are the first to analyse cross-level information flow between the layers by allowing information flow across different words in different layers. For this, we incorporate contextual information from the previous word to the current word in different layers, by adding contextual information obtained from morpheme tagging encoding and morpheme encoding of the previous word to POS and dependency layers of the current word. Similarly, we incorporate POS tagging encoding of the previous word into the dependency layer of the current word. This is shown in Figure 1 with PoSVerticalFlow, MorphTagVerticalFlow, and MorphVerticalFlow. The results show that such cross-level information flow improves the performance of the model especially in upper layers.

4.3 Semantic Parsing

We use the Universal Conceptual Cognitive Annotation (UCCA) (Abend and Rappoport, 2013) framework for semantic annotation, which is a cross-lingual semantic annotation framework. Since there is no Turkish UCCA dataset, the model is trained using a combination of English, German and French datasets (Hershcovich et al., 2017)[7], and the Turkish annotations are obtained in a zero-shot setting and manually revised. We annotated 50 sentences obtained from METU-Sabaci Turkish Treebank that is also publicly available[8].

We adopt an encoder/decoder model that tackles the semantic parsing task in the form of a chart-based constituency parsing (Bölücü and Can, 2021)[9]. Self-attention layers (Vaswani et al., 2017) are used in the encoder where the encoding is fed into an MLP with two fully-connected layers with ReLU activation function, and the CYK (Cocke-Younger-Kasami) algorithm (Chappelier and Rajman, 1998) is used within the decoder that generates the tree with the maximum score using the scores obtained from the encoder. Our Turkish UCCA-based semantic parser performs 81.11% F1 score on labeled evaluation and 90.24% F1 score on unlabeled evaluation in few shot learning.

4.4 Named Entity Recognition (NER)

We use a BiLSTM-CRF model where each word is encoded through a BiLSTM and decoded with a CRF layer to learn the named entities in a given text (Kağan Akkaya and Can, 2021). We feed the BiLSTM with character-level (learned through a character-level BiLSTM), character n-gram-level (fasttext), morpheme-level (morph2vec), and word-level word embeddings (word2vec), as well as orthographic embeddings that are learned either with a CNN or BiLSTM by encoding alphabetic characters similar to that of Aguilar et al. (2017).

[7] https://github.com/UniversalConceptualCognitiveAnnotation

[8] https://github.com/necvabolucu/semantic-dataset

[9] https://github.com/necvabolucu/ucca-parser

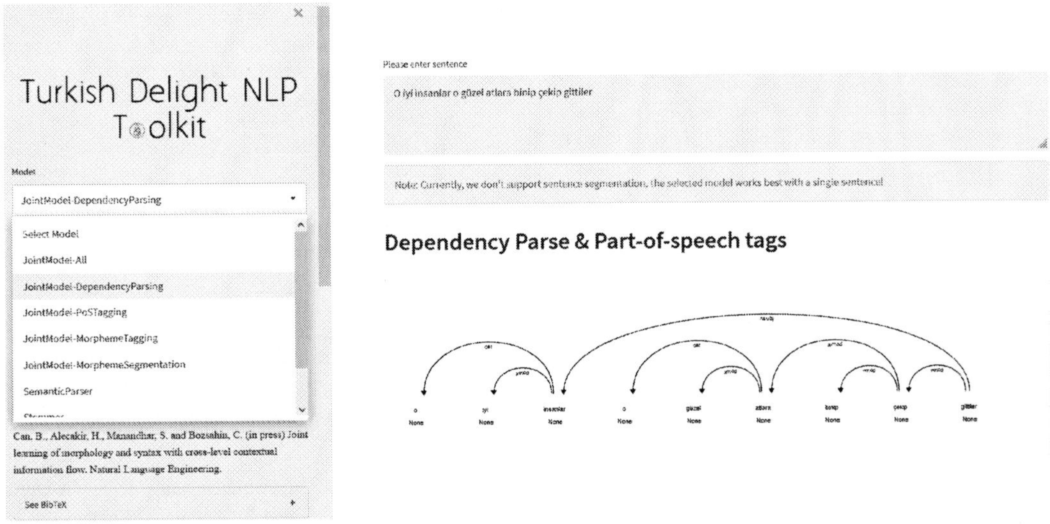

Figure 4: The user interface of the TurkishDelightNLP. The user selects a task from the dropdown menu on the left and populates an input sentence. The output is displayed on the right.

Since the particular target domain for NER in our study is noisy text especially obtained from social media, we use transfer learning to utilise any available information in a formal but possibly larger text to learn the named entities in an informal but usually a smaller text. Therefore, we adopt two CRF layers one of which is trained on the formal text (i.e. Turkish news corpus) and the other one is trained on an informal text (i.e. tweets) (Şeker and Eryiğit, 2017). Training is performed alternately between the two CRF layers which share the same BiLSTM layer. Our named entity recognition model outperforms the current state-of-art model on noisy text by Şeker and Eryiğit (2017) with 67.39% F1 score on DS-1 v4 (Şeker and Eryiğit, 2017). All source code and related material on NER are publicly available[10].

5 Web Interface

TurkishDelightNLP is a Streamlit application that provides a simple user interface for producing predictions for different tasks. We selected Streamlit since it is a low-code web framework that enables researchers to easily create a data-driven app. Streamlit has a relatively simple application programming interface and it is specifically designed for data science applications. In TurkishDelightNLP, in the backend, query and model are cached to avoid repeated calculations of the same input. Docker is used to increase portability and to be deployed in different operating systems and hardware platforms.

Figure 4 shows the user interface. In the left panel, there is a menu for the models. Whenever the user selects a model and populates a sentence, the result is displayed on the right panel.

We also provide a REST API that allows users to access the toolkit with HTTP requests. To be able to use the API, we provide an API token, so a user can access it from clients such as cURL and Postman. Moreover, with the help of Swagger and Redoc documentation, users can see how to consume API endpoints.

6 Conclusion and Future Work

We introduce a new Neural Turkish NLP toolkit that performs different levels of linguistic analysis from morphology to semantics, as well as other NLP applications such as NER. All source codes and relevant datasets are publicly available and we believe that this framework for Turkish NLP will be beneficial for other researchers in the area, and will eventually expedite the Turkish NLP research.

Acknowledgements

The joint model was funded by Scientific and Technological Research Council of Turkey (TUBITAK), project number EEEAG-115E464.

[10] `https://github.com/emrekgn/turkish-ner`

References

Omri Abend and Ari Rappoport. 2013. UCCA: A semantics-based grammatical annotation scheme. In *Proceedings of the 10th International Conference on Computational Semantics (IWCS 2013)–Long Papers*, pages 1–12.

Gustavo Aguilar, Suraj Maharjan, Adrian Pastor López Monroy, and Thamar Solorio. 2017. A multi-task approach for named entity recognition in social media data. In *Proceedings of the 3rd Workshop on Noisy User-generated Text*, pages 148–153.

Ahmet Afşın Akın and Mehmet Dündar Akın. 2007. Zemberek, an open source nlp framework for Turkic languages.

Zahra Azin and Gülşen Eryiğit. 2019. Towards Turkish Abstract Meaning Representation. In *Proceedings of the 57th Annual Meeting of the Association for Computational Linguistics: Student Research Workshop*, pages 43–47, Florence, Italy. Association for Computational Linguistics.

Dzmitry Bahdanau, Kyunghyun Cho, and Yoshua Bengio. 2015. Neural machine translation by jointly learning to align and translate. In *3rd International Conference on Learning Representations, ICLR 2015, San Diego, CA, USA, May 7-9, 2015*.

Piotr Bojanowski, Edouard Grave, Armand Joulin, and Tomas Mikolov. 2017. Enriching Word Vectors with Subword Information. *Transactions of the Association for Computational Linguistics*, 5:135–146.

Necva Bölücü and Burcu Can. 2019. Unsupervised joint PoS tagging and stemming for agglutinative languages. *ACM Transactions on Asian Low-Resource Language Information Processing*, 18(3).

Necva Bölücü and Burcu Can. 2021. A cascaded unsupervised model for PoS tagging. *ACM Transactions on Asian Low-Resource Language Information Processing*, 20(1).

Necva Bölücü and Burcu Can. 2021. Self-attentive constituency parsing for UCCA-based semantic parsing. *CoRR*, 2110(621).

Burcu Can. 2019. Stemming Turkish words with lSTM networks. *Bilişim Teknolojileri Dergisi*, 12:183 – 193.

Burcu Can, Hüseyin Aleçakır, Suresh Manandhar, and Cem Bozşahin. 2022. Joint learning of morphology and syntax with cross-level contextual information flow. *Natural Language Engineering*, page 1–33.

Burcu Can and Suresh Manandhar. 2009. Clustering morphological paradigms using syntactic categories. In *Proceedings of the 10th Cross-Language Evaluation Forum Conference on Multilingual Information Access Evaluation: Text Retrieval Experiments*, CLEF'09, page 641–648. Springer-Verlag.

Burcu Can and Suresh Manandhar. 2012. Probabilistic hierarchical clustering of morphological paradigms. In *Proceedings of the 13th Conference of the European Chapter of the Association for Computational Linguistics*, pages 654–663, Avignon, France. Association for Computational Linguistics.

Burcu Can and Suresh Manandhar. 2018. Tree structured Dirichlet processes for hierarchical morphological segmentation. *Computational Linguistics*, 44(2):349–374.

Kris Cao and Marek Rei. 2016. A joint model for word embedding and word morphology. In *Proceedings of the 1st Workshop on Representation Learning for NLP*, pages 18–26, Berlin, Germany. Association for Computational Linguistics.

J-C Chappelier and Martin Rajman. 1998. A generalized CYK algorithm for parsing stochastic CFG. In *Proceedings of 1st Workshop on Tabulation in Parsing and Deduction (TAPD'98)*, CONF, pages 133–137.

Wanxiang Che, Yijia Liu, Yuxuan Wang, Bo Zheng, and Ting Liu. 2018. Towards better UD parsing: Deep contextualized word embeddings, ensemble, and treebank concatenation. In *Proceedings of the CoNLL 2018 Shared Task: Multilingual Parsing from Raw Text to Universal Dependencies*, pages 55–64. Association for Computational Linguistics.

Çağrı Çöltekin. 2010. A freely available morphological analyzer for Turkish. In *Proceedings of the Seventh International Conference on Language Resources and Evaluation (LREC'10)*, Valletta, Malta. European Language Resources Association (ELRA).

Erenay Dayanık, Ekin Akyürek, and Deniz Yuret. 2018. MorphNet: A sequence-to-sequence model that combines morphological analysis and disambiguation. *CoRR*, abs/1805.07946.

Marie-Catherine de Marneffe, Christopher D. Manning, Joakim Nivre, and Daniel Zeman. 2021. Universal Dependencies. *Computational Linguistics*, 47(2):255–308.

Gözde Merve Demirci, Şeref Recep Keskin, and Gülüstan Doğan. 2019. Sentiment analysis in Turkish with deep learning. In *2019 IEEE International Conference on Big Data (Big Data)*, pages 2215–2221.

Jacob Devlin, Ming-Wei Chang, Kenton Lee, and Kristina Toutanova. 2019. BERT: pre-training of deep bidirectional transformers for language understanding. In *Proceedings of the 2019 Conference of the North American Chapter of the Association for Computational Linguistics: Human Language Technologies, NAACL-HLT 2019, Minneapolis, MN, USA, June 2-7, 2019, Volume 1 (Long and Short Papers)*, pages 4171–4186. Association for Computational Linguistics.

Bekir Dincer and Bahar Karaoğlan. 2003. Stemming in agglutinative languages: A probabilistic stemmer for Turkish. In *Lecture Notes in Computer Science book series*, volume 2869, pages 244–251. Springer.

Bekir Taner Dinçer, Bahar Karaoglan, and Tarik Kisla. 2008. A suffix based part-of-speech tagger for Turkish. *Fifth International Conference on Information Technology: New Generations (itng 2008)*, pages 680–685.

İlknur Durgar El-Kahlout, Ahmet Afşın Akın, and Ertuğrul Yılmaz. 2014. Initial explorations in two-phase Turkish dependency parsing by incorporating constituents. In *Proceedings of the First Joint Workshop on Statistical Parsing of Morphologically Rich Languages and Syntactic Analysis of Non-Canonical Languages*, pages 82–89, Dublin, Ireland. Dublin City University.

Jason M. Eisner. 1996. Three new probabilistic models for dependency parsing: An exploration. In *Proceedings of COLING 1996 Volume 1: The 16th International Conference on Computational Linguistics*, pages 340–345.

Fatih Ertam and Galip Aydin. 2021. Abstractive text summarization using deep learning with a new Turkish summarization benchmark dataset. *Concurrency and Computation: Practice and Experience*.

Gülşen Eryiğit. 2014. ITU Turkish NLP web service. In *Proceedings of the Demonstrations at the 14th Conference of the European Chapter of the Association for Computational Linguistics (EACL)*, Gothenburg, Sweden. Association for Computational Linguistics.

Gülşen Eryiğit, Joakim Nivre, and Kemal Oflazer. 2008. Dependency parsing of Turkish. *Computational Linguistics*, 34:627.

Yasin Eşref and Burcu Can. 2019. Using morpheme-level attention mechanism for Turkish sequence labelling. In *2019 27th Signal Processing and Communications Applications Conference (SIU)*, pages 1–4.

Jeffrey Flanigan, Sam Thomson, Jaime Carbonell, Chris Dyer, and Noah A. Smith. 2014. A discriminative graph-based parser for the Abstract Meaning Representation. In *Proceedings of the 52nd Annual Meeting of the Association for Computational Linguistics (Volume 1: Long Papers)*, pages 1426–1436, Baltimore, Maryland. Association for Computational Linguistics.

Bahar Gezici, Necva Bölücü, Ayça Tarhan, and Burcu Can. 2019. Neural sentiment analysis of user reviews to predict user ratings. In *2019 4th International Conference on Computer Science and Engineering (UBMK)*, pages 629–634.

Onur Güngör, Tunga Güngör, and Suzan üsküarlı. 2019. The effect of morphology in named entity recognition with sequence tagging. *Natural Language Engineering*, 25(1):147–169.

Sinan Göker and Burcu Can. 2018. Neural text normalization for Turkish social media. In *2018 3rd International Conference on Computer Science and Engineering (UBMK)*, pages 161–166.

Asim Güneş and A. Cüneyd Tantuğ. 2018. Turkish named entity recognition with deep learning. In *2018 26th Signal Processing and Communications Applications Conference (SIU)*, pages 1–4.

Coleman Haley. 2020. This is a BERT. Now there are several of them. Can they generalize to novel words? In *Proceedings of the Third BlackboxNLP Workshop on Analyzing and Interpreting Neural Networks for NLP*, pages 333–341, Online. Association for Computational Linguistics.

Daniel Hershcovich, Omri Abend, and Ari Rappoport. 2017. A Transition-Based Directed Acyclic Graph Parser for UCCA. In *Proceedings of the 55th Annual Meeting of the Association for Computational Linguistics (Volume 1: Long Papers)*, pages 1127–1138.

Emre Kağan Akkaya and Burcu Can. 2021. Transfer learning for Turkish named entity recognition on noisy text. *Natural Language Engineering*, 27(1):35–64.

Graham Neubig, Chris Dyer, Yoav Goldberg, Austin Matthews, Waleed Ammar, Antonios Anastasopoulos, Miguel Ballesteros, David Chiang, Daniel Clothiaux, Trevor Cohn, Kevin Duh, Manaal Faruqui, Cynthia Gan, Dan Garrette, Yangfeng Ji, Lingpeng Kong, Adhiguna Kuncoro, Gaurav Kumar, Chaitanya Malaviya, Paul Michel, Yusuke Oda, Matthew Richardson, Naomi Saphra, Swabha Swayamdipta, and Pengcheng Yin. 2017. Dynet: The dynamic neural network toolkit.

Linh The Nguyen and Dat Quoc Nguyen. 2021. Phonlp: A joint multi-task learning model for Vietnamese part-of-speech tagging, named entity recognition and dependency parsing. *CoRR*, abs/2101.01476.

Kemal Oflazer. 1993. Two-level description of Turkish morphology. In *Proceedings of the Sixth Conference on European Chapter of the Association for Computational Linguistics*, EACL '93, page 472, USA. Association for Computational Linguistics.

Kemal Oflazer and Ilker Kuruoz. 1994. Tagging and morphological disambiguation of Turkish text. In *Fourth Conference on Applied Natural Language Processing*, pages 144–149, Stuttgart, Germany. Association for Computational Linguistics.

Kemal Oflazer, Bilge Say, Dilek Zeynep Hakkani-Tür, and Gökhan Tür. 2003a. *Building a Turkish Treebank*, pages 261–277. Springer Netherlands, Dordrecht.

Kemal Oflazer, Bilge Say, Dilek Zeynep, and Gokhan Tur. 2003b. Building a turkish treebank. *Abeillé*.

Anil Ozdemir and Reyyan Yeniterzi. 2020. SU-NLP at SemEval-2020 task 12: Offensive language IdentifiCation in Turkish tweets. In *Proceedings of the*

Fourteenth Workshop on Semantic Evaluation, pages 2171–2176, Barcelona (online). International Committee for Computational Linguistics.

Adnan Ozturel, Tolga Kayadelen, and Isin Demirsahin. 2019. A syntactically expressive morphological analyzer for Turkish. In *Proceedings of the 14th International Conference on Finite-State Methods and Natural Language Processing*, pages 65–75, Dresden, Germany. Association for Computational Linguistics.

Haşim Sak, Tunga Güngör, and Murat Saraçlar. 2008. Turkish language resources: Morphological parser, morphological disambiguator and web corpus. In *Advances in Natural Language Processing*, pages 417–427, Berlin, Heidelberg. Springer Berlin Heidelberg.

Haşim Sak, Tunga Güngör, and Murat Saraçlar. 2009. A stochastic finite-state morphological parser for Turkish. In *Proceedings of the ACL-IJCNLP 2009 Conference Short Papers*, pages 273–276, Suntec, Singapore. Association for Computational Linguistics.

Gökhan Akın Şeker and Gülşen Eryiğit. 2017. Extending a CRF-based named entity recognition model for Turkish well formed text and user generated content 1. *Semantic Web*, 8(5):625–642.

Milan Straka. 2018. UDPipe 2.0 prototype at CoNLL 2018 UD shared task. In *Proceedings of the CoNLL 2018 Shared Task: Multilingual Parsing from Raw Text to Universal Dependencies*, pages 197–207, Brussels, Belgium. Association for Computational Linguistics.

Umut Sulubacak, Memduh Gokirmak, Francis Tyers, Çağrı Çöltekin, Joakim Nivre, and Gülşen Eryiğit. 2016. Universal Dependencies for Turkish. In *Proceedings of COLING 2016, the 26th International Conference on Computational Linguistics: Technical Papers*, pages 3444–3454, Osaka, Japan. The COLING 2016 Organizing Committee.

Umut Sulubacak and G. It. 2018. Implementing universal dependency, morphology, and multiword expression annotation standards for turkish language processing. *Turkish Journal of Electrical Engineering and Computer Sciences*, 26:1662–1672.

Meltem Tokgoz, Fatmanur Turhan, Necva Bolucu, and Burcu Can. 2021. Tuning language representation models for classification of Turkish news. In *2021 International Symposium on Electrical, Electronics and Information Engineering*, ISEEIE 2021, page 402–407, New York, NY, USA. Association for Computing Machinery.

Salih Tuç and Burcu Can. 2020. Self attended stack pointer networks for learning long term dependencies. In *Proceedings of the 17th International Conference on Natural Language Processing*, pages 90–100. NLP Association of India.

Ahmet Üstün, Murathan Kurfalı, and Burcu Can. 2018. Characters or morphemes: How to represent words? In *Proceedings of The Third Workshop on Representation Learning for NLP*, pages 144–153, Melbourne, Australia. Association for Computational Linguistics.

Ashish Vaswani, Noam Shazeer, Niki Parmar, Jakob Uszkoreit, Llion Jones, Aidan N Gomez, Łukasz Kaiser, and Illia Polosukhin. 2017. Attention is all you need. In *Advances in neural information processing systems*, pages 5998–6008.

Sait Can Yücebas and Rabia Tintin. 2017. Gövde-Türk: A Turkish stemming method. *2017 International Conference on Computer Science and Engineering (UBMK)*, pages 343–347.

Harun Resit Zafer. 2015. Resha stemmer. `https://github.com/hrzafer/resha-turkish-stemmer/`. [Online; accessed 6-Feb-2022].

ZS4IE: A toolkit for Zero-Shot Information Extraction with simple Verbalizations

Oscar Sainz[1,*], **Haoling Qiu**[2,*],
Oier Lopez de Lacalle[1], **Eneko Agirre**[1], and **Bonan Min**[2]

[1]HiTZ Basque Center for Language Technologies - Ixa NLP Group
University of the Basque Country (UPV/EHU)
[2]Raytheon BBN Technologies
oscar.sainz@ehu.eus, haoling.qiu@raytheon.com

Abstract

The current workflow for Information Extraction (IE) analysts involves the definition of the entities/relations of interest and a training corpus with annotated examples. In this demonstration we introduce a new workflow where the analyst directly verbalizes the entities/relations, which are then used by a Textual Entailment model to perform zero-shot IE. We present the design and implementation of a toolkit with a user interface, as well as experiments on four IE tasks that show that the system achieves very good performance at zero-shot learning using only 5–15 minutes per type of a user's effort. Our demonstration system is open-sourced at `https://github.com/BBN-E/ZS4IE`. A demonstration video is available at `https://vimeo.com/676138340`.

1 Introduction

Information Extraction (IE) systems are very costly to build. The current **define-then-annotate-and-train** workflow uses supervised machine learning, where the analyst first defines the schema with the entities and relations of interest and then builds a training corpus with annotated examples. Unfortunately, each new domain and schema requires starting from scratch, as there is very little transfer between domains.

We present an alternative **verbalize-while-defining workflow** where the analyst defines the schema interactively in a user interface using natural language verbalizations of the target entity and relation types. Figure 1 shows sample verbalization templates for a simple schema involving an employee relation and a passing away event, as well as a sample output annotated with the schema. The annotation of the EMPLOYEEOF relation requires performing Named Entity Recognition (NER) (Tjong Kim Sang and De Meulder, 2003) and Relation Extraction (RE) (Zhang et al., 2017), while annotating the LIFE.DIE event involves NER, Event Extraction (EE), and Event Argument Extraction (EAE) (Walker et al., 2006). Our toolkit is able to perform those four IE tasks using a single user interface, allowing the analyst to easily model and test the schema without the need to annotate examples.

Our toolkit leans on recent work which has successfully recast several IE tasks as Textual Entailment (TE) tasks (White et al., 2017; Poliak et al., 2018; Levy et al., 2017; Sainz et al., 2021). For instance, Sainz et al. (2021) model relation types between entity pairs using type-specific verbalization templates that describe the relation, generates a verbalization (hypothesis) automatically using those templates and then uses a pre-trained TE model to predict if the premise (the sentence where the pair appears) entails the hypothesis, therefore leading to a prediction of the relation or "no relation".

In this paper we thus present ZS4IE, a toolkit for zero-shot IE. We show that the four mainstream IE tasks mentioned above can be reformulated as TE problems, and that it is possible to achieve strong zero-shot performances leveraging pre-trained TE models and a small amount of templates curated by the user. Our toolkit allows a novice user to curate templates for each new types of entities, relations, events, and event argument roles, and validate their effectiveness online over any example. We also present strong results on widely used datasets with only 5-15 minutes per type of a user's effort.

2 Related Work

Textual Entailment has been shown to be a reasonable proxy for classification tasks like topic or sentiment analysis (Yin et al., 2019; Sainz and Rigau, 2021; Zhong et al., 2021). To reformulate a classification problem as TE, it often starts with defining templates to describe each class label, leading to a natural language text (a "verbalization" of a hypothesis) for each possible label. Inference is

*Denotes equal contribution.

Proceedings of the 2022 Conference of the North American Chapter of the Association for Computational Linguistics: Human Language Technologies: System Demonstrations, pages 27 - 38
July 10-15, 2022 ©2022 Association for Computational Linguistics

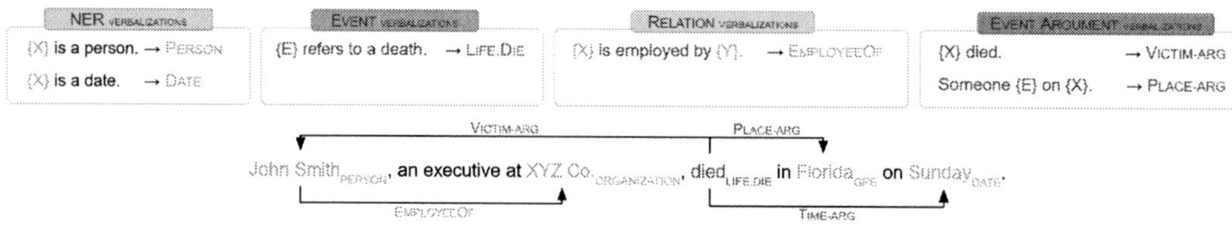

Figure 1: Verbalization templates for a sample schema involving four tasks (from left to right, NER, EE, RE, EAE), with example output (bottom). The schema contains a EMPLOYEEOF relation between PERSON and ORGANIZATION entities and a LIFE.DIE event with three argument types (VICTIM, PLACE and TIME) and PERSON, DATE and GPE entities as fillers. Due to space constraints, at most two verbalizations per task shown.

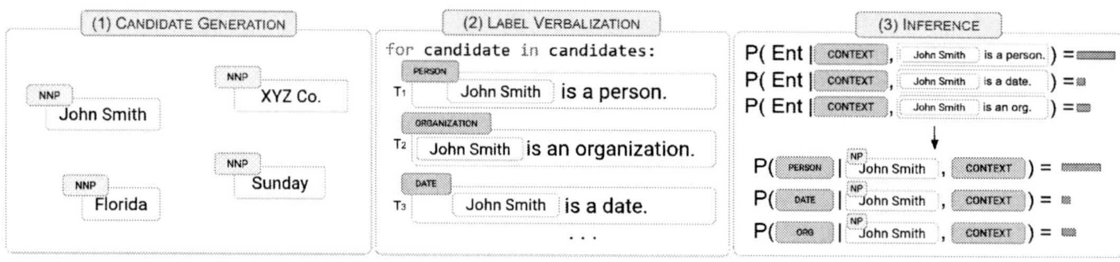

Figure 2: Three steps for entailment-based NER. The steps for the other IE tasks is analogous.

performed by selecting the most probable candidate hypothesis entailing the premise. TE is usually implemented with pre-trained language model fine-tuned on TE datasets, such as MNLI (Williams et al., 2018), SNLI (Bowman et al., 2015), FEVER (Thorne et al., 2018), ANLI (Nie et al., 2020) or XNLI (Conneau et al., 2018). The results on classification have been particularly strong for zero-shot and few-shot learning, with Wang et al. (2021b) hypothesizing that entailment is a true language understanding task, where a model that performs entailment well is likely to succeed on similarly-framed tasks.

Sainz et al. (2021) reformulated relation extraction as a TE task surpassing the state-of-the-art in zero- and few-short learning. A similar approach was previously explored by Obamuyide and Vlachos (2018), using TE models that are not based on pre-trained language models. Similar to TE, (Clark et al., 2019) performs yes/no Question Answering, in which a model is asked about the veracity of some fact given a passage. Lyu et al. (2021) recast the zero-shot event extraction as a TE task, using TE model to check whether a piece of text is about a type of event. Lastly, Sainz et al. (2022) showed that TE allows to leverage the knowledge from other tasks and schemas.

3 IE via Textual Entailment

We first describe how to recast each of the IE tasks (NER, RE, EE, EAE) as TE independently, and leave the workflow between the tasks for the next section. At a high level, the zero-shot TE reformulation consists of three steps: candidate generation, label verbalization and TE inference (Figure 2 illustrates the steps for NER). The first step, candidate generation, identifies text spans (e.g., proper nouns for NER) or span pairs (a pair of entity mentions for relation extraction) in the input sentence as the focus of the prediction. Taking a text span (or span pair) as input, the label verbalization step applies a verbalization template to generate a *hypothesis*, which is a natural language sentence describing the span (or span pair) being an instance of a type of entity, relation, event, or event argument. The verbalization generates hypothesis for each of the target types. Finally, the TE inference step takes the original sentence (the *premise*) and each *hypothesis* as input, and uses a pre-trained TE model to predict if the *premise* entails, contradicts, or is neutral to the *hypothesis*. The type with the verbalization having the highest entailment probability is selected. We next describe each step in detail.

3.1 Candidate Generation

We describe the candidate generation for each of the task below.

Named Entity Recognition (NER): Candidates are extracted using specific patterns of PoS tags as returned by Stanza (Qi et al., 2020). For instance, for the simple example in Figure 1 it suffices to select proper nouns (shown in Figure 2), which are easily extended with other PoS patterns if needed. The toolkit also allows the usage of a constituency parser (Kitaev and Klein, 2018).

Relation Extraction (RE): Each relation requires a pair of entities that satisfy specific type constraints, e.g. the EMPLOYEEOF relation requires a PERSON and an ORGANIZATION. A NER module is used to extract all candidate entities that follow the required entity types according to the target schema. The toolkit uses the TE based NER module, although it also allows usage of a supervised NER system (Qi et al., 2020).

Event (Trigger) Extraction (EE): The main goal of this task is to detect whether the input sentence contains a mention of any of the target event types in the schema, e.g. LIFE.DIE. This task can be formulated as a multi-label text classification task, and in this case the full sentence is the candidate. Alternatively, the textual span that most likely expresses the event (the so-called trigger) can be extracted. In this case, the candidates are generated using specific PoS tags, e.g. verbs like *died* (cf. Figure 1). Our toolkit allows both options.

Event Argument Extraction: Given a sentence containing an event type (as detected by EE above), the goal is to extract entity mentions that are fillers of the target arguments in the schema. For example, the schema in Figure 1 involves three target arguments. Each of the arguments requires specific entity types, e.g. PERSON for the VICTIM argument. The candidates of the required types are extracted using the same NER module as for RE.

3.2 Label Verbalization

For each of the IE tasks, the label verbalization process takes a sentence, a set of candidates and the set of target types (e.g. NER types), and generates a natural language text (the hypothesis) describing the existence of the type in the sentence (the premise) using verbalization templates. Each candidate is a span (or pair of spans) that can belong to a specific type (e.g. being a PERSON in NER). Therefore, the textual verbalization is generated to express each potential type for the span or the pair of spans. For the NER and event extraction tasks, each verbalization expresses one potential entity (or event type) for the target candidate. For the relation and event argument extraction tasks, the verbalization template combines the information from the text spans of the candidate pair and produces a text that expresses a relation (or event argument role). The analyst just needs to write the verbalization templates for each target type, and they are applied to the candidates to generate the hypothesis, as shown in the second step in Figure 2 for NER.

Figure 1 shows sample TE verbalization templates for entity, relation, event, and event argument types corresponding to the 4 IE tasks, as well as sample example as output. The templates for **NER** and **event extraction** (leftmost part of the figure) are applied over a single candidate as extracted in the previous step (the candidate entity or event trigger, respectively). Note that for event extraction it is also possible to produce hypothesis using templates with no slots, e.g. "A person died" for LIFE.DIE. In the case of **relation extraction**, the verbalization templates contain two slots for the two entity spans potentially holding the relation. Finally, templates for **event argument extraction** can be more varied. The figure shows two examples: a template using a single slot for the candidate filler, and a template which, in addition to the filler slot, uses the trigger ("died" in this case, for PLACE).

3.3 Inference

Given a premise (the original sentence) and a hypothesis (an verbalization generated by label verbalization templates), we use a pre-trained TE model to decide whether the hypothesis is entailed by, contradicted with, or is neutral to the premise. In principle, any model trained on an entailment dataset can be used. The inference is mainly determined by three key factors: the TE probabilities for the verbalizations of all templates for all labels, the type-specific input span constraints, and a threshold that decides if the probability is high enough to consider the candidate a positive instance. The type-specific input span constraints are enforced to make sure we don't have candidates that violates the constraints. We return the class label of the hypothesis with highest entailment probability. If none of the hypothesis is higher than the threshold, we return the negative class, that is the class that represents that there is not a valid entity, relation, event, or event argument role type for the input candidate. The threshold for minimal entailment probability is set by default to 0.5.

4 ZS4IE toolkit

ZS4IE comprises a pipeline and a user interface.

4.1 The ZS4IE Pipeline

As described in Section 3.1 and illustrated in Figure 3, there are inter-task dependencies between the four IE tasks (e.g., relation extraction requires that entity mentions have already been tagged in the input sentence). Some task also require external NLP tools for generating candidates. To address these issues and to allow maximal flexibility for the users, we support the following two workflows.

The End-to-End (E2E) Mode: This mode will run the ZS4IE modules in a pipeline: we allow the users to start from raw text, and perform customization (e.g., develop templates for new types of interest) for all four IE tasks. The user has to follow the inter-task dependencies as illustrated in Figure 3: the user must finish NER customization before moving on to relation extraction or the event argument extraction task, because the later two tasks needs NER to generate their input candidates. Similarly, the user must finish customization for the event trigger classification task, before working on the event argument extraction task.

The end-to-end pipeline also runs a customizable pre-processing step including a POS tagger and a constituency parser, before any of the later modules.

The Task Mode: In this mode, the user can choose to work on each of the four IE tasks independently. In order to address the inter-dependencies, the user can choose to run an independent NER module instead, as part of the pre-processing step. The user interface allows the user to tag any spans for entity or event trigger types, before running customization for the more complex tasks such as relation extraction or event argument extraction. This option allows to explore additional entity and event trigger types before actually implementing them

4.2 User Interface (UI)

Figure 4 shows the User Interface. It allows the user to add new types of entities, relations, events and event argument roles, and then develop templates (along with input type constraints for each type). Figure 5 shows the NER extraction results on an user-input sentence. It also displays the likelihood scores produced by the TE model of those

Figure 3: An illustration of the dependencies between the four IE tasks.

templates that are above the threshold, to allow the user to validate templates.

To show why it extracts each entity, it displays a ranked list of likely entity types, the template that led to that type, along with the entailment probability produced by the pre-trained TE model. The user can click on "+" and "-" sign next to each extraction to label its correctness. Our system will track the total number of extractions and and accuracy for each task, each type and each template, to allow the user to quickly validate the effectiveness of the templates and to spot any low-precision template.

Supplying Input Text: The user can supply a text snippet, one at a time, to test writing templates. As described in Section 4.1, when using the task mode, the user can label spans in the input text for the more complex relation extraction and event argument extraction tasks, so that the text already has the right entity or event trigger spans and types to begin with.

Develop Templates for New Types: The user can add new types of entities, relations, events, and event argument role. For each type, the user can create templates along with the input span type constraints, and then run inference interactively on the input text, to see whether these templates

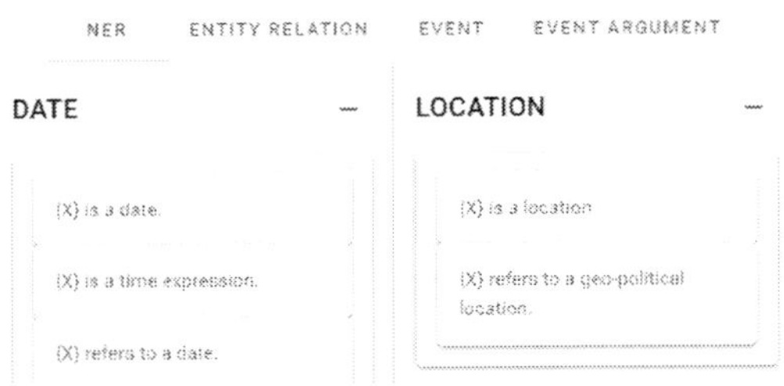

Figure 4: The UI for curating templates for types of interests for NER, relation extraction, event extraction and event argument extraction tasks. The NER tab is partially shown with two types.

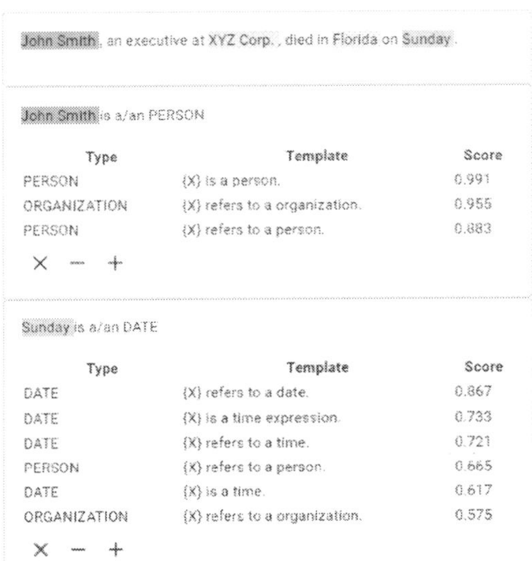

Figure 5: The UI for displaying NER extraction results on an user-input sentence. We show the extractions and the likelihood scores of the templates above the threshold (e.g. $\mathcal{T} = 0.5$).

can be used for extract the instances. The user can label the correctness of the extracted instances, resulting a small development dataset (the *dev* set) to help measuring the precision and relative recall for each template, and to tune the threshold for the TE inference.

Display Metrics: The UI displays the accuracy and yield for each template and each type in real-time, to allow the user to monitor the progress and make adjustments on the fly.

More screenshots and details of our UI are describe in Appendix A.

5 Experiments

We evaluated our system using publicly available datasets. We use CoNLL 2003 (Tjong Kim Sang and De Meulder, 2003) for NER evaluation, TACRED (Zhang et al., 2017) for RE, and ACE for EE and EAE (Walker et al., 2006). We evaluate each task independently (not as a pipeline) to make as comparable as possible to existing zero-shot systems. In order to apply our toolkit we made some adaptations as follows: We consider only proper nouns as candidates for NER, and we ignore the MISC label because it is not properly defined in the task [1]. We evaluate EE as event classification, where the task is to output the events mentioned in the sentence without extracting the trigger words, as we found that deciding which is the trigger word is in many cases an arbitrary decision [2]. In the case of RE we used the templates from (Sainz et al., 2021), which are publicly available. We will release the templates used on the experiments as additional material along with the paper. The analysts spent between 5-15 minutes per type, depending on the task, with NER and EE being the fastest.

Table 1 shows the zero-shot results for NER, RE, EE, and EAE tasks. We report the results of three entailment models: RoBERTa (Liu et al., 2019) trained on MNLI, RoBERTa* trained on MNLI, SNLI, FEVER and ANLI; and DeBERTa (He et al., 2021) trained on MNLI. The main results (top three rows) use the default threshold ($\mathcal{T} = 0.5$), we selected the $\mathcal{T}$ blindly, without checking any development result.

The results show strong zero-shot performance. Note that there is no best entailment model, suggesting that there still exists margin for improvement. However, we see that RoBERTa* performs relatively well in all scenarios except EE (see Section 6 for further discussion).

The table also shows in the middle three rows the results where we optimize the threshold on development. The results improve in most of the cases, and allow comparison to other zero-shot systems which sometimes optimize a threshold in development data.

Furthermore, we compare our system with zero-shot task specific approaches from other authors when available. For RE, Wang et al. (2021a) propose a text-to-triple translation method that given a text and a set of entities returns the existing relations. For EE, Lyu et al. (2021) propose, similar

[1] More specifically, we re-labeled the MISC instances to O label.

[2] Note that EAE can be addressed without an explicit mention of the trigger since we used templates that do not require the trigger

Model	NER			RE			EE			EAE			AVG
	Pre	Rec	F1	Prec	Rec	F1	Prec	Rec	F1	Prec	Rec	F1	F1
RoBERTa	53.3	54.5	53.9	32.8	75.5	45.7	**23.8**	**63.0**	**34.5**	20.5	60.9	30.7	46.7
RoBERTa*	**73.5**	**76.3**	**74.9**	36.8	76.7	49.8	23.5	60.8	33.9	**30.1**	**63.2**	**40.8**	**49.0**
DeBERTa	58.0	50.2	53.8	**40.3**	**77.7**	**53.0**	12.9	60.3	21.2	20.0	31.9	24.6	45.1
RoBERTa (+ $\mathcal{T}$ opt)	49.3	61.8	↑ 54.9	56.1	55.8	↑ 55.9	32.0	52.9	↑ 39.9	25.8	40.1	↑ 31.4	↑ 50.9
RoBERTa* (+ $\mathcal{T}$ opt)	71.9	77.8	↓ 74.8	54.2	59.5	↑ 56.8	25.1	58.6	↑ 35.1	31.1	58.3	↓ 40.6	↑ 51.9
DeBERTa (+ $\mathcal{T}$ opt)	56.3	63.1	↑ 59.5	66.3	59.7	↑ 62.8	13.0	55.8	↓ 21.1	28.9	17.5	↓ 21.8	↑ 51.3
Other authors	-	-	-	-	-	49.2	36.2†	69.1†	47.5†	38.2	35.8	37.0	-

Table 1: Results for NER, RE, EE and EAE experiments results. Three top rows for zero-shot systems with default parameters. Middle rows for threshold optimized on development. The best scores among our results obtained with default thresholds are marked in **bold**. The † indicates non-comparable results due to additional SRL preprocessing.

to us, the use of an entailment model, but in their case the input sentence is split in clauses according to the output of a Semantic Role Labelling system. In order to compare their results with ours, we only use the event types, not the trigger information[3]. The results from our system can be seen as an ablation where we do not make use of any SRL preprocessing. For EAE, Liu et al. (2020) perform zero-shot EAE by recasting the task as QA. Some of these approaches also optimize a threshold on development data, although it is not always clear. We show that our toolkit with default threshold obtains excellent results despite being an all-in-one method.

6 Discussion

Towards post-editing on IE. Our internal evaluation suggest that verbalizing-while-defining workflow can have similar impact as post-editing machine translated text, where human translators obtain quality translations with less effort (Toral et al., 2018). The idea of this new framework will bring down the effort required to create larger and higher quality datasets. Current IE system are subject to a predefined schema and are useless to classify new types of entities, relations and events. The use interface of ZS4IE brings to the annotators the opportunity of defining the schema interactively and manually annotating the dataset with the help of the entailment model. In the future we would like to use the manual annotations to fine-tune the TE model, which would further improve the performance, as shown by the excellent few-shot results of Sainz et al. (2021).

Implicit events extraction. During the development of the EE verbalizations we found out that the entailment model is prone to predict implicit events that are implied by other events. For example, an event type of JUSTICE:JAIL implies an event of JUSTICE:CONVICT where as the same time it implies event type of JUSTICE:TRIAL-HEARING. As the entailment models are not specifically trained for a particular IE task (e.g. EE) they are not limited to the extraction of **explicit** mentions of types (e.g. event types) annotated in the dataset. We think that this phenomenon might have penalized the RoBERTa* model on the EE task, as ACE dataset only contains annotations of explicit events. On the contrary, rather than a limitation of our approach, we believe that this is a positive feature that can be exploited by the users.

7 Conclusions

The ZS4IE toolkit allows a novice user to model complex IE schemas, curating simple yet effective templates for a target schema with new types of entities, relations, events, and event arguments. Empirical validation showed that reformulating the IE tasks as an entailment problem is easy and effective, as spending only 5-15 minutes per type allows to achieve very strong zero-shot performance. ZS4IE brings to the users the opportunity of defining the desired schema on the fly. In addition it allows to annotate examples, similar to post editing MT output. Rather than being a finalized toolkit, we envision several exciting directions, such as including further NLP tasks, allowing the user to select custom pre-processing steps for candidate generation and allowing the user to interactively improve the system annotating examples that are used to fine-tune the TE model.

More generally, we would like to extend the inference capability of our models, perhaps acquired from other tasks or schemas (Sainz et al., 2022),

[3]Output kindly provided by the authors.

in a research avenue where entailment and task performance improve in tandem.

Acknowledgements

Oscar is funded by a PhD grant from the Basque Government (PRE_2020_1_0246). This work is based upon work partially supported via the IARPA BETTER Program contract No. 2019-19051600006 (ODNI, IARPA), and by the Basque Government (IXA excellence research group IT1343-19).

References

Samuel R. Bowman, Gabor Angeli, Christopher Potts, and Christopher D. Manning. 2015. A large annotated corpus for learning natural language inference. In *Proceedings of the 2015 Conference on Empirical Methods in Natural Language Processing*, pages 632–642, Lisbon, Portugal. Association for Computational Linguistics.

Christopher Clark, Kenton Lee, Ming-Wei Chang, Tom Kwiatkowski, Michael Collins, and Kristina Toutanova. 2019. BoolQ: Exploring the surprising difficulty of natural yes/no questions. In *Proceedings of the 2019 Conference of the North American Chapter of the Association for Computational Linguistics: Human Language Technologies, Volume 1 (Long and Short Papers)*, pages 2924–2936, Minneapolis, Minnesota. Association for Computational Linguistics.

Alexis Conneau, Ruty Rinott, Guillaume Lample, Adina Williams, Samuel Bowman, Holger Schwenk, and Veselin Stoyanov. 2018. XNLI: Evaluating cross-lingual sentence representations. In *Proceedings of the 2018 Conference on Empirical Methods in Natural Language Processing*, pages 2475–2485, Brussels, Belgium. Association for Computational Linguistics.

Pengcheng He, Xiaodong Liu, Jianfeng Gao, and Weizhu Chen. 2021. Deberta: Decoding-enhanced bert with disentangled attention. In *International Conference on Learning Representations*.

Nikita Kitaev and Dan Klein. 2018. Constituency parsing with a self-attentive encoder. In *Proceedings of the 56th Annual Meeting of the Association for Computational Linguistics (Volume 1: Long Papers)*, pages 2676–2686, Melbourne, Australia. Association for Computational Linguistics.

Omer Levy, Minjoon Seo, Eunsol Choi, and Luke Zettlemoyer. 2017. Zero-shot relation extraction via reading comprehension. In *Proceedings of the 21st Conference on Computational Natural Language Learning (CoNLL 2017)*, pages 333–342, Vancouver, Canada. Association for Computational Linguistics.

Jian Liu, Yubo Chen, Kang Liu, Wei Bi, and Xiaojiang Liu. 2020. Event extraction as machine reading comprehension. In *Proceedings of the 2020 Conference on Empirical Methods in Natural Language Processing (EMNLP)*, pages 1641–1651, Online. Association for Computational Linguistics.

Yinhan Liu, Myle Ott, Naman Goyal, Jingfei Du, Mandar Joshi, Danqi Chen, Omer Levy, Mike Lewis, Luke Zettlemoyer, and Veselin Stoyanov. 2019. Roberta: A robustly optimized bert pretraining approach. *arXiv preprint arXiv:1907.11692*.

Qing Lyu, Hongming Zhang, Elior Sulem, and Dan Roth. 2021. Zero-shot event extraction via transfer learning: Challenges and insights. In *Proceedings of the 59th Annual Meeting of the Association for Computational Linguistics and the 11th International Joint Conference on Natural Language Processing (Volume 2: Short Papers)*, pages 322–332, Online. Association for Computational Linguistics.

Yixin Nie, Adina Williams, Emily Dinan, Mohit Bansal, Jason Weston, and Douwe Kiela. 2020. Adversarial NLI: A new benchmark for natural language understanding. In *Proceedings of the 58th Annual Meeting of the Association for Computational Linguistics*, pages 4885–4901, Online. Association for Computational Linguistics.

Abiola Obamuyide and Andreas Vlachos. 2018. Zero-shot relation classification as textual entailment. In *Proceedings of the First Workshop on Fact Extraction and VERification (FEVER)*, pages 72–78, Brussels, Belgium. Association for Computational Linguistics.

Adam Poliak, Aparajita Haldar, Rachel Rudinger, J. Edward Hu, Ellie Pavlick, Aaron Steven White, and Benjamin Van Durme. 2018. Towards a unified natural language inference framework to evaluate sentence representations. *CoRR*, abs/1804.08207.

Peng Qi, Yuhao Zhang, Yuhui Zhang, Jason Bolton, and Christopher D. Manning. 2020. Stanza: A python natural language processing toolkit for many human languages. In *Proceedings of the 58th Annual Meeting of the Association for Computational Linguistics: System Demonstrations*, pages 101–108, Online. Association for Computational Linguistics.

Oscar Sainz, Itziar Gonzalez-Dios, Oier Lopez de Lacalle, Bonan Min, and Agirre Eneko. 2022. Textual entailment for event argument extraction: Zero- and few-shot with multi-source learning. In *Findings of the Association for Computational Linguistics: NAACL-HLT 2022*, Online and Seattle, Washington. Association for Computational Linguistics.

Oscar Sainz, Oier Lopez de Lacalle, Gorka Labaka, Ander Barrena, and Eneko Agirre. 2021. Label verbalization and entailment for effective zero and few-shot relation extraction. In *Proceedings of the 2021 Conference on Empirical Methods in Natural Language Processing*, pages 1199–1212, Online and Punta Cana, Dominican Republic. Association for Computational Linguistics.

Oscar Sainz and German Rigau. 2021. Ask2Transformers: Zero-shot domain labelling with pretrained language models. In *Proceedings of the 11th Global Wordnet Conference*, pages 44–52, University of South Africa (UNISA). Global Wordnet Association.

James Thorne, Andreas Vlachos, Christos Christodoulopoulos, and Arpit Mittal. 2018. FEVER: a large-scale dataset for fact extraction and VERification. In *Proceedings of the 2018 Conference of the North American Chapter of the Association for Computational Linguistics: Human Language Technologies, Volume 1 (Long Papers)*, pages 809–819, New Orleans, Louisiana. Association for Computational Linguistics.

Erik F. Tjong Kim Sang and Fien De Meulder. 2003. Introduction to the CoNLL-2003 shared task: Language-independent named entity recognition. In *Proceedings of the Seventh Conference on Natural Language Learning at HLT-NAACL 2003*, pages 142–147.

Antonio Toral, Martijn Wieling, and Andy Way. 2018. Post-editing effort of a novel with statistical and neural machine translation. *Frontiers in Digital Humanities*, 5:9.

Christopher Walker, Stephanie Strassel, Julie Medero, and Kazuaki Maeda. 2006. Ace 2005 multilingual training corpus. *Linguistic Data Consortium, Philadelphia*, 57:45.

Chenguang Wang, Xiao Liu, Zui Chen, Haoyun Hong, Jie Tang, and Dawn Song. 2021a. Zero-shot information extraction as a unified text-to-triple translation. In *Proceedings of the 2021 Conference on Empirical Methods in Natural Language Processing*, pages 1225–1238, Online and Punta Cana, Dominican Republic. Association for Computational Linguistics.

Sinong Wang, Han Fang, Madian Khabsa, Hanzi Mao, and Hao Ma. 2021b. Entailment as few-shot learner.

Aaron Steven White, Pushpendre Rastogi, Kevin Duh, and Benjamin Van Durme. 2017. Inference is everything: Recasting semantic resources into a unified evaluation framework. In *Proceedings of the Eighth International Joint Conference on Natural Language Processing (Volume 1: Long Papers)*, pages 996–1005, Taipei, Taiwan. Asian Federation of Natural Language Processing.

Adina Williams, Nikita Nangia, and Samuel Bowman. 2018. A broad-coverage challenge corpus for sentence understanding through inference. In *Proceedings of the 2018 Conference of the North American Chapter of the Association for Computational Linguistics: Human Language Technologies, Volume 1 (Long Papers)*, pages 1112–1122, New Orleans, Louisiana. Association for Computational Linguistics.

Wenpeng Yin, Jamaal Hay, and Dan Roth. 2019. Benchmarking zero-shot text classification: Datasets, evaluation and entailment approach. In *Proceedings of the 2019 Conference on Empirical Methods in Natural Language Processing and the 9th International Joint Conference on Natural Language Processing (EMNLP-IJCNLP)*, pages 3914–3923, Hong Kong, China. Association for Computational Linguistics.

Yuhao Zhang, Victor Zhong, Danqi Chen, Gabor Angeli, and Christopher D. Manning. 2017. Position-aware attention and supervised data improve slot filling. In *Proceedings of the 2017 Conference on Empirical Methods in Natural Language Processing*, pages 35–45, Copenhagen, Denmark. Association for Computational Linguistics.

Ruiqi Zhong, Kristy Lee, Zheng Zhang, and Dan Klein. 2021. Adapting language models for zero-shot learning by meta-tuning on dataset and prompt collections. In *Findings of the Association for Computational Linguistics: EMNLP 2021*, pages 2856–2878, Punta Cana, Dominican Republic. Association for Computational Linguistics.

A User Interface

We present more details on our user interface (UI) in this section. Our system supports all 4 IE tasks into a single integrated interface.

Template development. Figure 6a shows the main template development UI, in which each tab on the top represents one of the entity, relation, event, and event argument tasks. The user switch between tasks by simply clicking on a different tab (the tabs for the other 3 tasks are shown in Figure 6b, 6c, and 6d, respectively).

Take the NER task as an example (Figure 6a), it shows an overview of all entity types along with the templates defined for each type (e.g., "X is a person" for the type PERSON, in which "X" is a placeholder that can be replaced with a noun phrase "New York City"). If the user clicks on the edit button (the pen-shaped button), the pop-up window for adding a new entity type (the right-hand side figure in Figure 6a) shows up. The user can add a template by clicking on "+" sign, and then input the template to the left (the user can repeat this several times to add more templates). The user can remove a template by clicking on "-". The user can also click on the big "+" card to the left to add a new entity type.

Template development for the relation extraction task is similar to NER, except for two differences: first, as shown in Figure 6b (right), we can further add a set of "allowed type" pairs, that are the set of entity pairs each relation is defined over. For example, the "per:date_of_death" relation is only valid between a pair of PERSON and DATE mentions. Our UI allows the user to specify the "LeftEntityType" (left entity type) and the "RightEntityType" (right entity type) for each relation type under "allowed type". These type constraints are show on the top box for each relation card on the left figure in Figure 6b (e.g., "PERSON->DATE" under "per:date_of_death"). Second, a relation involves a pair of entity mentions. Therefore, each pattern has two placeholders, "X" and "Y", which can be replaced with two entity candidates that are likely to participate in the relationship.

Template development for the event extraction task (Figure 6c) is also similar to NER, except that the template may not contain any trigger. For example, "Someone died" is a template for the "Death" event (Figure 6c). This template would allow the TE approach to classify whether an extent (e.g., a sentence) expresses a type of event.

Template development for the event argument extraction task (Figure 6d) is similar to relation extraction, except that the template can include either two placeholders "X" and "Y" in which "X" is an event trigger and "Y" is an event argument candidate filler (an entity), or only one placeholder "Y" which is the event argument candidate filler. The later would require the template to implicitly describes the event type as well (for example, "Someone died in Y" for the LOCATION event argument role in Figure 6d).

Template validation. We developed an interactive workflow to allow the user to quickly develop templates and validate their effectiveness in our TE-based framework. To support this workflow, our UI allows the user to run inference over any free text supplied by the user herself/himself. For simplicity, we omit the UI where we allow the user type in free text. We show the UI that displays the extraction output on the free text, that also allows the user to label the correcness of the extractions. Based on those labeled examples, the UI also automatically calculate a few metrics to help the user to find the effectiveness of the templates curated so far.

Figure 7 shows the UI for displaying NER extraction outputs (left) and automatically calculated metrics (right). Taken the user-supplied sentence "John Smith, an executive at XYZ Corp., died in Florida on Sunday" as input, the UI on the left-hand side shows the extracted named entities. It shows extractions such as "John Smith is a/an PERSON", "Sunday is a/an DATE", and so on. To provide rationale for each extraction, it displays a rank list of possible entity types, the template led to that type, along with the entailment probability produced by the pre-trained TE model. The user can click on "+" and "-" sign next to each extraction to label its correctness. In Figure 7, all extractions are green (labeled by the user as correct) except that "Florida is a/an CITY" is in red (labeled as incorrect by the user). Based on these user-labeled extractions, the system calculated a number of metrics to facilitate template validation: the total number of extracted named entities (shown under "total"), the number of correct and incorrect extractions under "correct" and "incorrect", respectively (the accuracy number is also shown in the parenthesis next to "correct") for the overall task, each type, and each pattern. The right-hand side UI in Figure 7 displays these metrics, and allows the user to sort patterns/types by each of the metric. The user can quickly identify some templates are low-precision (e.g., "X is a location" for the entity type CITY), and can revise them to improve precision.

Figure 8a, 8b, and 8c shows the UI for displaying extraction results for the relation extraction, event extraction, and event argument extraction, respectively. Similar to the NER task. Similarly, our system also includes metric board (the metrics above) for the other 3 IE tasks. To view the metric boards for these tasks, please refer to our demonstration video.

(a) NER

(b) Relation extraction

(c) Event extraction

(d) Event argument extraction

Figure 6: The UI for developing templates for the 4 IE tasks. For each task, we show the overall UI on the left, and the pop-up window for adding a new entity type PERSON on the right.

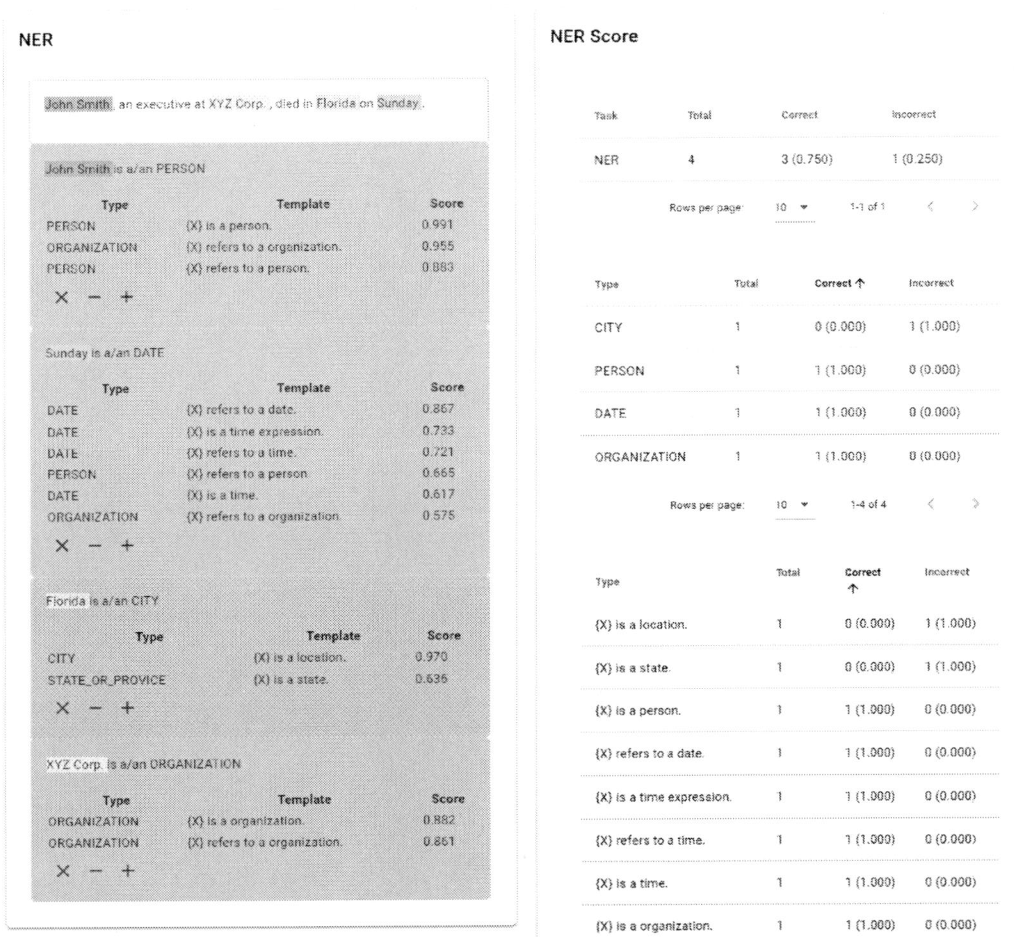

Figure 7: The UI for displaying NER extraction outputs (left) and automatically calculated metrics (right). The left-hand side shows the named entities extracted from an user-input sentence (shown on the top). The user can click on "+" and "-" sign next to each extraction to label its correctness. The right-hand side shows the total number of extracted named entities (total), the number of correct and incorrect extractions (the accuracy number is also shown in the parenthesis next to "correct") for the overall task, each type, and each pattern. These metrics are calculated based on the set of user labels.

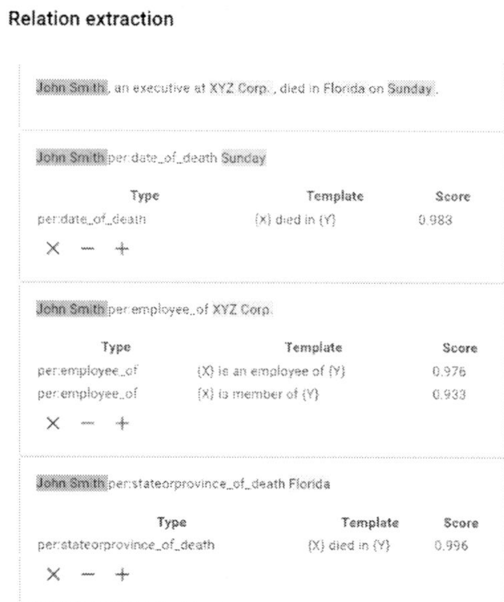

(a) Relation extraction

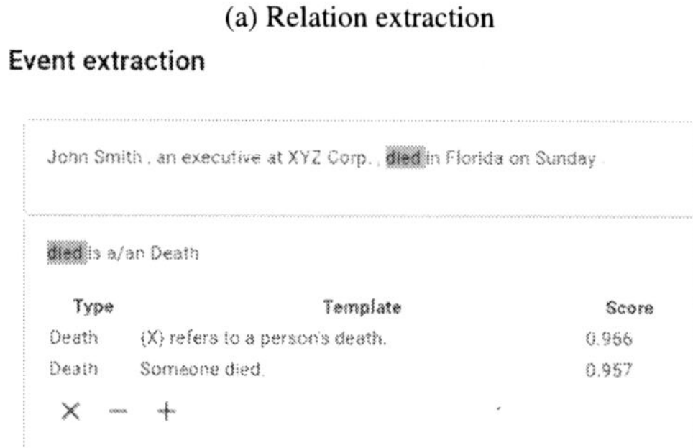

(b) Event extraction

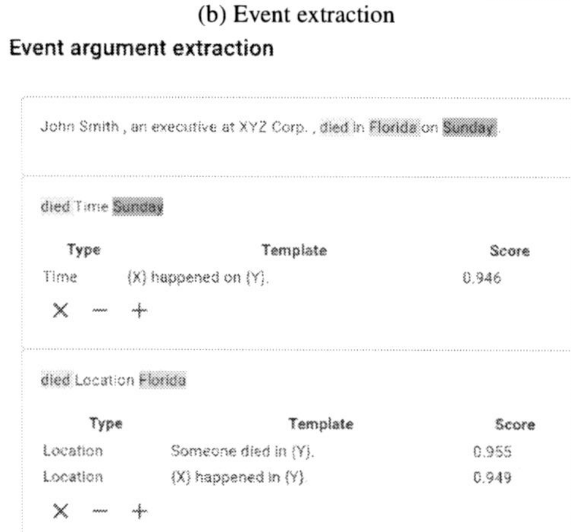

(c) Event argument extraction

Figure 8: The UI for displaying extractions for relation extraction, event extraction, and event argument extraction, respectively. The user an click on the "+" or "-" sign next to each extraction to label the extraction as correct or incorrect.

Flowstorm: Open-Source Platform with Hybrid Dialogue Architecture

Jan Pichl,[12] **Petr Marek,** [12] **Jakub Konrád** [12] **Petr Lorenc** [12]
Onřej Kobza[1] **Tomáš Zajíček** [2] **Jan Šedivý** [32]
[1] Faculty of Electrical Engineering, Czech Technical University, Prague, Czech Republic
[2] PromethistAI, Prague, Czech Republic
[3] CIIRC, Czech Technical University, Prague, Czech Republic
{pichljan,marekp17,konrajak,lorenpe2,kobzaond}@fel.cvut.cz,
{tomas.zajicek,jan.sedivy}@promethist.ai

Abstract

This paper presents a conversational AI platform called Flowstorm. Flowstorm is an open-source SaaS project suitable for creating, running, and analyzing conversational applications. Thanks to the fast and fully automated build process, the dialogues created within the platform can be executed in seconds. Furthermore, we propose a novel dialogue architecture that uses a combination of tree structures with generative models. The tree structures are also used for training NLU models suitable for specific dialogue scenarios. However, the generative models are globally used across applications and extend the functionality of the dialogue trees. Moreover, the platform functionality benefits from out-of-the-box components, such as the one responsible for extracting data from utterances or working with crawled data. Additionally, it can be extended using a custom code directly in the platform. One of the essential features of the platform is the possibility to reuse the created assets across applications. There is a library of prepared assets where each developer can contribute. All of the features are available through a user-friendly visual editor.

1 Introduction

With the increasing popularity of conversational systems in various areas, there is an increasing demand for human-like aspects of the systems. The human-like aspects cover not only the content of the conversation but also the conversational style and tone of voice. Moreover, many conversational constructs are applicable to various situations and are therefore suitable for sharing and reusing. We introduce the Flowstorm platform[1], where conversational designers can easily design an application using shared assets created by a community, create an application on their own, or use a combination of both approaches. The platform does not require any installation as it can be used as a web app. However, advanced developers can use the open-source code[2] to run and modify their own version of the platform.

Our platform works with a novel dialogue architecture we have proposed. It uses a combination of dialogue trees/graphs (scenarios) specific to a domain (or only a part of the domain) and generative models handling the aspects of the conversation that are not domain-specific. The Flowstorm platform targets users with limited coding skills and conversational AI knowledge as well as the experts in the area who can easily extend an out-of-the-box functionality with custom logic. Using the provided tools, documentation[3], and library of the shared assets, one can create a dialogue application in minutes. The Alquist (Konrád et al., 2021) socialbot, which was the first place winner in the Alexa Prize Socialbot Grand Challenge 4 (Hu et al., 2021), was created using the Flowstorm platform, proving the platform to be suitable even for such a complex system.

Flowstorm platform supports English, Czech, German and Spanish languages.

2 Related Work

There are two categories of related software: open-source frameworks or libraries and online platforms. Rasa (Bocklisch et al., 2017) and DeepPavlov (Burtsev et al., 2018) are the most famous representatives of the framework category. They provide the developer with a set of programmatic and declarative interfaces for defining and training natural language understanding (NLU) and dialogue management (DM) models. They also allow creating a pipeline of the components where the developer can create a sequence of models or components for utterance processing. Both libraries require a local installation and, in addition, inte-

[1] https://app.flowstorm.ai

[2] https://gitlab.com/promethistai/flowstorm

[3] https://docs.flowstorm.ai/

Proceedings of the 2022 Conference of the North American Chapter of the Association for Computational Linguistics: Human Language Technologies: System Demonstrations, pages 39 - 45
July 10-15, 2022 ©2022 Association for Computational Linguistics

grating either of them with the rest of the conversational application requires considerable effort.

Alexa Skills Kit (ASK)[4], Google Dialogflow[5], and Voiceflow[6] are representatives of the category of online platforms. ASK and Dialogflow offer an online application for the definition of NLU models (intents and slots/entities). For dialogue management, ASK introduced Alexa Conversations (Acharya et al., 2021) allowing the developer to specify the conversation flow using sample conversations. Dialogflow CX (a part of Dialogflow providing a new way of working with conversational agents) offers a visual view of the conversation agents to see the possible flows of the conversation. Voiceflow uses a visual dialogue editor as an approach to building a conversational application. Dialogue blocks can be connected via transitions to create a flow of blocks where each block represents a specific functionality such as keyword matching or API calls.

The comparison of the key aspects of the described libraries and platforms is shown in Table 1.

	Flowstorm	Rasa	DeepPavlov	Amazon ASK	Google Dialogflow	Voiceflow
SaaS	✓			✓	✓	✓
Open-source	✓	✓	✓			*p*
Visual editor	✓				*p*	*p*
Custom code	✓	✓				
ML-based NLU	✓	✓	✓	✓	✓	✓
Sub-dialogues	✓					
Sharing assets	✓					✓
Built-in NRG	✓					
Analytic tools	✓			✓	✓	✓

Table 1: Comparison of frameworks and online conversational platforms, *p* means partial functionality.

3 Architecture

The Flowstorm platform combines two sets of functions—design and analytics. The design functions allow users to create individual sub-dialogues, train entity models, write shared code, and combine the sub-dialogues into complex conversational applications. Each of the created assets can then be shared with the community. The analytic functions can be used to inspect the applications' traffic and show basic metrics such as session transcripts or visualizations of specific parameters.

The following sections describe a novel conversational system architecture. The novel aspect consists of a combination of manually created sub-dialogues (that can be easily combined into a complex dialogue structure) and neural generative models. First, we describe the blocks essential for creating an application, and then we describe each component used in runtime in detail.

3.1 Conversational Application

Conversational application is a set of dialogue trees we call sub-dialogues. Each sub-dialogue is focused on a small subset of a domain (e.g., in the movie domain, one sub-dialogue can be focused on a user's favorite movie). Each application has at least one sub-dialogue, but typically consists of several sub-dialogues. The sub-dialogue which is triggered when the application is launched is called "main". The other sub-dialogues are triggered when a specific situation occurs during the conversation. It depends on the specific design of the application, and it is described in detail in the following subsection.

Additionally, each application has configurable parameters such as language, Skimmer rules, or voice.

3.2 Sub-dialogue

Sub-dialogue is a graph structure consisting of connected nodes representing the flow of the conversation. The key node types are described in the following list. The basic structure and node types are shown in Figure 1.

Enter – Entry point of the sub-dialogue. Each sub-dialogue must have exactly one Enter.

Speech – Speech node contains one or more natural language responses that are presented to a user. If there are multiple responses, one is randomly selected. It can also contain slots that are eventually filled with variables based on the context. The responses can be customized using Kotlin-based DSL language.

User Input – Point in a conversation where the bot waits for the user utterance. It is typically connected to multiple intent nodes. Each User Input node has its own underlying intent recognition model trained separately. It has as many intent classes as there are intent nodes connected

[4]https://developer.amazon.com/alexa/alexa-skills-kit

[5]https://cloud.google.com/dialogflow

[6]https://www.voiceflow.com/

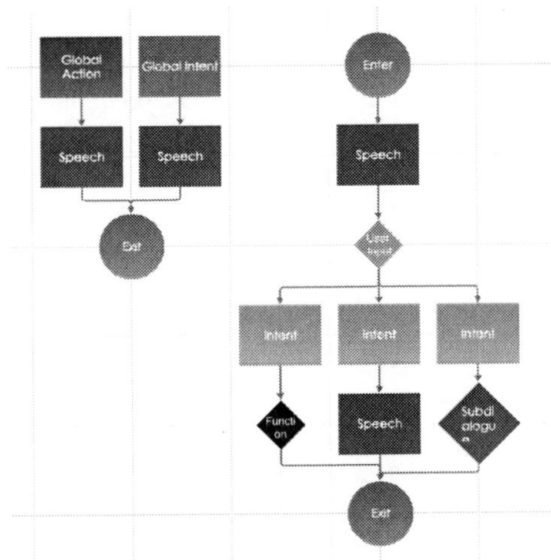

Figure 1: Nodes connected to the sub-dialogue structure. The names of the node types are shown in the corresponding boxes in the picture.

to it. The default behavior can be customized using Kotlin-based DSL language.

(Global) Intent – Intent node contains examples of the users' possible utterances which serve as training data for the intent recognition model. Each intent represents a single class in the intent recognition model. There are two types of intent nodes: contextual Intent and Global Intent. Contextual intents can be recognized only at a specific point of the conversation—when the conversation flow reaches the User Input node they are connected to. Global Intents, however, can be recognized at any point of the conversation.

Function – Function node contains code written in the Kotlin language (JetBrains, 2011). The code can contain arbitrary logic (usually working with attributes — see the attributes subsection). The function returns the transition to the next dialogue node. It is suitable for branching the dialogue based on the attribute values, API results, etc.

(Global) Action – Actions represent specific situations in the conversation flow. There are several predefined situations: *Silence*, *Error* and *Out of domain*. *Silence* action is triggered when no speech is recognized. *Error* action is triggered when the logic written in the Function nodes fails (connection errors or bad design). *Out of domain* action represents the utterance that does not belong to any of the intent classes. This will be described in detail in the following sections.

Sub-dialogue – Sub-dialogue node introduces the ability to reference another sub-dialogue. When the conversation flow reaches this node, it triggers the referenced sub-dialogue, processing its logic from the Enter node to the Exit.

Exit – Exit node represents the end of the sub-dialogue flow. If the sub-dialogue is the "main" dialogue, the session is ended. If it is a lower-level sub-dialogue, the conversation flow jumps to the parent sub-dialogue (i.e., the one where the current sub-dialogue was referenced).

Init code – Each sub-dialogue has a declarative code part that typically serves as a place to define attributes (see below) and methods that can be called from the function nodes. As the code is written in the Kotlin language, the type control is done in the build phase, which lowers runtime errors.

Attributes – There are four scopes of the attributes that can be defined in the Init code. The attribute stores values that can be used to modify the conversation flow, or they can be presented directly as part of a response. Each attribute must have its default value which is used to initialize the attribute based on its scope.

1. *Turn* – the value is reset to default at the beginning of each turn.
2. *Session* – the value is reset to default at the beginning of each session.
3. *User* – the default value is used for each new user. Once the value of a user attribute is set, it is valid for all sessions of the user.
4. *Community* – the default value is used for each community namespace. Once the value of a community attribute is set, it is valid for all users using the same community namespace.

4 System Components

The Flowstorm conversational platform consists of several components crucial for processing the user utterance and driving the dialogue. First, NLU gathers the information required by the DM. Afterward, DM traverses the corresponding sub-dialogue tree structure based on the NLU output.

4.1 Natural Language Understanding

The NLU consists of the main components—entity recognition and intent recognition—that are commonly used in conversational systems. Additionally, the out-of-domain detection enhances the intent recognition, allowing the system to handle a situation that was not expected during dialogue design.

4.1.1 Entity Recognition

There are two modules used for Entity Recognition. Regex-based tool Duckling[7] and a sequence labeling neural network. The neural network uses the Bi-LSTM-CRF architecture (Huang et al., 2015). The architecture is simple enough to provide reasonable response time when run on CPU. Duckling is used to recognize such entities that have a specific structure and can be easily described using regular expressions (date, time, numbers, URLs, amount of money, etc.). Additionally, it parses (not only) the date and time values from natural language representation into a structured format. We enhanced the Duckling component with rules for numbers and time values in the Czech language.

During the process of dialogue creation, one can define custom entity types that can be recognized in the conversation. The entities are defined using example sentences where they can occur, e.g. `My favorite movie is [Matrix]{movie}`, meaning the word `Matrix` is an entity with type `movie`. These examples are used as training data for the sequence labeling model.

4.1.2 Entity Masking

The recognized entities are masked out in the user utterance prior to the intent recognition phase. This step allows the intent recognition model to focus only on the types of entities rather than the actual values. The intent recognition module receives, for example, the sentence `My favorite movie is {movie}` instead of `My favorite movie is Matrix`. Only the entity types included in the intent examples (in the intent nodes) are masked out.

4.1.3 Intent Recognition

A key part of each sub-dialogue are the intent nodes. Each sub-dialogue may contain multiple global intents and multiple user input nodes with various numbers of local intents connected to it. Let the $\mathcal{G} = (g_1, \ldots, g_n)$ be a set of global intents of the sub-dialogue S and let the $\mathcal{U} = (u_1, \ldots, u_m)$ be the set of User Input nodes where each node u_i has its own set of local intents $\mathcal{L}_i = (l_1, \ldots, l_{k_i})$. There is one model trained for each $u_i \in \mathcal{U}$ that classifies the user utterance into $|\mathcal{L}_i|$ classes. Additionally, there is one extra model trained for global intents which has $|\mathcal{G}|$ classes.

[7]https://github.com/facebook/duckling

When the conversation flow reaches the User Input node, the system starts listening to the user (or waits for a text input). Then the actual intent recognition process consists of two steps:

First, the user utterance is embedded using the Universal Sentence Encoder (Cer et al., 2018) and the embedding is compared with the training examples from both global and local intent classes. This step only decides whether the final intent will be selected from local intents, global intents or whether the utterance is out of domain given the context of the current User Input node (see Subsection *Out of Domain Detection* and Figure 2). Note that not only global intents from the current sub-dialogue are considered but also the global intents from all parent sub-dialogues which are on the path from the current sub-dialogue to the main dialogue.

Second, the corresponding model (either global intent model or a model corresponding to the current User Input node) is selected. This model classifies the utterance into the final class.

The intent recognition experiments and a comparison with other NLU tools is described in the paper by Lorenc et al. (2021).

4.1.4 Out of Domain Detection

During each dialogue turn, the utterance is classified into one of the intent classes. However, the utterance does not have to correspond to either of the classes. We call such utterances out of domain (OOD). Whether the utterance is OOD or not depends purely on the sample utterances in the global intents and the corresponding local intent classes given in the current User Input node. The OOD is triggered using the confidences of the corresponding intent classes and the empirically estimated threshold. When the OOD is recognized, the dialogue flow continues with a local OOD action (if connected to the current User input node) or with a global OOD action.

4.2 Skimmer

The Skimmer is a component that extracts relevant data from the user utterance and stores it for later usage. It is done on a turn basis regardless of the dialogue context. An example of such information is: the information about the user having a brother mentioned "by the way" in the conversation (e.g., in a movie-related conversation, the user may mention *"I went to the cinema with my brother yesterday."*). The component skims through each utterance and saves the values into the attributes.

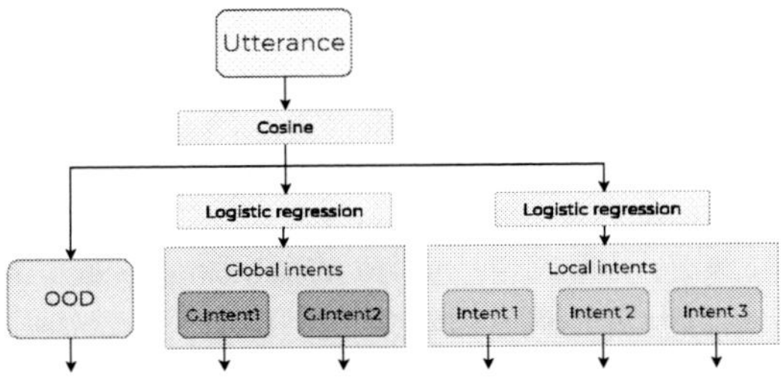

Figure 2: Classification algorithm for intent and OOD detection. The utterance is first classified by a cosine similarity into a class of local intents or a class of global intents. Next, the corresponding logistic regression makes the final intent classification. Additionally, cosine similarity can predict the OOD class if the similarity score falls below the threshold.

The dialogue creator can then use the information in the conversation. The Skimmer is defined by a set of rules containing the following attributes:

- *Regular expression* - a set of patterns which must be contained in the utterance.
- *Attribute name* - the name of the attribute where the value will be stored.
- *Value* - the value stored in the attribute, typically *true*, *false*, or a matched group of the regular expression.

This component is inspired by a similar functionality used in the Alquist socialbot (Konrád et al., 2021).

4.3 Dialogue Management

Dialogue management (DM) of a conversational application created in Flowstorm is divided into two stages: *Sub-dialogue DM* and *Dialogue selection*. The former stage operates on the graph structure of the corresponding sub-dialogue. The DM simply follows the directed edges beginning in the *Start* node. There are two types of nodes that may have multiple outgoing edges: User Inputs and Functions. In the User Input nodes, the next edge is selected using Intent Recognition results, i.e., the edge leading to the most probable intent or global intent is selected. The Function nodes contain code that returns one of the connected edges.

4.3.1 Dialogue selector

The dialogue selector stage is triggered whenever a previous sub-dialogue is ended, and there is not a direct transition to a different one. The overall goal is to select a sub-dialogue that is related to the context of the conversation. The most suitable sub-dialogue is selected from a list of eligible sub-dialogues, which is defined by the developer who creates the dialogue application. Each sub-dialogue has several properties that are considered during the process of the dialogue selection.

- *Label* – one or more labels can be assigned to each sub-dialogue.
- *Entity* – a sub-dialogue can use the information about an entity and work with the entity attributes. E.g., a sub-dialogue works with the information about a person, including the information about their birth date, occupation, etc. In that case, the sub-dialogue is tagged with the entity type Person.
- *Starting conditions* is a custom logic that tells whether the corresponding sub-dialogue can be selected given the current context. E.g., in the case of the sub-dialogue discussing the user's favorite movie, it needs to check whether the information about the favorite movie is already stored. Additionally, most of the sub-dialogue can be triggered only once per session. Hence, the starting condition typically checks that as well.

The intuition behind the dialogue selector is to choose a dialogue whose starting condition is met, and its label and entity sets have the biggest overlap with the label and entity sets currently being discussed in the session. Formally, let $\mathcal{D}$ be a set of eligible sub-dialogues, S be the current session. $\text{label}(d, S)$ returns the overlapping labels between the dialogue d and session S, and, analogically, $\text{entity}(d, S)$ returns overlapping entities, and C is a set of starting conditions. Then the dialogue selector selects a sub-dialogue as follows:

$$\arg\max_{d \in \mathcal{D}} |\,\text{label}(d, S) \cup \text{entity}(d, S)| \\ s.t.\ \ \forall\, \text{cond}_i \in C : \text{cond}_i(d, S)$$

4.4 Neural Response Generation

All the principles described in the previous sections are suitable for creating high-quality content for various scenarios with maximum control over the conversation flow. A natural language conversation can, however, easily deviate from these scenarios. The Flowstorm platform comes with a novel approach using a combination of manually created content and generated content for this type of situation. During the dialogue creation process, the user may plug the generated response into any part of the sub-dialogue.

The platform currently uses a GPT-2-based (Radford et al., 2019) architecture for generating responses. The model takes a sequence of user utterances and bot responses as input. Additionally, the input contains the information about the dialogue act of the desired response. Since the model expects only natural language as the input, it is suitable for situations where the next response cannot be determined using only the tree-like dialogue structure.

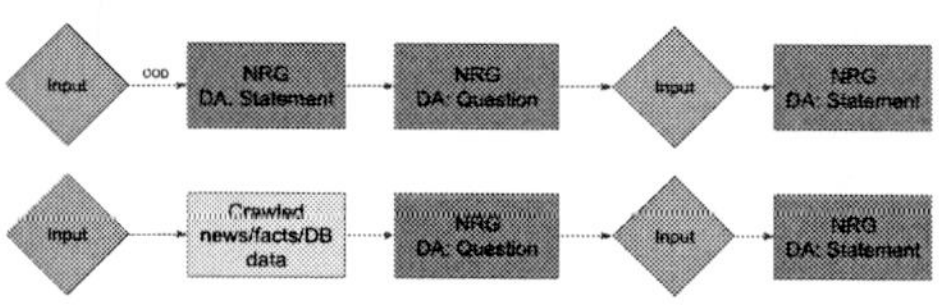

Figure 3: Two basic NRG usage scenarios. The upper part uses NRG response when OOD is detected. NRG generates a statement and a question, and then the system waits for the user's utterance. Afterward, another NRG statement is used, and the flow is returned to the dialogue graph. The lower part illustrates the scenario where the crawled text or information from a DB is used. A single NRG generated question follows it. The next turn starts with the NRG statement, and the flow is returned to the dialogue graph.

A typical use case for a generative model is to use it whenever an out-of-domain utterance is recognized. Since the dialogue designer cannot easily predict all out-of-domain variants and design a proper reaction, the generative approach is a suitable solution as it operates purely with the dialogue history.

In Figure 3, we show two typical use cases of the generative model—generating response after an out-of-domain utterance is detected and asking additional questions based on free text (news article, fun-fact, etc.).

5 Analytics

The set of analytic tools allows developers to inspect the traffic on their conversational applications. There are tools for inspecting session transcripts, community and user attributes, and creating metric visualizations. The *Session transcripts* contains a list of the dialogue turns of each session with all the annotations and log messages. One can easily watch the NLU results, identify a weak part of the corresponding application, inspect the Automatic Speech Recognition (ASR) hypotheses, duration of each turn, and session attributes stored during the conversation. The community and user attributes can be viewed in individual tables to watch the values gathered during conversations.

The metric visualization tool allows creating plots of values defined as a metric. One can easily filter the specific values, time ranges, applications, users and specify the granularity of the visualization. An example visualization is shown in Figure 4.

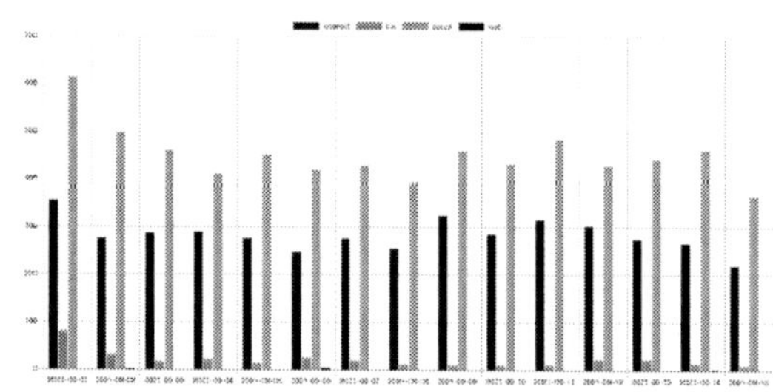

Figure 4: Example metric visualization. The columns show the count of sessions per client (Android, iOS, web and total).

6 Conclusion

The open-source platform Flowstorm allows users to easily create conversational applications with low effort while allowing them to modify each part with custom functionality. Developers can visually design an application and extend it with custom code thanks to an easy-to-use interface. A library of shared assets contains common dialogue structures that can be used in various use cases. A novel hybrid architecture allows the system to handle unexpected utterances and make the conversation more robust. Analytic tools show the conversation transcripts, attributes, and metrics directly in the Flowstorm app. Based on the analytic data, the developer can quickly identify the weak parts of the application and fix them by modifying the dialogue structure or intent examples.

The Flowstorm platform is in active development, and we are primarily focusing on the generative part of the dialogue architecture to make it more suitable for various dialogue situations.

References

Anish Acharya, Suranjit Adhikari, Sanchit Agarwal, Vincent Auvray, Nehal Belgamwar, Arijit Biswas, Shubhra Chandra, Tagyoung Chung, Maryam Fazel-Zarandi, Raefer Gabriel, et al. 2021. Alexa conversations: An extensible data-driven approach for building task-oriented dialogue systems. In *Proceedings of the 2021 Conference of the North American Chapter of the Association for Computational Linguistics: Human Language Technologies: Demonstrations*, pages 125–132, Online. Association for Computational Linguistics.

Tom Bocklisch, Joey Faulkner, Nick Pawlowski, and Alan Nichol. 2017. Rasa: Open source language understanding and dialogue management.

Mikhail Burtsev, Alexander Seliverstov, Rafael Airapetyan, Mikhail Arkhipov, Dilyara Baymurzina, Nickolay Bushkov, Olga Gureenkova, Taras Khakhulin, Yurii Kuratov, Denis Kuznetsov, et al. 2018. Deeppavlov: Open-source library for dialogue systems. In *Proceedings of ACL 2018, System Demonstrations*, pages 122–127.

Daniel Cer, Yinfei Yang, Sheng-yi Kong, Nan Hua, Nicole Limtiaco, Rhomni St John, Noah Constant, Mario Guajardo-Céspedes, Steve Yuan, Chris Tar, et al. 2018. Universal sentence encoder. *arXiv preprint arXiv:1803.11175*.

Shui Hu, Yang Liu, Anna Gottardi, Behnam Hedayatnia, Anju Khatri, Anjali Chadha, Qinlang Chen, Pankaj Rajan, Ali Binici, et al. 2021. Further advances in open domain dialog systems in the fourth alexa prize socialbot grand challenge. In *4th Proceedings of Alexa Prize (Alexa Prize 2021)*.

Zhiheng Huang, Wei Xu, and Kai Yu. 2015. Bidirectional lstm-crf models for sequence tagging. *arXiv preprint arXiv:1508.01991*.

JetBrains. 2011. Kotlin programming language. `https://kotlinlang.org/`. Accessed on 14.09.2021.

Jakub Konrád, Jan Pichl, Petr Marek, Petr Lorenc, Van Duy Ta, Ondřej Kobza, Lenka Hýlová, and Jan Šedivý. 2021. Alquist 4.0: Towards social intelligence using generative models and dialogue personalization. In *4th Proceedings of Alexa Prize (Alexa Prize 2021)*.

Petr Lorenc, Petr Marek, Jan Pichl, Jakub Konrád, and Jan Šedivý. 2021. Benchmark of public intent recognition services. *Language Resources and Evaluation*, pages 1–19.

Alec Radford, Jeff Wu, Rewon Child, David Luan, Dario Amodei, and Ilya Sutskever. 2019. Language models are unsupervised multitask learners.

Contrastive Explanations of Text Classifiers as a Service

Lorenzo Malandri[1,3], **Fabio Mercorio**[1,3], **Mario Mezzanzanica**[1,3], **Navid Nobani**[2], **Andrea Seveso**[2,3]
[1]Dept of Statistics and Quantitative Methods, University of Milano Bicocca, Italy
[2]Dept of Informatics, Systems and Communication, University of Milano Bicocca, Italy
[3]CRISP Research Centre crispresearch.eu, University of Milano Bicocca, Italy

Abstract

The recent growth of black-box machine-learning methods in data analysis has increased the demand for explanation methods and tools to understand their behaviour and assist human-ML model cooperation. In this paper, we demonstrate `ContrXT` , a novel approach that uses natural language explanations to help users to comprehend how a back-box model works. `ContrXT` provides time contrastive (t-contrast) explanations by computing the differences in the classification logic of two different trained models and then reasoning on their symbolic representations through Binary Decision Diagrams. `ContrXT` is publicly available at `ContrXT.ai` as a python pip package.

1 Introduction and Contribution

Consider a text classifier ψ_1, retrained with new data and resulting into ψ_2. The underlying learning function of the newly trained model might lead to outcomes considered as contradictory by the end users when compared with the previous ones, as the system does not explain why the logic is changed. Hence, such a user might wonder *"why do the criteria used by ψ_1 result in class c, but ψ_2 does not classify on c anymore?"*. This is posed as a *T-contrast* question, namely, *"Why does object A have property P at time t_i, but property Q at time t_j?"* (Miller, 2019; Van Bouwel and Weber, 2002).

1.1 Contribution

In this paper we demonstrate `ContrXT` as a service, built on top of the approach we presented in (Malandri et al., 2022). `ContrXT` (Contrastive eXplainer for Text classifier) is a tool that computes model-agnostic global T-contrast explanations from any black box text classifiers. `ContrXT`, as a novelty, (i) encodes the differences in the classification criteria over multiple training phases through symbolic reasoning, and (ii) estimates to what extent the retrained model is congruent with the past. `ContrXT` is available as an off-the-shelf Python tool on Github, a pip package, and as a service through REST-API.[1] We present a system to deliver `ContrXT` as a service, together with detailed insights and metrics. Among them, we introduce an explanation of how - and to what extent - the single classification rules differ through time, along with examples of instances with the the rules used by classifiers highlighted in the text.

To date, there is no work (other than `ContrXT`) that the authors are aware of that computes T-contrast explanation globally, as clarified by the most recent state-of-the-art surveys on XAI for supervised ML (see (Burkart and Huber, 2021; Mueller et al., 2019)).

2 `ContrXT` in a nutshell

`ContrXT` aims at explaining how a classifier changes its predictions through time. Below we describe the five building blocks composing `ContrXT`, as in Fig.1: (A) the two text classifiers, (B) their post-hoc interpretation using global, rule-based surrogate models, (C) the Trace step, (D) the eXplain step and, finally, (E) the generation of the final explanations through indicators and Natural Language Explanations (NLE).

(A) Text classifiers. `ContrXT` takes as input two *text* classifiers $\psi_{1,2}$ on the same target class set C, and the corresponding training datasets $D_{1,2}$.As clarified in (Sebastiani, 2002), classifying $\mathcal{D}_i$ under C consists of $|C|$ independent problems of classifying each $d \in \mathcal{D}_i$ under a class c_i for $i = 1, \ldots, |C|$. Hence, a *classifier* for c_i is a function $\psi : \mathcal{D} \times C \to \mathbb{B}$ approximating an unknown target function $\dot{\psi}$.
Output: Two black-box classifiers on the same class set.

(B) Post-hoc interpretation. Following the study about ML post-hoc explanation methods

[1]http://ContrXT.ai

Proceedings of the 2022 Conference of the North American Chapter of the Association for Computational Linguistics: Human Language Technologies: System Demonstrations, pages 46 - 53
July 10-15, 2022

of (Burkart and Huber, 2021), one of the approaches consists in explaining a black box model globally by approximating it to a suitable interpretable model (i.e., the *surrogate*) solving the following:

$$p_g* = \arg\max_{p_g \in I} \frac{1}{X} \sum_{x \in X} S(p_g(x), \psi(x)) \qquad (1)$$
$$s.t. \Omega(p_g) \leq \Gamma$$

where I represents a set of possible white box models to be chosen as surrogates, and S is the fidelity of the surrogate p_g, that measures how well it fits the predictions of the black box model ψ. In addition to (Burkart and Huber, 2021), `ContrXT` adds $\Omega(p_g) \leq \Gamma$ as a constraint to Eq. 1 to keep the surrogate simple enough to be understandable while maximising the fidelity score. The constraint measures the complexity of the model whilst Γ is a bounding parameter. In the global case, the surrogate model p_g approximates ψ over the whole training set X taken from $\mathcal{D}$ which is representative of the distribution of the predictions of ψ.[2]

Output: Two white-box, rule based surrogates $p_{1,2}$ of $\psi_{1,2}$

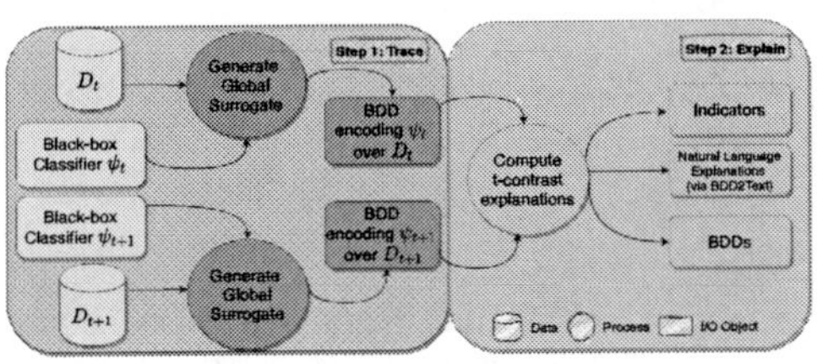

Figure 1: Overview of `ContrXT`, taken from (Malandri et al., 2022)

(C) Trace. This step aims at tracing the logic of the models $p_{1,2}$ while working on a datasets $D_{1,2}$. It generates the classifiers' patterns through a global interpretable predictor (i.e., the surrogate), then it is encoded into the corresponding Binary Decision Diagram (BDD) (Bryant, 1986). A BDD is a rooted, directed acyclic graph with one or two terminal nodes of out-degree zero, labelled 0 or 1. BDDs are usually reduced to canonical form, which means that given an identical ordering of input variables, equivalent Boolean functions will always reduce to the same BDD. Reduced ordered BDDs allow `ContrXT` to (i) compute compact representations of Boolean expressions, (ii) apply efficient algorithms for performing all kinds of logical operations, and (iii) guarantee that for any function $f : \mathbb{B}^n \rightarrow \mathbb{B}$ there is one BDD representing it, testing whether it is true or false in constant time.

Output: two BDDs $b_{1,2}$ representing the logic of $p_{g1,2}$.

[2]in case the surrogate is a decision tree, $\Omega(p_g)$ might be the number of leaf nodes whilst it could be the number of non-zero coefficients in case of a logistic regression

(D) eXplain. This step takes as input the BDDs $b_{1,2}$, that formalise the logic of the surrogates $p_{g1,2}$, and computes the BDDs encoding the *differences* between the two. Step D manipulates the BDDs generated from the Trace step to explain how ψ_1 and ψ_2 differ (i) *quantitatively* by calculating the distance metric defined below (*aka*, Indicators), and (ii) *qualitatively* by generating the BDDs of the added/deleted patterns over multiple datasets D_{t_i}. As this is the key idea of `ContrXT`, we formalise the following.

Definition: T-contrast explanations using BDDs Given $f_1 : \mathbb{B}^n \rightarrow \mathbb{B}$ and $f_2 : \mathbb{B}^m \rightarrow \mathbb{B}$ we define:

$$f_1 \obslash f_2 = \neg f_1 \wedge f_2 \quad (2) \qquad f_1 \oslash f_2 = f_1 \wedge \neg f_2 \quad (3)$$

The goal of the operator $\oslash$ ($\obslash$) is to obtain a boolean formula that is true iff a variables assignment that satisfies (falsifies) f_1 is falsified (satisfied) in f_2 given f_1 (f_2). Let b_1 and b_2 be two BDDs generated from f_1 and f_2 respectively, we synthesise the following BDDs:

$$b_{\obslash}^{b_1,b_2} = b_1 \obslash b_2 \quad (4) \qquad b_{\oslash}^{b_1,b_2} = b_1 \oslash b_2 \quad (5)$$

where $b_{\obslash}$ ($b_{\oslash}$) is the BDD that encodes the reduced ordered classification paths that are falsified (satisfied) by b_1 and satisfied (falsified) by b_2. We also denote as

- $var(b)$ the variables of b;
- $sat(b_{\obslash}^{b_1,b_2})$ all the true (satisfied) paths of $b_{\obslash}^{b_1,b_2}$ removing $var(b_1) \setminus var(b_2)$;
- $sat(b_{\oslash}^{b_1,b_2})$ all the true (satisfied) paths of $b_{\oslash}^{b_1,b_2}$ removing $var(b_2) \setminus var(b_1)$.

Both $b_{\obslash}^{b_1,b_2}$ and $b_{\oslash}^{b_1,b_2}$ encode the differences in the logic used by b_1 and b_2 in terms of feature presence (i.e., classification paths). Indeed, $b_{\obslash}^{b_1,b_2}$ ($b_{\oslash}^{b_1,b_2}$) can be queried to answer a T-contrast question like *"Why did a path on b_1 have a true (false) value, but now it is false (true) in b_2?"*. Clearly, features discarded (added) by b_2 are removed from paths of $b_{\obslash}^{b_1,b_2}$ ($b_{\oslash}^{b_1,b_2}$) as they are used by ψ_1.

Output: Two BDDs $b_{\obslash}^{b_1,b_2}$ and $b_{\oslash}^{b_1,b_2}$ encoding the rules used by b_2 but not by b_1 and vice-versa.

(E) Generation of final explanations: Starting from $b_{\oslash}^{b_1,b_2}$ and $b_{\obslash}^{b_1,b_2}$, the final explanations are provided through a set of *indicators* and *Natural Language Explanations.*

Indicators estimate the differences between the classification paths of the two BDDs through the Add and Del values (see Eq. 6 and 7). To compare *add* and *del* across classes, we compute the *Add_Global* (*Del_Global*) as the number of paths to true in $b_{\oslash}$ ($b_{\obslash}$) over the corresponding maximum among all the $b_{\oslash}^{c}$ ($b_{\obslash}^{c}$) with $c \in C$.

In the case of a multiclass classifier, as for 20newsgroup, `ContrXT` suggests focusing on classes that changed more with respect the indicators distribution.

$$Add(b_{\oslash}^{b_1,b_2}) = \frac{|sat(b_{\oslash}^{b_1,b_2})|}{|sat(b_{\oslash}^{b_1,b_2})| + |sat(b_{\obslash}^{b_1,b_2})|} \tag{6}$$

$$Del(b_{\obslash}^{b_1,b_2}) = \frac{|sat(b_{\obslash}^{b_1,b_2})|}{|sat(b_{\oslash}^{b_1,b_2})| + |sat(b_{\obslash}^{b_1,b_2})|} \tag{7}$$

Natural Language Explanations (NLE) exhibits the added/deleted paths derived from $b_{\oslash}$ and $b_{\obslash}$ to final users through natural language. `ContrXT` uses the last four steps of *six NLG tasks* described by (Gatt and Krahmer, 2018), responsible for *microplanning* and *realisation.* In our case, the structured output of BDDs obviates the necessity of *document planning* which is covered by the first two steps.

The explanation is composed of two main parts, corresponding to Add and Del paths. Content of each part is generated by parsing the BDDs, extracting features, aggregating them using Frequent Itemsets technique (Rajaraman and Ullman, 2011) to reduce the redundancy, inserting the related parts in the predefined sentences (Rosenthal et al., 2016).

2.1 `ContrXT` as a Service

`ContrXT` has been implemented through Python as a pip package, using scikit-learn for generating surrogates and pyEDA package for synthesising BDDs. It takes as input the training data and the predicted labels by the classifier.

The user can specify (i) the coverage of the dataset to be used (default: 100%), otherwise a sampling procedure is used; (ii) to obtain explanations either for the multiclass case (default: one class vs all) or the two-class case (class vs class, by restricting the surrogate generation to those classes); (iii) the Γ value as a measure of complexity of the surrogate.

`ContrXT` can be used either as a pip Python package[3] or as a service through REST API. In the former case, `ContrXT` can be easily installed via `pip install contrxt`. Then, it can be executed as in Code 1. A python notebook ready to use is available on the Google Colab platform.[4]

```
from contrxt.contrxt import ContrXT
exp = ContrXT(
    X_t1, predicted_labels_t1,
    X_t2, predicted_labels_t2,
    save_path='results/',
    hyperparameters_selection=True,
)
exp.run_trace()
exp.run_explain()
exp.explain.BDD2Text()
```

Code 1: Invoke `ContrXT` with few lines of code.

The API is written using Python and the Flask library (Grinberg, 2018) and can be invoked using a few lines code shown in Code 3. Users are required to upload two csv files for time 1 and 2 Each csv is expected to have two columns respectively for corpus (texts to be classified) and predicted (the outcome of the classifier) for which the schema is shown in the following JSON.

```
schema = {
    "type": "csv",
    "columns": {
        "corpus": {"type": "string"},
        "predicted": {"type": "string"},
    },
}
```

Code 2: API schema

A load testing has been performed using locust.io to measure the quality of service of the `ContrXT`'s API, adding a virtual user every 10 seconds, executing the whole `ContrXT` process for the *20newsgroups* dataset for each. Time needed to upload/download datasets and to generate PDF versions of the BDDs are not considered. We followed (Menascé, 2002) to determine the number of users/requests our API web server can tolerate in order to guarantee an acceptable response time (set to 5 minutes) while increasing the throughput, i.e., requests per second.

Our architecture reached a throughput of 2.55 users per second, as seen in Fig. 2. Beyond this value, the API service keeps working, putting additional requests into a queue.

```
import requests, io
from zipfile import ZipFile
```

[3]https://pypi.org/project/contrxt/

[4]https://tinyurl.com/ContrXT-pyn

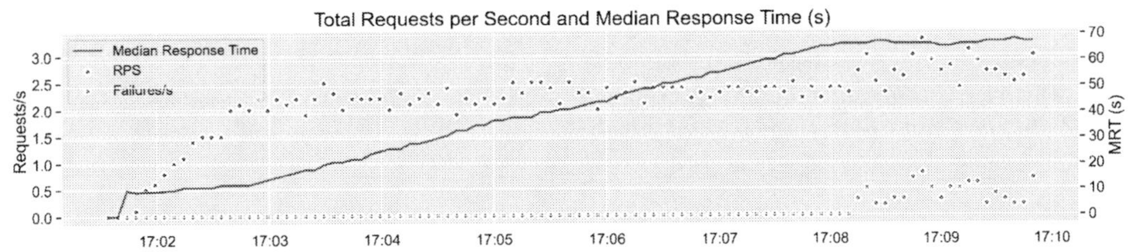

Figure 2: Load testing provided by Locust.io: MRT (median response time, green), Request per Seconds (throughput, green) and the number of failures (requests reached the 5 min timeout, red).

```python
files = {
    'time_1': open(t1_csv_path, 'rb'),
    'time_2': open(t2_csv_path, 'rb')
    }
r = requests.post('[see details on
    github repo]',files=files)
result = ZipFile(io.BytesIO(r.content))
```

Code 3: Complete Python code to call `ContrXT` API

3 Experimental Evaluation

`ContrXT` was evaluated in terms of approximation quality to the input model to be explained (i.e., the fidelity of the surrogate) on 20newsgroups, a well-known benchmark used in (Jin et al., 2016) to build a reproducible text classifier, and in (Ribeiro et al., 2016), to evaluate LIME's effectiveness in providing local explanations.

We ran `ContrXT` over different classifiers, trained using popular classifiers such as linear regression (LR), random forest (RF), support vector machines (SVM), Naive Bayes (NB), Bidirectional Gated Recurrent Unit (bi-GRU) (Cho et al., 2014), and BERT (Devlin et al., 2019) *(bert-base-uncased)* with a sequence classification layer on top. Results are shown in Table 1. We considered and evaluated *all* the global surrogate models surveyed by (Burkart and Huber, 2021), representing the state of the art. Approaches falling outside the goal of `ContrXT` (e.g., SP-LIME (Ribeiro et al., 2016) and k-LIME (Hall et al., 2017) whose outcome is limited to the feature importance values) and papers that did not provide the code were discarded.

To date, `ContrXT` relies on decision trees to build the surrogate, though it can employ any surrogate algorithms.

3.1 Results Comment for 20newsgroup

One might inspect how the classification changes from ψ_1 to ψ_2 for each class, i.e., which are the paths leading to class c at time t_1 (before) that lead to other classes at time t_2 (now) (*added paths*) and those who lead to c at t_2 that were leading to other classes at time t_1 (*deleted paths*). Focusing on the class *atheism* of Fig. 3 the number of deleted paths is higher than the added ones. Fig. 4 reveals that the presence of the word *bill* leads the ψ_2 to assign the label *atheism* whilst the presence of such a feature was not a criterion for ψ_1. Conversely, ψ_1 used the feature *keith* to assign the label, whilst ψ_2 discarded this rule. Actually, both terms refer to the name of the posts' authors.

The example of Fig. 4 sheds light on the goal of `ContrXT`, which is providing to the final user a way to investigate why ψ_2 classified documents to a different class with respect to ψ_1, as well as monitoring future changes. NLE allows the user to discover that -though the accuracy of ψ_1 and ψ_2 is high[5]- the underlying learning functions (i) learned

Table 1: `ContrXT` on 20newgroups (D_{t_1}, D_{t_2} from (Jin et al., 2016)) varying the ML algorithm. • indicates the best surrogate.

ML Algo	**Model F1-w** D_{t_1}	D_{t_2}	**Surrogate Fidelity F1-w** D_{t_1}	D_{t_2}
LR	.88	.83	.76 (±.06)	.78 (±.07)
RF	.78	.74	.77 (±.06)	.79 (±.07)
SVM	.89	.84	.76 (±.06)	.78 (±.06)
NB	.91	.87	.76 (±.06)	.78 (±.06)
bi-GRU	.79	.70	.77 (±.06)	.78 (±.06)
BERT	.84	.72	.78 (±.05) •	.83 (±.06) •

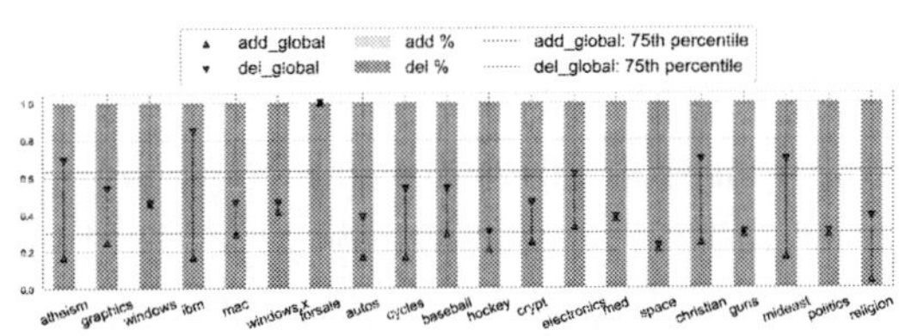

Figure 3: Indicators for the changes in classification paths from t_1 to t_2 for each *20newsgroup* class. On the x-axis, we present the classification classes, and on the y-axis the ADD/DEL indicators

[5]The Spearman correlation test revealed the accuracy is not correlated with the ADD/DEL indicators, confirming they

terms that should have been discarded during the preprocessing, (ii) ψ_2 persists in relying on those terms, which are changed after retraining (using *bill* instead of *keith*), and (iii) having *political_atheist* is no longer enough to classify in the class.

The model now uses the following classification rules for this class:
This class has 4 added classification rules, but only 3 are used to classify the 80% of the items.

- Having **Bill** but not **PoliticalAtheists**, and **Atheists**.
- Having **ManyPeople** but not **PoliticalAtheists**, **Atheists**, and **Bill**.
- Having **Though** but not **PoliticalAtheists**, **Atheists**, **Bill**, and **ManyPeople**.

The model is not using the following classification rules anymore:
This class has 5 deleted classification rules, but only 3 are used to classify the 80% of the items.

- Having **Atheism** but not **PoliticalAtheists**, and **Atheists**.
- Having **Islam** but not **PoliticalAtheists**, **Atheism**, and **Atheists**.
- Having **Keith** but not **PoliticalAtheists**, **Atheism**, **Atheists**, and **Islam**.

The following classification rules are unchanged throughout time:
This class has 1 unchanged classification rule.

- Having **PoliticalAtheists**.

Figure 4: NLE for *alt.atheism* using the BERT model of Tab. 1

Get Rule Examples. The NLE shows the differences between the two models. However, a user might also wish to see example instances in the datasets where these rules apply.

To do so, `ContrXT` provides the *get_rule_examples* function, which requires the user to specify a rule to be applied and the number of examples to show. `ContrXT` applies the rule to D_1 and D_2, specifying the number of document classified by that rule and provides some examples, highlighting in the text the portion in which the rule applies, as in Fig. 5.

Notice this function is also useful to check the consistency of a specific rule, that is, for an *add* rule, its prevalence should be higher in D_1, for a *del* rule the opposite, while for a *still* rule the should be roughly equivalent in both D_1 and D_2.

3.2 Evaluation through Human Subjects

We designed a study to assess if - and to what extent - final users can understand and describe what differs in the classifiers' behaviour by looking at NLE outputs. We recruited 15 participants from *prolific.co* (Palan and Schitter, 2018), an online service that provides participants for research

provide additional insights beyond the quality of the trained models

```
Rule add: {Bill: 1, PoliticalAtheists: 0, Atheists: 0}
Overall, the rule appeared 199 times in time 1.
Out of these, 15 (7.54%) belong to the class Alt.Atheism.
Some example instances:
- [...] Statement Properly Analysed Venue Bill
- [...] Think Relates Anything IveSaid Bill
- [...] Consequences True Truth Irrelevent Bill
- [...] Annoy Us Like Bobby Bill Wish Command Bill [...]
- [...] Untainted Biases Scientist Nonsense Bill One Argue Ob
jectiveValues MoralSense [...]
-------------------------------
Rule add: {Bill: 1, PoliticalAtheists: 0, Atheists: 0}
Overall, the rule appeared 112 times in time 2.
Out of these, 13 (11.61%) belong to the class Alt.Atheism.
Some example instances:
- [...] Statement Properly Analysed Venue Bill Think Misunder
standing Atheism Lack [...]
- [...] Maddi Saves Everything Write Bill
- [...] Comment Especially Time PeopleLike Bill Projector Con
ner Complaining Posting [...]
- [...] Disbelieve Incredulity Admit Fallacy Bill Suppose Rea
sonBelieve Gods Different [...]
- [...] Need Read Friendly Christian Bill Conners Posts JimHa
lat Bearstearns [...]
```

Figure 5: `ContrXT` shows examples in which a rule applies for the class *alt.atheism*.

studies. Participants were asked to look at NLE textual explanations and to select one (or more) statements according to the meaning they catch from NLEs. Results showed that the participants understood the NLE format and answered with an 89% accuracy on average, and an F1-score of 87%. Finally, we computed Krippendorff's alpha coefficient, a statistical measure of the extent of agreement among users. We reached an alpha value of 0.7, which Krippendorff (2004) considers as acceptable to positively assess the subjects consensus.

```
The model now uses the following classification rules for this class:
This class has 6 added classification rules, but only 3 are used to classify
the 80%
of the items.

 - Having Consultant but not Analyst.
 - Having BusinessAnalyst but not Analyst, and Consultant.
 - Having DataScientist, and MachineLearning but not Analyst, Consultant, an
d BusinessAnalyst.

The model is not using the following classification rules anymore:
This class has 6 deleted classification rules, but only 3 are used to classi
fy the
80% of the items.

 - Having Systems but not Analyst.
 - Having TestAnalyst but not Analyst, and Systems.
 - Having System but not Analyst, Systems, and TestAnalyst.

The following classification rules are unchanged throughout time:
This class has 1 unchanged classification rule.

 - Having Analyst.
```

Figure 6: NLE for *2511, Systems Analysts* using the RF model.

```
Rule add: {DataScientist: 1, MachineLearning: 1, Analyst: 0,
Consultant: 0, BusinessAnalyst: 0}
Overall, the rule appeared 0 times in time 1.
-------------------------------
Rule add: {DataScientist: 1, MachineLearning: 1, Analyst: 0,
Consultant: 0, BusinessAnalyst: 0}
Overall, the rule appeared 6 times in time 2.
Out of these, 6 (100.0%) belong to the class 2511.
Some example instances:
- Senior DataScientist Etl Bi Python Java Sql MachineLearning
- DataScientist Sql Hadoop Alteryx MachineLearning
- DataScientist MachineLearning Ai AwsCloud Banking
- DataScientist MachineLearning Ai
- Visual DataScientist MachineLearning University Bradford
```

Figure 7: `ContrXT` shows examples in which a rule applies for the class *2511, Systems Analysts* .

3.3 `ContrXT` in a real-life scenario

In the last years, the problem of extracting knowledge from online job ads (OJA, aka, online job vacancies) in terms of occupations and skills is growing in interest in academic, industrial, and government organisations to monitor and understanding labour market changes (i) timely and (ii) at a very fine-grained geographical level, (iii) catching novelties in terms of novel occupations and skills as soon as they emerge in the real-labour market. This is the goal of labour market intelligence (aka, skill intelligence) which refers to the use and design of AI algorithms and frameworks to analyse labour market data for supporting decision making (see, e.g., (Giabelli et al., 2021a,c; Turrell et al., 2018; Zhang et al., 2019)).

From a statistical perspective, in late 2020 EUROSTAT and Cedefop have joined forces announcing a call for tender (EuroStat, 2020) aimed at establishing results from (CEDEFOP, 2016a,b) fostering AI and Statistics to build up the European Hub of Online Job Ads. In such a scenario, training an ML model would be helpful to support questions such as: *Which occupations will grow in the future and where? What skills will be demanded the most in the next years?* However, once such an ML model has been trained and deployed (see, e.g., (Colombo et al., 2019; Boselli et al., 2018)) it needs to be periodically re-trained as the labour market demand constantly changes through time, mainly due to rise of new emerging occupations and skills (Giabelli et al., 2021a,b). This, in turn, leads policy makers to ask if - and to what extent - the re-trained model is coherent in classifying new job ads with respect to the past criteria.

As an example, let us consider the *systems analysts*, an occupation that changed a lot in the last years driven by technological progresses (Malandri et al., 2021). A policy maker might ask: *"how systems analysts are now classified by the updated model, and how the updated model differs with respect to the previous one?"*

Figure 6 shows the difference in the criteria between the two classifiers for the class *"Systems Analysts"*. The Figure shows that the updated model considers *business analysts* as *Systems Analysts*. Furthermore, the user can easily discover that a novel occupation, i.e., *"data scientist"*, is considered as a system analyst by the updated model. On the other side, Fig. 6 clarifies to the user that the updated model changed its criterion in regard to the term "test analyst", that now does not characterise the class anymore. Being able to catch those differences -class by class- is helpful to end users as it allows understanding to what extent the updated model is coherent with past predictions, as well as its ability to catch the novelty in the domain and terms that might lead the model to misclassification. Furthermore, the Get Rule function provides samples to the user, as shown in Fig. 7.

4 Conclusion, Limitations and Future Work

In this demonstration we presented a system to deliver contrastive explanations of text classifiers as a service. The system is built on top of `ContrXT` (Malandri et al., 2022), a novel model-agnostic tool to globally explain how a black box text classifier change its learning criteria with regard to the past (T-contrast) by manipulating BDDs. Given two classifiers trained on the same target class set, the system we presented provides time contrastive explanations of their behaviour, together with detailed insights and metrics. Among them, we presented the possibility to highlight how and how much the classification rules differ along time. A load test demonstrated that our architecture has a throughput of 2.55 users per second. Beyond this value, the API service puts the additional requests into a queue but keeps working.

To date, `ContrXT` is bounded to explain text classifiers. We are working to extend `ContrXT` to tabular classifiers.

4.1 Demonstration of `ContrXT`

Video to see `ContrXT` in action through a video demonstration at https://tinyurl.com/ContrXT-NAACL.

Google Colab to run `ContrXT` directly on a python notebook, using Google Colab resources at at https://tinyurl.com/ContrXT-pyn

REST-API to embed `ContrXT` into a third-party application. Notice, it is required to ask for credential at https://tinyurl.com/contrxt-request-form

GitHub to download as well as to contribute to this project, at https://ContrXT.ai

Impact Statement and Ethical Considerations

AI-based decision systems interact with humans in many application domains, including sensitive ones like credit-worthiness, education and law enforcement. An unmitigated data-driven decision-making algorithm can systematically make unfair decisions against certain population subgroups with specific attributes (e.g. race or gender) due to the inherited biases encoded in the data. Even a system which has been carefully trained in order to mitigate such effects can change its behaviour over time, due to changes in the underlying data. The opaque nature of machine learning models can hide those unfair behaviours to the end user.

In this context, `ContrXT` might reveal itself extremely useful in tracing and explaining how the model, which was designed to be fair at time 1, changed its behaviour and rules after being re-trained at time 2. This allows one to check whether the model kept fair over time.

An interesting example of application in such sense is the paper *Towards Fairness Through Time (Castelnovo et al., 2021)*, presented at the *2nd Workshop on Bias and Fairness in AI (BIAS)*[6] at ECML-PKDD, which uses `ContrXT` to observe the evolution of a ML model for credit lending over time. Understanding the changing of the gaps between different population subgroups, like gender or race, allows observing whether the mitigation strategies in place are bringing benefits to society, favoring the convergence between individual and group fairness.

References

Roberto Boselli, Mirko Cesarini, Stefania Marrara, Fabio Mercorio, Mario Mezzanzanica, Gabriella Pasi, and Marco Viviani. 2018. Wolmis: a labor market intelligence system for classifying web job vacancies. *Journal of Intelligent Information Systems*, 51(3).

Randal E Bryant. 1986. Graph-based algorithms for boolean function manipulation. *IEEE Transactions on Computers*.

Nadia Burkart and Marco F Huber. 2021. A survey on the explainability of supervised machine learning. *JAIR*, 70:245–317.

Alessandro Castelnovo, Lorenzo Malandri, Fabio Mercorio, Mario Mazzanzanica, and Andrea Cosentini. 2021. Towards fairness through time. *ECML PKDD, CCIS 1524*, page 1–17.

[6]https://sites.google.com/view/bias2021/

CEDEFOP. 2016a. Real-time labour market information on skill requirements: Setting up the eu system for online vacancy analysis. https://goo.gl/5FZS3E.

CEDEFOP. 2016b. Real-time labour market information on skill requirements: Setting up the eu system for online vacancy analysis. https://goo.gl/5FZS3E.

Kyunghyun Cho, Bart Van Merriënboer, Dzmitry Bahdanau, and Yoshua Bengio. 2014. On the properties of neural machine translation: Encoder-decoder approaches. *arXiv preprint arXiv:1409.1259*.

Emilio Colombo, Fabio Mercorio, and Mario Mezzanzanica. 2019. AI meets labor market: exploring the link between automation and skills. *Information Economics and Policy*, 47.

Jacob Devlin, Ming-Wei Chang, Kenton Lee, and Kristina Toutanova. 2019. Bert: Pre-training of deep bidirectional transformers for language understanding. In *NAACL*, pages 4171–4186.

EuroStat. 2020. Towards the european web intelligence hub — european system for collection and analysis of online job advertisement data (wih-oja), available at https://tinyurl.com/y3xqzfhp.

Albert Gatt and Emiel Krahmer. 2018. Survey of the state of the art in natural language generation: Core tasks, applications and evaluation. *JAIR*, 61.

Anna Giabelli, Lorenzo Malandri, Fabio Mercorio, Mario Mezzanzanica, and Andrea Seveso. 2021a. NEO: A system for identifying new emerging occupation from job ads. In *Thirty-Fifth AAAI Conference on Artificial Intelligence, AAAI 2021*, pages 16035–16037. AAAI Press.

Anna Giabelli, Lorenzo Malandri, Fabio Mercorio, Mario Mezzanzanica, and Andrea Seveso. 2021b. Neo: A system for identifying new emerging occupation from job ads. In *AAAI - Demo track*.

Anna Giabelli, Lorenzo Malandri, Fabio Mercorio, Mario Mezzanzanica, and Andrea Seveso. 2021c. Skills2job: A recommender system that encodes job offer embeddings on graph databases. *Appl. Soft Comput.*, 101:107049.

Miguel Grinberg. 2018. *Flask web development: developing web applications with python*. " O'Reilly Media, Inc.".

Patrick Hall, Navdeep Gill, Megan Kurka, and Wen Phan. 2017. Machine learning interpretability with h2o driverless ai. *H2O. ai. URL: http://docs. h2o. ai/driverless-ai/latest-stable/docs/booklets/MLIBooklet. pdf*.

Peng Jin, Yue Zhang, Xingyuan Chen, and Yunqing Xia. 2016. Bag-of-embeddings for text classification. In *IJCAI*, pages 2824–2830.

Klaus Krippendorff. 2004. Reliability in content analysis: Some common misconceptions and recommendations. *Human communication research*, 30(3).

Lorenzo Malandri, Fabio Mercorio, Mario Mezzanzanica, and Navid Nobani. 2021. MEET-LM: A method for embeddings evaluation for taxonomic data in the labour market. *Comput. Ind.*, 124:103341.

Lorenzo Malandri, Fabio Mercorio, Mario Mezzanzanica, Navid Nobani, and Andrea Seveso. 2022. ContrXT: Generating contrastive explanations from any text classifier. *Information Fusion*, 81:103–115.

Daniel A Menascé. 2002. Load testing of web sites. *IEEE internet computing*, 6(4):70–74.

Tim Miller. 2019. Explanation in artificial intelligence: Insights from the social sciences. *Artificial Intelligence*, 267.

Shane T Mueller, Robert R Hoffman, William Clancey, Abigail Emrey, and Gary Klein. 2019. Explanation in human-ai systems: A literature meta-review, synopsis of key ideas and publications, and bibliography for explainable ai. *arXiv preprint arXiv:1902.01876*.

Stefan Palan and Christian Schitter. 2018. Prolific. ac—a subject pool for online experiments. *Journal of Behavioral and Experimental Finance*, 17:22–27.

Anand Rajaraman and Jeffrey David Ullman. 2011. *Mining of massive datasets*. Cambridge University Press.

Marco Tulio Ribeiro, Sameer Singh, and Carlos Guestrin. 2016. Why should i trust you?: Explaining the predictions of any classifier. In *ACM-SIGKDD*.

Stephanie Rosenthal, Sai P Selvaraj, and Manuela M Veloso. 2016. Verbalization: Narration of autonomous robot experience. In *IJCAI*, volume 16, pages 862–868.

Fabrizio Sebastiani. 2002. Machine learning in automated text categorization. *CSUR*, 34(1).

Arthur Turrell, Bradley Speigner, Jjyldy Djumalieva, David Copple, and James Thurgood. 2018. Using job vacancies to understand the effects of labour market mismatch on uk output and productivity.

Jeroen Van Bouwel and Erik Weber. 2002. Remote causes, bad explanations? *JTSB*, 32(4).

Denghui Zhang, Junming Liu, Hengshu Zhu, Yanchi Liu, Lichen Wang, Pengyang Wang, and Hui Xiong. 2019. Job2vec: Job title benchmarking with collective multi-view representation learning. In *CIKM*.

RESIN-11: Schema-guided Event Prediction for 11 Newsworthy Scenarios

Xinya Du[1], Zixuan Zhang[1], Sha Li[1], Ziqi Wang[1], Pengfei Yu[1], Hongwei Wang[1], Tuan Manh Lai[1], Xudong Lin[2], Iris Liu[3], Ben Zhou[4], Haoyang Wen[1], Manling Li[1], Darryl Hannan[5], Jie Lei[5], Hyounghun Kim[5], Rotem Dror[4], Haoyu Wang[4], Michael Regan[3], Qi Zeng[1], Qing Lyu[4], Charles Yu[1], Carl Edwards[1], Xiaomeng Jin[1], Yizhu Jiao[1], Ghazaleh Kazeminejad[3], Zhenhailong Wang[1], Chris Callison-Burch[4], Carl Vondrick[2], Mohit Bansal[5], Dan Roth[4], Jiawei Han[1], Shih-Fu Chang[2], Martha Palmer[3], Heng Ji[1]

[1] University of Illinois Urbana-Champaign [2] Columbia University [3] University of Colorado, Boulder
[4] University of Pennsylvania [5] University of North Carolina at Chapel Hill
{xinyadu2,zixuan11,shal2,hengji}@illinois.edu

Abstract

We introduce RESIN-11, a new schema-guided event extraction and prediction system that can be applied to a large variety of newsworthy scenarios. The framework consists of two parts: (1) an open-domain end-to-end multimedia multilingual information extraction system with weak-supervision and zero-shot learning-based techniques. (2) a schema matching and schema-guided event prediction system based on our curated schema library. We build a demo website[1] based on our dockerized system and schema library publicly available for installation[2]. We also include a video demonstrating the system.[3]

1 Introduction

If the evening news discusses a migration of people due to drought and the infrastructure cannot handle the population influx, what will happen next? While annotated datasets have fueled progress in machine intelligence, the knowledge required for event forecasting is vast and potentially ambiguous. For example, to predict that a rebellion is likely in the future, models need to integrate background events (drought), abstractions (strained infrastructure causes unrest), and event schemas (structure and duration of rebellion). Existing link prediction (Zhang and Chen, 2018; Wang et al., 2018; Lei et al., 2019) or knowledge graph completion methods (Zhang et al., 2019; Goel et al., 2020; Wang et al., 2021a) cannot meet this goal because the event instance graphs extracted from news are often incomplete and noisy. Recent work (Li et al., 2020b, 2021a) proposes to leverage complex event schemas (stereotypical evolution pattern of complex events) for event prediction. However, these methods are often limited to a few scenarios due to the lack of high-quality, open-domain information extraction systems to construct event instance graphs needed for schema induction.

To tackle these challenges, in this paper we use the event schemas discovered at scale to guide the learning of predictive models. We first identify 11 newsworthy scenarios, and construct comprehensive hierarchical schemas through the combination of automatic schema induction and manual curation. Then we develop an open-domain end-to-end multimedia multilingual information extraction system that can extract entities, relations, events, and temporal orders for all of these scenarios, based on a series of weak supervision based methods, including few-shot learning and lifelong learning. Compared with previous event tracking systems (Wen et al., 2021) that conduct graph matching on a linearized sequence, we propose a new schema matching algorithm that directly operates on graphs. We also proposed a event prediction model trained with self-supervision to predict possible missing events to form a coherent story. Our contributions include:

- We induce and curate hierarchical schemas for 11 scenarios, capturing a wide coverage of newsworthy events.
- We extend our multi-lingual multi-media information extraction techniques (Wen et al., 2021) to handle the open-domain extraction setting.
- We develop a new schema matching and prediction algorithm that is capable of recovering missing events and predicting events that will likely to happen in the future.

[1]Demo: `http://18.221.187.153:11000`

[2]Github: `https://github.com/RESIN-KAIROS/RESIN-11`

[3]Video: `https://screencast-o-matic.com/watch/c3nlhnVbeyg`

Proceedings of the 2022 Conference of the North American Chapter of the Association for Computational Linguistics: Human Language Technologies: System Demonstrations, pages 54 - 63
July 10-15, 2022

2 Methodology

Overview Figure 1 illustrates the overall architecture of our framework. It includes three parts: (1) schema library construction (Section 2.1); (2) open-domain multimedia multilingual Information Extraction (IE) system (Section 2.2-2.3) ; (3) schema matching and prediction component (Section 2.4).

We first perform schema induction and curation for 11 identified newsworthy scenarios. Specifically, we use GPT-3 generated results as an outline, enrich the schema with the help of the WikiData ontology and expand the steps for better coverage.

On the IE side, we assume our input consists of multilingual multimedia document clusters about a specific scenario (e.g., disease outbreak). Each document cluster contains documents about a specific complex event scenario (e.g., COVID-19 pandemic). Our textual IE pipeline takes documents and transcribed speech as input and extracts entity, relation and event mentions (Section 2.2). In order to extend IE to open-domain, we have adopted weak supervision and zero-shot transfer learning techniques. Then we perform cross-document cross-lingual entity and event coreference resolution, and link them to WikiData. The extracted events are then ordered by temporal relation extraction. Our visual pipeline extracts events and arguments from visual signals (i.e., images and videos), and link the extracted knowledge elements to our extracted graph using cross-media event coreference resolution (Section 2.3). Finally, our system automatically selects the schema from a schema library that best matches the extracted IE graph and new events are predicted (Section 2.4).

2.1 Schema Induction and Curation

For our schema library creation, we first start with creating schemas with a zero-shot approach utilizing GPT-3. Given a scenario for which we want to create a schema, we generate multiple texts that discuss the topically-related complex events using the OpenAI GPT-3 API[4] with the Davinci-instruct-beta-v3 model. We use three prompting methods to generate documents of diverse genres such as news articles, Wikihow-style documents, and step-by-step event description. One example of such a prompt and the generated output is shown in Figure 2. Then we identify the events mentioned in the texts and link the events to WikiData Qnodes. We use generated documents instead of real documents because we observe that generated documents are generally cleaner and contain a higher percentage of events that can be linked. For instance, comparing the generated text and the crawled news articles for IED attacks, the generated text contains 0.13 events per token and the news articles only contain 0.06 events per token. From there we add arguments to the events, and identify the temporal and hierarchical relations between the events effectively converting each text into a graph structure (Figure 3).

Note that the automatic induced schema is often noisy and has limited coverage. Some of such mistakes come from the GPT3 generation, e.g., in the generated output in Figure 2, it omits how the disease was discovered. Other mistakes root from incorrect prediction of temporal relations, such as the "Kill" → "Come (Attack)" edge in Figure 3.

To improve coverage, human curators further check Wikipedia and news articles on the related topics and add more events. Three other crucial aspects of human curation are (1) entity coreference resolution, (2) temporal ordering and (3) hierarchical structure construction. Entity coreference chains in schemas often involve implicit entities, such as the "area where the sick live" in step 2. This location entity is futher coreferential with the "contaminated areas" entity mentioned later in step 4. The generated output is a list of steps, which can be converted to a linear ordering of events. However, some events can happen concurrently such as the "Educate" event in step 4 and all other events. In addition, some events have strong semantic coherence involving the same set of entities and thus can be grouped together. For example, this chain of "Identify-Quarantine-Disinfect" can be seen as a medical response to one batch of infections. We refer to this as a sub-schema and this medical response sub-schema can be repeated with a different set of patients and medical agents. An example of the human curated schema is shown in Figure 4.

In the curation process, we use a web-based graphical interface (Mishra et al., 2021) to help visualize and assess schemas.

2.2 Open Domain IE from Speech and Text

We first convert speech data into text using the Amazon Transcribe API[5]. When the language is not specified, it is automatically detected from the audio signal. It returns the transcription with start-

[4] `https://openai.com/blog/openai-api/`

[5] `https://aws.amazon.com/transcribe/`

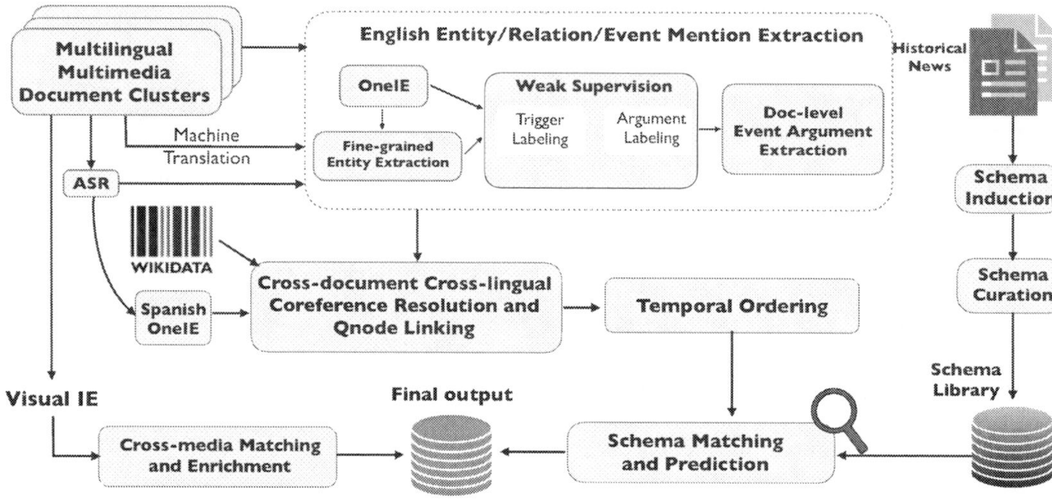

Figure 1: The architecture of RESIN-11 framework: including (1) open-domain multimedia multilingual information extraction; and (2) schema matching and prediction.

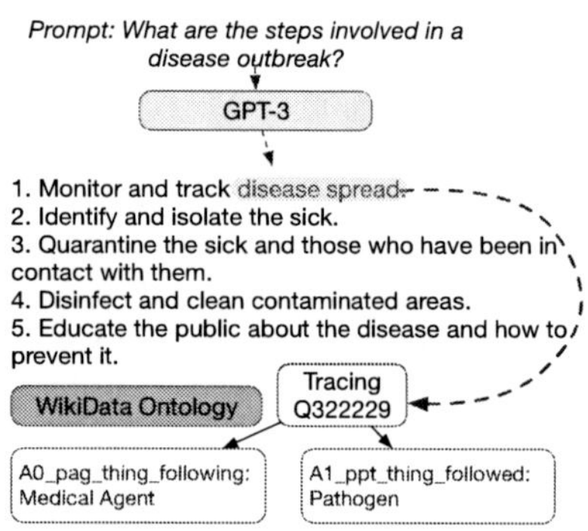

Figure 2: An illustration of the schema curation process. The steps are actual output from GPT-3.

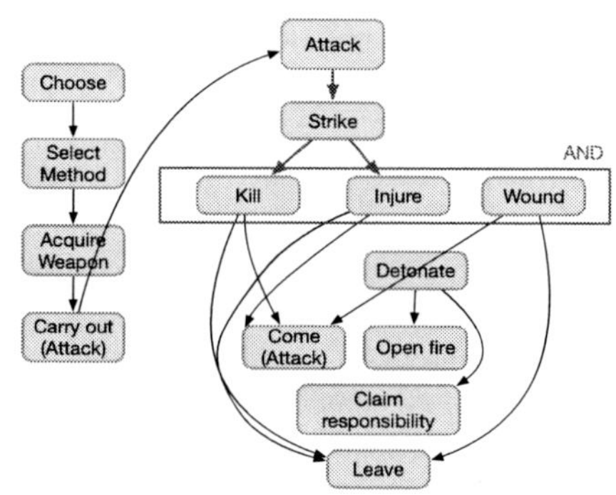

Figure 3: An automatically induced schema for the terrorist attack scenario with model predicted temporal order, hierarchical relations and logical relations. Arguments are omitted for clarity.

ing and ending times for each detected words, as well as potential alternative transcriptions.

To achieve wide coverage of event types from 11 scenarios, our information extraction system consists of 3 components: (1) the supervised joint entity, relation and event extraction model OneIE (Lin et al., 2020); (2) weakly supervised keyword-guided event extraction; and (3) zero-shot generation-based argument extraction (Li et al., 2021b).

OneIE is a joint neural model for sentence-level information extraction. Given a sentence, the goal of this module is to extract an information graph $G = (V, E)$, where V is the node set containing entity mentions and event triggers and E is the edge set containing entity relations and event-argument links. In order to capture the interactions among knowledge elements, we incorporate schema-guided global features when decoding information graphs. After we extract these mentions, we apply a syntactic parser (Honnibal et al., 2020) to extend mention head words to their extents. Based on OneIE relations output, we perform rule-based relation enrichment to obtain fine-grained relation subsubtypes. We collect keywords for various fine-grained types, then we construct rules by checking keywords in Shortest Dependency Paths (SDP) between two relation entities.

To extract emergent event types for which we do not have large-scale annotation, we employ a keyword-based event detection system. Specifically, we select a list of keywords for each new

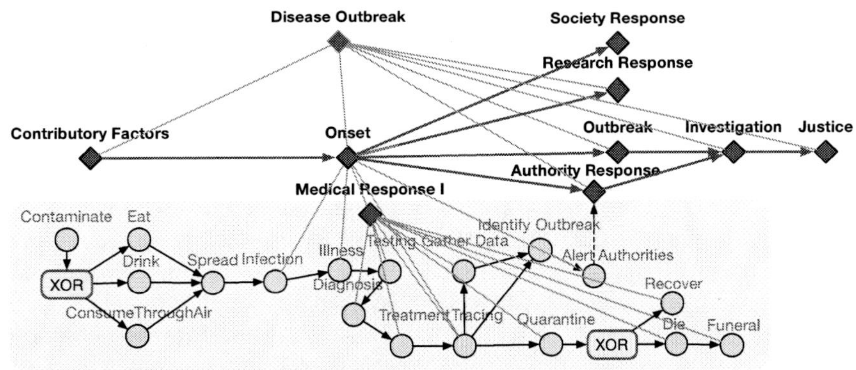

Figure 4: The curated schema for the disease outbreak scenario. Blue diamond shapes represent sub-schemas and yellow circles represent primitive events. Black arrows between primitive events represent temporal order, light blue lines between the primitive events and the sub-schema node represent event-subevent hierarchical relationship. Here we only show the primitive events under the Onset sub-schema.

event type, and search for the occurrences of these keywords in a text corpus. We compute keyword representations by averaging the contextualized representations from BERT (Devlin et al., 2019) of keyword occurrences, and cluster keyword representations for the same event type to get a set of cluster representations for each event type. For event trigger detection, we first compute BERT representations of all the tokens in a sentence, and consider a token as an event trigger if its cosine similarity with some cluster representations of an event type is larger than a threshold. We tuned the threshold using a few example event mentions.

After identifying the event triggers, we further employ a document-level event argument extraction model (Li et al., 2021b) to improve the recall of event argument role labeling. This model formulates the argument extraction problem as conditional text generation. The condition consists of the original document and a blank event template. For example, the template for `Transportation` event type is *arg1 transported arg2 in arg3 from arg4 place to arg5 place*. To apply this model in a zero-shot setting, we create new templates for the emerging event types and use them as input.

For entity linking over Wikidata, we directly use the EPGEL system proposed in Lai et al. (2022). For cross-document cross-lingual coreference resolution, we follow the approach of (Wen et al., 2021). After the coreference resolution/entity linking stage, we conduct temporal ordering for all of the extracted events. First we provide two independent temporal ordering results from two learning-based pairwise event order classification systems (Zhou et al., 2021; Wen and Ji, 2021). To make the prediction consistent and valid over each document cluster, we use a greedy algorithm that selects conflict-free predicted temporal relations to the final instance graph sequentially based on their confidence scores. Similar to Wen et al. (2021), these two results will be used for schema matching and event prediction and only the best prediction will be used in the final output.

2.3 Cross-media Info Grounding and Fusion

Visual event and argument role extraction Our goal is to extract structured visual events and entities. Specifically, given an image or a video segment, the desired output are its event type and the associated argument roles. Due to the expensive cost of event annotation for images and videos, it is not feasible to perform annotation for each new type. Unlike existing systems leveraging supervised training (Chen et al., 2021a), we propose an open-domain framework to enable the visual event extraction for a broader spectrum of event types.

Our proposed system is composed of two complementary models. The first model is a supervised model based on a large-scale image dataset, Situation with Groundings (SWiG) (Pratt et al., 2020). We manually define the mapping that covers 16 event types and use the model pretrained on the SWiG dataset to extract event and argument roles. The second model is an unsupervised model by leveraging large-scale vision-language pretrained model (Li et al., 2022; Radford et al., 2021). We conduct further pretraining on an event-rich corpus (Li et al., 2022) by adding an additional pre-training task of event structure alignment between two modalities. In detail, we extract event structures from captions and utilize them as the supervision for image event extraction. The pretraining corpus comprises multiple scenarios, providing support for the extraction of events for a wide range of scenarios. To process images and videos in a unified manner, we follow Wen et al. (2021) to sample frames at a frame rate of 1 frame per second from videos and process these key-frames as individual images.

Cross-media event coreference resolution To augment the text event graph, we leverage a weakly-supervised coreference resolution model (Chen et al., 2021a) that is trained based on the alignment between video frames and speech texts on a large collection of news videos to predict the relevance between a textual cvent and the extracted visual event. Once the relevance is higher than a threshold, we leverage a rule-based approach to decide whether the visual event mention and a textual event mention are coreferential: (1) Matched event types; (2) No contradiction of entity types for the same argument role in different modalities. This pipeline enables adding provenance of visual-only arguments into the event graph, which provides more comprehensive event understanding.

2.4 Schema Matching and Prediction

After obtaining a large-scale library of schema graphs for various scenarios, our goal is to instantiate the schema graphs with extracted events, and then use it for schema-guided event prediction.

Schema Matching To match the event nodes between the IE graphs and schema graphs, previous work (Wen et al., 2021) first linearizes graphs into event sequences and then conducts event matching using longest common subsequences (LCS). However, such a sequence-based matching algorithm cannot well capture some global dependencies in a graph point of view, and the performance largely depends on the quality of event temporal ordering results. Also, the LCS based matching algorithm can only handle the cases where the events in schema graph and IE graph use an identical ontology (i.e., the same category of event types), which is however not applicable for open-domain settings since the names of events could be diverse and multifarious.

To tackle these problems, we propose a new schema matching algorithm that directly operates on each pair of instance graph I and schema graph S. We formulate schema matching as an integer programming problem, where we can use an assignment matrix $X \in \mathbb{R}^{|I|\times|S|}$ to represent the matching results. To enable matching between events with different names, we compute the pairwise Synsets similarities from WordNet[6] and store it into a node similarity matrix A. For each event e_i in a given instance graph I, we obtain the set of all reachable event nodes $\mathcal{R}_I(i) = \{e \mid P_I(e_i, e) = 1, e \in I\}$, where $P_I(e_i, e)$ denotes whether there exists a path from e_i to e in the instance graph I. Similarly, we can also obtain the reachable event sets $\mathcal{R}_S$ and P_S for the schema graph S. For edge similarity between each pair of events e_i and e_j, instead of strictly judging whether they are temporal neighbors (i.e., whether there exists an event-event temporal link between e_i and e_j) , we only use the reachability as temporal constraints (i.e., whether $e_j \in \mathcal{R}_I(i)$) to mitigate the high dependence on the quality of event temporal ordering results. Specifically, we aim to find the optimal solution X_{opt}

$$X_{opt} = \arg\max_{X} \sum_{i,j} A_{i,j} X_{i,j} - c \cdot \mathcal{Q}(X), \qquad (1)$$

where c is a hyper-parameter and $\mathcal{Q}(X)$ denotes the penalty term for the violation of temporal constraints. The penalty term $\mathcal{Q}(X)$ is defined as the total number of event pairs that violates the temporal constraints.

Schema-guided Event Prediction After schema matching, an instance graph I is mapped to a subgraph of the schema graph, i.e., $I' \subseteq S$. The next step is to determine whether a candidate event node $e \in S \backslash I'$ is a missing node for I'. Specifically, we aim to learn a function $f(e, I') : S \times 2^S \mapsto [0, 1]$, which outputs the probability that event node e is missing for subgraph I'. We consider two factors when designing the function $f(e, I')$: (1) Neighbors of e and I'. We use a graph neural network (GNN) to aggregate neighbor information and learn embedding vectors for nodes in S, then aggregate embeddings of nodes in I' to obtain the embedding of I'. The embeddings of e and I' are concatenated, followed by an MLP to output the predicted probability. (2) Paths. We identify all paths that connect e and each node in I' in the schema graph S, then aggregate the paths together to obtain the bag-of-path feature for the pair of (e, I'). The bag-of-path feature is fed into another MLP to output

[6] https://www.nltk.org/howto/wordnet.html

Scenario	# Episodes	# Events	# Ents	# Rels
Business Change	18	81	24	54
Civil Unrest	6	34	18	24
Disease Outbreak	19	102	27	93
Election	8	35	14	33
International Conflict	17	95	56	50
Kidnapping	9	66	15	56
Mass Shooting	8	37	13	31
Sports Events	4	17	14	19
Terrorist Attacks	8	36	11	26
Disaster/Manmade Disaster	8	38	10	29
Disaster/Natural Disaster	4	23	8	18
IED/General Attack	19	52	40	22
IED/General IED	10	48	18	39
IED/Drone Strikes	10	50	19	43
IED/Backpack IED	10	49	18	40
IED/Roadside IED	10	48	19	39
IED/Car IED	10	50	19	43

Table 1: Statistics of our schema library.

the predicted probability. Finally, the outputs of the above two modules are averaged as the final prediction.

3 Schema and Experiments

The overall statistics of our schema library are presented in Table 1. The performance of each component is shown in Table 2. We evaluate the performance of our full system on a complex event corpus (LDC2022E02), which contains multi-lingual multi-media document clusters. We train our mention extraction component on ACE05 (Walker et al., 2006) and ERE (Song et al., 2015); document-level argument extraction on ACE05 and RAMS (Ebner et al., 2020); coreference component on ACE05, EDL 2016 (LDC2017E03), EDL 2017 (LDC2017E52), OntoNotes (Pradhan et al., 2012), ERE, CoNLL 2002 (Tjong Kim Sang, 2002), DCEP (Dias, 2016) and SemEval10 (Recasens et al., 2010); temporal ordering component on MATRES (Ning et al., 2018); weakly supervised event extraction on ACE05; schema matching and prediction on LDC2022E03; visual event and argument extraction on M2E2 (Li et al., 2020a) and cross-media event coreference on Video M2E2 (Chen et al., 2021a). For coreference resolution, similar to previous work (Wen et al., 2021), we use the CoNLL metric.

Component			Benchmark	Metric	Score
Weakly-supervised IE		Trigger	ACE	F1	63.3
		Argument	ACE	F1	41.5
Mention Extraction	En	Trigger	ACE+ERE	F1	64.1
		Argument	ACE+ERE	F1	49.7
		Relation	ACE+ERE	F1	49.5
	Es	Trigger	ACE+ERE	F1	63.4
		Argument	ACE+ERE	F1	46.0
		Relation	ACE+ERE	F1	46.6
Document-level Argument Extraction			ACE	F1	66.7
			RAMS	F1	48.6
Coreference Resolution	En	Entity	OntoNotes	CoNLL	92.4
		Event	ACE	CoNLL	84.8
	Es	Entity	SemEval 2010	CoNLL	67.6
		Event	ERE-ES	CoNLL	81.0
Wikidata QNode Linking			TACKBP-2010	Acc.	90.9
Temporal Ordering	RoBERTa		MATRES	F1	81.7
	T5		MATRES-b	Acc.	89.6
Visual Event Extraction			M2E2	F1	52.7
Cross-media Event Coreference			Video M2E2	F1	51.5

	Benchmark	Metric	Score
Schema Matching	LDC2022E03	Recall	63.2
Schema Prediction	WikiEvents	F1	45.5

Table 2: Performance (%) of each component our open-domain multimedia multilingual IE system (upper) and schema matching and prediction component (bottom).

4 Related Work

Event Schema Induction and Curation Event schemas, or otherwise known as scripts, are structures that represent typical event progressions (Schank and Abelson, 1975). Prior to this work, there has been some effort in creating schema databases through crowdsourcing (Regneri et al., 2010; Modi et al., 2016; Wanzare et al., 2016; Sakaguchi et al., 2021). The key characteristics that separate our schema library from exiting resources include (1) focus on diverse newsworthy scenarios instead of everyday events; (2) highly structured multi-level schema organization.

In addition to schema resources, there has also been work on automating the schema induction process, through the use of probabilistic graphical models (Chambers, 2013; Cheung et al., 2013; Nguyen et al., 2015; Weber et al., 2018) and event-based language models (Pichotta and Mooney, 2016; Modi and Titov, 2014; Rudinger et al., 2015; Li et al., 2020b, 2021a). We hope that our schema library can serve as a resource for the development of better automatic schema induction methods.

Weakly-Supervised Event Extraction Due to the high cost of annotating event instances, low resource event extraction has received much attention in recent years. There are a variety of settings explored, including zero-shot transfer learning (Lyu et al., 2021; Huang et al., 2018), cross-lingual transfer (Subburathinam et al., 2019), inducing event types (Huang et al., 2016; Wang et al., 2021b), keyword-based supervision (Zhang et al., 2021) and few-shot learning (Peng et al., 2016; Lai et al., 2020; Shen et al., 2021; Cong et al., 2021; Chen et al., 2021b).

Schema-Guided Event Prediction Our schema-guided event prediction model is also related to link prediction (Zhang and Chen, 2018; Wang et al., 2018; Lei et al., 2019) and graph completion (Zhang et al., 2019; Goel et al., 2020; Wang et al., 2021a) methods. The advantages of our schema-guided method are that: (1) Our method is specially designed for multiple small event graphs, rather than a single large graph as studied in previous work. Therefore, using event schema enables us to model the common pattern of instance event graphs. (2) An event schema can be seen as a pool of inter-connected candidate events, which provides new event nodes that can be added into an incomplete instance event graph. However, existing work can only predict missing links rather than missing nodes.

5 Conclusions and Future Work

We build an open-domain schema-guided event prediction system that is capable of extracting and predicting structured information regarding events from various scenarios. In the future, we plan to further improve both the extraction quality and portability to cover even more scenarios, and use the automatic zero-shot schema induction algorithm to iteratively extend our curated schemas. The hierarchy structure of our event schemas can also be further utilized to improve future event prediction.

6 Broader Impact

The goal of this project is to advance the state-of-the-art schema-guided information extraction and event prediction from real-world multi-modal news sources. We believe that grounding our work in real-world applications will help us make progress in event-centric natural language understanding. However, this work is not void of possible improper use that may have adverse social impacts.

One major distinction between beneficial use and harmful use depends on the data sources. Proper use of the technology requires that input sources are legally and ethically obtained. As an instance of beneficial use, our demo may contribute to disease outbreak monitoring and disaster emergency response, which is included in our chosen scenarios. Besides, we should also be aware of the possible biases that may exists in the datasets. Our system components, as well as pretrained language models that we use, are trained and evaluated on specific benchmark datasets, which could be affected by such biases. For example, as is observed in Abid et al. (2021), the text generated by GPT-3 might include undesired social biases. Our careful human curators' effort involved in the schema library building can mitigate this issue.

Generally, increasing transparency and explainability of models can help prevent social harm, such as over-estimation of the model ability. We plan to make our software fully open source for public audition and verification. We are also open to explore countermeasures to prevent unintended consequences.

The event prediction part of our model is able to forecast the future trend of the current complex event, which enables us to better understand the structure and semantics of complex events. Moreover, it is particularly helpful for us to analyze and predict the public opinion.

Acknowledgement

We thank the anonymous reviewers helpful suggestions. This research is based upon work supported by U.S. DARPA KAIROS Program No. FA8750-19-2-1004, U.S. DARPA AIDA Program No. FA8750-18-2-0014 and LORELEI Program No. HR0011-15-C-0115. The views and conclusions contained herein are those of the authors and should not be interpreted as necessarily representing the official policies, either expressed or implied, of DARPA, or the U.S. Government. The U.S. Government is authorized to reproduce and distribute reprints for governmental purposes notwithstanding any copyright annotation therein.

References

Abubakar Abid, Maheen Farooqi, and James Zou. 2021. Large language models associate muslims with violence. *Nature Machine Intelligence*, 3(6):461–463.

Nathanael Chambers. 2013. Event schema induction with a probabilistic entity-driven model. In *Proceedings of the 2013 Conference on Empirical Methods in Natural Language Processing (EMNLP2013)*, volume 13, pages 1797–1807.

Brian Chen, Xudong Lin, Christopher Thomas, Manling Li, Shoya Yoshida, Lovish Chum, Heng Ji, and

Shih-Fu Chang. 2021a. Joint multimedia event extraction from video and article. In *Findings of the Association for Computational Linguistics: EMNLP 2021*, pages 74–88, Punta Cana, Dominican Republic. Association for Computational Linguistics.

Jiawei Chen, Hongyu Lin, Xianpei Han, and Le Sun. 2021b. Honey or poison? solving the trigger curse in few-shot event detection via causal intervention. *EMNLP*.

Jackie Chi Kit Cheung, Hoifung Poon, and Lucy Vanderwende. 2013. Probabilistic frame induction. In *Proceedings of the 2013 Conference of the North American Chapter of the Association for Computational Linguistics: Human Language Technologies*, pages 837–846, Atlanta, Georgia. Association for Computational Linguistics.

Xin Cong, Shiyao Cui, Bowen Yu, Tingwen Liu, Wang Yubin, and Bin Wang. 2021. Few-Shot Event Detection with Prototypical Amortized Conditional Random Field. In *Findings of the Association for Computational Linguistics: ACL-IJCNLP 2021*, pages 28–40, Online. Association for Computational Linguistics.

Jacob Devlin, Ming-Wei Chang, Kenton Lee, and Kristina Toutanova. 2019. BERT: Pre-training of deep bidirectional transformers for language understanding. In *Proceedings of the 2019 Conference of the North American Chapter of the Association for Computational Linguistics: Human Language Technologies, Volume 1 (Long and Short Papers)*, pages 4171–4186, Minneapolis, Minnesota. Association for Computational Linguistics.

Francisco Dias. 2016. Multilingual Automated Text Anonymization. Msc dissertation, Instituto Superior Técnico, Lisbon, Portugal, May.

Seth Ebner, Patrick Xia, Ryan Culkin, Kyle Rawlins, and Benjamin Van Durme. 2020. Multi-sentence argument linking. In *Proceedings of the 58th Annual Meeting of the Association for Computational Linguistics*.

Rishab Goel, Seyed Mehran Kazemi, Marcus Brubaker, and Pascal Poupart. 2020. Diachronic embedding for temporal knowledge graph completion. In *Proceedings of the AAAI Conference on Artificial Intelligence*, volume 34, pages 3988–3995.

Matthew Honnibal, Ines Montani, Sofie Van Landeghem, and Adriane Boyd. 2020. spaCy: Industrial-strength Natural Language Processing in Python. *Zenodo*.

Lifu Huang, Taylor Cassidy, Xiaocheng Feng, Heng Ji, Clare R. Voss, Jiawei Han, and Avirup Sil. 2016. Liberal event extraction and event schema induction. In *Proceedings of the 54th Annual Meeting of the Association for Computational Linguistics (Volume 1: Long Papers)*, pages 258–268, Berlin, Germany. Association for Computational Linguistics.

Lifu Huang, Heng Ji, Kyunghyun Cho, Ido Dagan, Sebastian Riedel, and Clare Voss. 2018. Zero-shot transfer learning for event extraction. In *Proceedings of the 56th Annual Meeting of the Association for Computational Linguistics (Volume 1: Long Papers)*, pages 2160–2170, Melbourne, Australia. Association for Computational Linguistics.

Tuan Manh Lai, Heng Ji, and ChengXiang Zhai. 2022. Improving candidate retrieval with entity profile generation for wikidata entity linking. *arXiv preprint arXiv:2202.13404*.

Viet Dac Lai, Thien Huu Nguyen, and Franck Dernoncourt. 2020. Extensively matching for few-shot learning event detection. In *Proceedings of the First Joint Workshop on Narrative Understanding, Storylines, and Events*, pages 38–45, Online. Association for Computational Linguistics.

Kai Lei, Meng Qin, Bo Bai, Gong Zhang, and Min Yang. 2019. Gcn-gan: A non-linear temporal link prediction model for weighted dynamic networks. In *IEEE INFOCOM 2019-IEEE Conference on Computer Communications*, pages 388–396. IEEE.

Manling Li, Sha Li, Zhenhailong Wang, Lifu Huang, Kyunghyun Cho, Heng Ji, Jiawei Han, and Clare Voss. 2021a. The future is not one-dimensional: Complex event schema induction by graph modeling for event prediction. In *Proceedings of the 2021 Conference on Empirical Methods in Natural Language Processing*, pages 5203–5215.

Manling Li, Ruochen Xu, Shuohang Wang, Luowei Zhou, Xudong Lin, Chenguang Zhu, Michael Zeng, Heng Ji, and Shih-Fu Chang. 2022. Clip-event: Connecting text and images with event structures. *arXiv preprint arXiv:2201.05078*.

Manling Li, Alireza Zareian, Qi Zeng, Spencer Whitehead, Di Lu, Heng Ji, and Shih-Fu Chang. 2020a. Cross-media structured common space for multimedia event extraction. In *Proceedings of the 58th Annual Meeting of the Association for Computational Linguistics*, pages 2557–2568, Online. Association for Computational Linguistics.

Manling Li, Qi Zeng, Ying Lin, Kyunghyun Cho, Heng Ji, Jonathan May, Nathanael Chambers, and Clare Voss. 2020b. Connecting the dots: Event graph schema induction with path language modeling. In *Proceedings of the 2020 Conference on Empirical Methods in Natural Language Processing (EMNLP)*, pages 684–695.

Sha Li, Heng Ji, and Jiawei Han. 2021b. Document-level event argument extraction by conditional generation. In *Proc. The 2021 Conference of the North American Chapter of the Association for Computational Linguistics - Human Language Technologies (NAACL-HLT2021)*.

Ying Lin, Heng Ji, Fei Huang, and Lingfei Wu. 2020. A joint end-to-end neural model for information extraction with global features. In *Proc. The 58th Annual*

Meeting of the Association for Computational Linguistics (ACL2020).

Qing Lyu, Hongming Zhang, Elior Sulem, and Dan Roth. 2021. Zero-shot event extraction via transfer learning: Challenges and insights. In *Proceedings of the 59th Annual Meeting of the Association for Computational Linguistics and the 11th International Joint Conference on Natural Language Processing (Volume 2: Short Papers)*, pages 322–332, Online. Association for Computational Linguistics.

Piyush Mishra, Akanksha Malhotra, Susan Windisch Brown, Martha Palmer, and Ghazaleh Kazeminejad. 2021. A graphical interface for curating schemas. In *Proceedings of the 59th Annual Meeting of the Association for Computational Linguistics and the 11th International Joint Conference on Natural Language Processing: System Demonstrations*, pages 159–166, Online. Association for Computational Linguistics.

Ashutosh Modi, Tatjana Anikina, Simon Ostermann, and Manfred Pinkal. 2016. InScript: Narrative texts annotated with script information. In *Proceedings of the Tenth International Conference on Language Resources and Evaluation (LREC'16)*, pages 3485–3493, Portorož, Slovenia. European Language Resources Association (ELRA).

Ashutosh Modi and Ivan Titov. 2014. Inducing neural models of script knowledge. In *Proceedings of the Eighteenth Conference on Computational Natural Language Learning*, pages 49–57.

Kiem-Hieu Nguyen, Xavier Tannier, Olivier Ferret, and Romaric Besançon. 2015. Generative event schema induction with entity disambiguation. In *Proceedings of the 53rd Annual Meeting of the Association for Computational Linguistics and the 7th International Joint Conference on Natural Language Processing (Volume 1: Long Papers)*, pages 188–197.

Qiang Ning, Hao Wu, and Dan Roth. 2018. A multi-axis annotation scheme for event temporal relations. In *Proceedings of the 56th Annual Meeting of the Association for Computational Linguistics (Volume 1: Long Papers)*, pages 1318–1328, Melbourne, Australia. Association for Computational Linguistics.

Haoruo Peng, Yangqiu Song, and Dan Roth. 2016. Event detection and co-reference with minimal supervision. In *Proceedings of the 2016 Conference on Empirical Methods in Natural Language Processing*, pages 392–402, Austin, Texas. Association for Computational Linguistics.

Karl Pichotta and Raymond J Mooney. 2016. Learning statistical scripts with lstm recurrent neural networks. In *Thirtieth AAAI Conference on Artificial Intelligence*.

Sameer Pradhan, Alessandro Moschitti, Nianwen Xue, Olga Uryupina, and Yuchen Zhang. 2012. Conll-2012 shared task: Modeling multilingual unrestricted coreference in ontonotes. In *Joint Conference on Empirical Methods in Natural Language Processing and Computational Natural Language Learning - Proceedings of the Shared Task: Modeling Multilingual Unrestricted Coreference in OntoNotes, EMNLP-CoNLL 2012, July 13, 2012, Jeju Island, Korea*, pages 1–40. ACL.

Sarah Pratt, Mark Yatskar, Luca Weihs, Ali Farhadi, and Aniruddha Kembhavi. 2020. Grounded situation recognition. In *European Conference on Computer Vision*, pages 314–332. Springer.

Alec Radford, Jong Wook Kim, Chris Hallacy, Aditya Ramesh, Gabriel Goh, Sandhini Agarwal, Girish Sastry, Amanda Askell, Pamela Mishkin, Jack Clark, et al. 2021. Learning transferable visual models from natural language supervision. In *International Conference on Machine Learning*, pages 8748–8763. PMLR.

Marta Recasens, Lluís Màrquez, Emili Sapena, M. Antònia Martí, Mariona Taulé, Véronique Hoste, Massimo Poesio, and Yannick Versley. 2010. Semeval-2010 task 1: Coreference resolution in multiple languages. In *Proceedings of the 5th International Workshop on Semantic Evaluation, SemEval@ACL 2010, Uppsala University, Uppsala, Sweden, July 15-16, 2010*, pages 1–8. The Association for Computer Linguistics.

Michaela Regneri, Alexander Koller, and Manfred Pinkal. 2010. Learning script knowledge with web experiments. In *ACL*.

Rachel Rudinger, Pushpendre Rastogi, Francis Ferraro, and Benjamin Van Durme. 2015. Script induction as language modeling. In *Proceedings of the 2015 Conference on Empirical Methods in Natural Language Processing*, pages 1681–1686.

Keisuke Sakaguchi, Chandra Bhagavatula, Ronan Le Bras, Niket Tandon, Peter Clark, and Yejin Choi. 2021. proScript: Partially ordered scripts generation. In *Findings of the Association for Computational Linguistics: EMNLP 2021*, pages 2138–2149, Punta Cana, Dominican Republic. Association for Computational Linguistics.

Roger C Schank and Robert P Abelson. 1975. Scripts, plans, and knowledge. In *IJCAI*, volume 75, pages 151–157.

Shirong Shen, Tongtong Wu, Guilin Qi, Yuan-Fang Li, Gholamreza Haffari, and Sheng Bi. 2021. Adaptive knowledge-enhanced Bayesian meta-learning for few-shot event detection. In *Findings of the Association for Computational Linguistics: ACL-IJCNLP 2021*, pages 2417–2429, Online. Association for Computational Linguistics.

Zhiyi Song, Ann Bies, Stephanie Strassel, Tom Riese, Justin Mott, Joe Ellis, Jonathan Wright, Seth Kulick, Neville Ryant, and Xiaoyi Ma. 2015. From light to rich ere: annotation of entities, relations, and events. In *Proceedings of the the 3rd Workshop on EVENTS: Definition, Detection, Coreference, and Representation*, pages 89–98.

Ananya Subburathinam, Di Lu, Heng Ji, Jonathan May, Shih-Fu Chang, Avirup Sil, and Clare Voss. 2019. Cross-lingual structure transfer for relation and event extraction. In *Proceedings of the 2019 Conference on Empirical Methods in Natural Language Processing and the 9th International Joint Conference on Natural Language Processing (EMNLP-IJCNLP)*, pages 313–325, Hong Kong, China. Association for Computational Linguistics.

Erik F. Tjong Kim Sang. 2002. Introduction to the CoNLL-2002 shared task: Language-independent named entity recognition. In *COLING-02: The 6th Conference on Natural Language Learning 2002 (CoNLL-2002)*.

Christopher Walker, Stephanie Strassel, Julie Medero, and Kazuaki Maeda. 2006. Ace 2005 multilingual training corpus. *Linguistic Data Consortium, Philadelphia*, 57.

Hongwei Wang, Hongyu Ren, and Jure Leskovec. 2021a. Relational message passing for knowledge graph completion. In *Proceedings of the 27th ACM SIGKDD Conference on Knowledge Discovery & Data Mining*, pages 1697–1707.

Hongwei Wang, Fuzheng Zhang, Min Hou, Xing Xie, Minyi Guo, and Qi Liu. 2018. Shine: Signed heterogeneous information network embedding for sentiment link prediction. In *Proceedings of the Eleventh ACM International Conference on Web Search and Data Mining*, pages 592–600.

Ziqi Wang, Xiaozhi Wang, Xu Han, Yankai Lin, Lei Hou, Zhiyuan Liu, Peng Li, Juanzi Li, and Jie Zhou. 2021b. CLEVE: Contrastive Pre-training for Event Extraction. In *Proceedings of the 59th Annual Meeting of the Association for Computational Linguistics and the 11th International Joint Conference on Natural Language Processing (Volume 1: Long Papers)*, pages 6283–6297, Online. Association for Computational Linguistics.

Lilian D. A. Wanzare, Alessandra Zarcone, Stefan Thater, and Manfred Pinkal. 2016. A crowdsourced database of event sequence descriptions for the acquisition of high-quality script knowledge. In *Proceedings of the Tenth International Conference on Language Resources and Evaluation (LREC'16)*, pages 3494–3501, Portorož, Slovenia. European Language Resources Association (ELRA).

Noah Weber, Leena Shekhar, Niranjan Balasubramanian, and Nathanael Chambers. 2018. Hierarchical quantized representations for script generation. *ACL*.

Haoyang Wen and Heng Ji. 2021. Utilizing relative event time to enhance event-event temporal relation extraction. In *Proceedings of the 2021 Conference on Empirical Methods in Natural Language Processing*, pages 10431–10437, Online and Punta Cana, Dominican Republic. Association for Computational Linguistics.

Haoyang Wen, Ying Lin, Tuan Lai, Xiaoman Pan, Sha Li, Xudong Lin, Ben Zhou, Manling Li, Haoyu Wang, Hongming Zhang, et al. 2021. Resin: A dockerized schema-guided cross-document cross-lingual cross-media information extraction and event tracking system. In *Proceedings of the 2021 Conference of the North American Chapter of the Association for Computational Linguistics: Human Language Technologies: Demonstrations*, pages 133–143.

Hongming Zhang, Haoyu Wang, and Dan Roth. 2021. Zero-shot Label-aware Event Trigger and Argument Classification. In *Findings of the Association for Computational Linguistics: ACL-IJCNLP 2021*, pages 1331–1340, Online. Association for Computational Linguistics.

Muhan Zhang and Yixin Chen. 2018. Link prediction based on graph neural networks. *Advances in Neural Information Processing Systems*, 31:5165–5175.

Shuai Zhang, Yi Tay, Lina Yao, and Qi Liu. 2019. Quaternion knowledge graph embeddings. In *Advances in Neural Information Processing Systems*, pages 2735–2745.

Ben Zhou, Kyle Richardson, Qiang Ning, Tushar Khot, Ashish Sabharwal, and Dan Roth. 2021. Temporal reasoning on implicit events from distant supervision. In *Proceedings of the 2021 Conference of the North American Chapter of the Association for Computational Linguistics: Human Language Technologies*, pages 1361–1371, Online. Association for Computational Linguistics.

A Human-machine Interface for Few-shot Rule Synthesis for Information Extraction

Robert Vacareanu, George C. G. Barbosa, Enrique Noriega-Atala, Gus Hahn-Powell, Rebecca Sharp, Marco A. Valenzuela-Escárcega, Mihai Surdeanu
University of Arizona
Tucson, AZ, USA
{rvacareanu, gcgbarbosa, enoriega, hahnpowell, msurdeanu}@email.arizona.edu
{bsharpataz, marcovalenzuelaescarcega}@gmail.com

Abstract

We propose a system that assists a user in constructing transparent information extraction models, consisting of patterns (or rules) written in a declarative language, through program synthesis. Users of our system can specify their requirements through the use of examples, which are collected with a search interface. The rule-synthesis system proposes rule candidates and the results of applying them on a textual corpus; the user has the option to accept the candidate, request another option, or adjust the examples provided to the system. Through an interactive evaluation, we show that our approach generates high-precision rules even in a 1-shot setting. On a second evaluation on a widely-used relation extraction dataset (TACRED), our method generates rules that outperform considerably manually written patterns. Our code, demo, and documentation is available at `https://clulab.github.io/odinsynth/`.

1 Introduction

Rule-based methods for information extraction address the opacity of neural architectures by producing models that are completely transparent, i.e., they are usually a collection of rules written in a declarative language. Such models are better suited for incremental improvements, as each individual rule can be explicitly interpreted. However, these benefits do not come for free: users of such systems must be familiar with the underlying declarative rule language, and, potentially, with representations of syntax such as syntactic dependencies. None of these are trivial to users outside of natural language processing (NLP), which, we argue, should be the target users of these systems.

To mitigate the above limitation, we propose a human-machine interface (HMI) that: (a) lets users synthesize rules from natural language examples, and correct them *without necessarily understanding the rule syntax* (although expert users who do have access to the actual rule produced), (b) generates rules in a *few-shot setting*, i.e., from a very small number of examples. The latter contribution is possible because our rule synthesis engine has been pretrained on a large collection of rules that were automatically generated from a large text corpus (Vacareanu et al., 2022). In other words, our rule synthesis approach is akin to prompting for language models (Liu et al., 2021). That is, we first train an open-domain rule synthesis model, and then we guide its predictions to the task of interest using a small number of examples of the desired extractions (the "prompt").

We include two types of evaluations that prove the value of the proposed approach. The first evaluation focuses on interactive sessions where users generate rules that extract mentions of named entity classes, e.g., `CITY` or `ACADEMIC INSTITUTION` from a *single example extraction.* Using six different users, we show that, despite the minimal supervision, the tool produces named entities in the corresponding classes with high precision, e.g., precision at 20 (P@20) at over 75% for the `CITY` class. This suggests that the proposed HMI is useful to domain scientists that need to perform information extraction quickly, without understanding the underlying NLP technology. For completeness, we also include a traditional, non-interactive evaluation, on the TACRED dataset (Zhang et al., 2017), through which we show that the rules synthesized by our approach outperform the manually-written rules by over 4 F1 points, even though our synthesis component is *not* re-trained on the TACRED data.

Proceedings of the 2022 Conference of the North American Chapter of the Association for Computational Linguistics: Human Language Technologies: System Demonstrations, pages 64 - 70
July 10-15, 2022

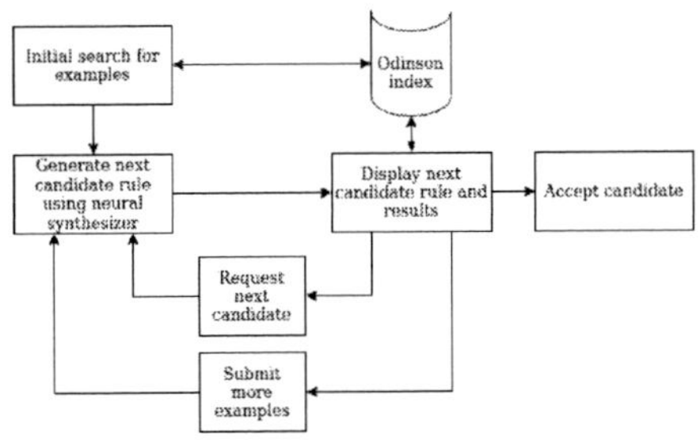

Figure 1: The architecture of our proposed system.

2 Architecture

At a high level, the proposed system consists of two main modules: a rule synthesis component, and an UI module to facilitate rapid rule prototyping with minimal programming or linguistic knowledge. The rule synthesis component consists of: (a) a searcher that explores the possible rule space, and (b) a neural scorer that prioritizes next steps during rule generation. Figure 1 summarizes the overall architecture. The user selects a handful of examples after an initial query. Then, our system proposes a rule, together with its potential extractions. The user then decides if this rule is satisfactory. If not, the user can either ask for a new rule or add new examples (positive or negative). This process repeats until the generated rule is accepted. We describe these components in detail in the next two sections.

3 Rule Synthesis

Our proposed approach for rule generation follows closely the method proposed in (Vacareanu et al., 2022). For completeness, we summarize it here as well. Our rule synthesis method uses enumerative search that is guided by a transformer-based scoring mechanism, and is optimized using search-space pruning heuristics. Our transformer model scores each potential next state (where a **state** contains the incompletely generated rule up to this point), given the current state, such that the number of states to be explored is minimized. Specifically, our system consists of two main components:

A **searcher**, with Branch and Bound (Land and Doig, 1960) as the underlying algorithm. The searcher uses the scores assigned by the scorer (below) to determine the order of exploration, choosing the state with the highest score, *regardless of its position in the search tree*. As such, it is important for the scorer to assign high scores to states that are in the sub-tree that leads to the desired final rule, and lower scores to all other states;

A **scorer**, with a transformer backbone that is initialized with a pretrained model, but fine-tuned through self-supervision, i.e., over *automatically generated rules* (see Section 3.2). The scorer uses the current state and the **specification**, i.e., the natural language examples to be matched by the generated rule, to score each potential next state.

The searcher is responsible for exploring the states in priority order (as determined by the scorer), and deciding if a given state is successful (i.e., it is a valid query and correctly extracts the requested highlighted words and nothing more). The search space can be interpreted as a tree, where the root is the initial candidate solution and the children of a node n are the candidate solutions that the node n could expand into. Given this, the searcher can be seen as iteratively applying a sequence of three operations: (a) **Expand** the current state according to the domain-specific language grammar, (b) **Score** each expanded candidate next state and insert them into the priority queue, and (c) **Select** from the queue the state with the highest score to be the next state. We repeat this process until we find a solution or we reach our step limit.

The scorer assigns a numerical value to states to establish the order of exploration. We explore two variants: a **static** variant, which assigns static weights to states based on their components, and a **contextual** neural variant based on a self-supervised method that assigns contextual state scores based on the current context.

As a simple example, consider a user that wants to learn named entities belonging to the class CITY. She may start with a specification based on the sentence "Regina Romero is the mayor of Tucson, Arizona, having been elected after...", in which she highlights "mayor of" as the relevant *context* representative of this class, and "Tucson" as the desired entity to be extracted. From this specification, our method would generate the rule: [lemma=mayor] [tag=IN] (?<arg>

[tag=NNP]+),[1] which picks up "mayor" followed by a preposition (part-of-speech tag IN) as the context, and a sequence of 1 or more proper nouns as the entity to be extracted.

3.1 Multiple sentences

Our system can handle specifications that contain multiple sentences and their highlights. We require the enumerative searcher to find a rule that would satisfy *all* the constraints for all sentences in the specification. When scoring, we score a (current state, next potential state, single-sentence specification) triple, and then average over all sentences in the specification to obtain a final score for the (current state, next potential state) transition.

3.2 Training the neural scorer

Unlike the static scorer, the neural guiding function of the contextual scorer needs to be trained, which we do with self-supervision. Because there is no large corpus of Odinson rules, we artificially generate one with random spans of text that we randomly manipulate into rules. Our random-length text spans are chosen from the UMBC corpus (Han et al., 2013). Each token in this span is then randomly manipulated into an Odinson token constraint based on either word, lemma, or part-of-speech. For example, a span such as *the dog barked* might be converted to [tag=DT] [word=dog] [lemma=bark]. Then, to expose the model to additional rule components (e.g., alternation, quantifiers), we add further manipulations, again with randomization. To add alternations, we build a temporary query by replacing one of the token constraints with a wildcard that can match *any* token and query the corpus for an additional sentence that has different content in that position. This new content is added as an alternation. For example, with the temporary version of the above query [tag=DT] [word=dog] [],[2] we might find *A dog runs*, resulting in the following alternation: [tag=DT] [word=dog] ([lemma=bark]|[lemma=run]). To add a quantifier (i.e., *, +, or ?), we select a token to modify and a quantifier to add, and check the corpus to ensure that the addition of the quantifier yields additional results.

After generating each random rule, we build a corresponding specification by querying the UMBC corpus: the retrieved sentences and their matched spans constitute specifications. However, having a specification and the corresponding rule is not enough to train our model. We also need a correct sequence of transitions from the initial placeholder to the final rule. For this, we use an Oracle to generate the shortest sequence of transitions, which we consider to be the correct sequence for our purposes. This sequence of transitions, together with the specification, forms the training data for our model. Note that we train *only* on this data, i.e., after this self-supervised training process the transformer's weights are fixed. We train using the cross-entropy loss and with a cyclical learning rate, as suggested by (Smith, 2017). Further, we employ a curriculum learning approach (Bengio et al., 2009; Platanios et al., 2019), splitting the training data by sentence length and by pattern length. We did not tune our hyperparameters.

4 User Interface

We accompany the above rule synthesis component with a user interface (UI) to facilitate rapid prototyping with minimal programming or linguistic knowledge. We showcase the UI in Figure 2, split into 5 blocks (a–e). Initially, the user has to do an initial search for sentences of interest (a). Then, she selects any relevant sentence, highlighting the parts for which she wishes to obtain a rule, e.g., highlighting *the capital city of* as the context and *Amman* as the entity of interest (b). The system then returns a potential rule which satisfies the current constraints, together with what the rule extracts (c). Note that we display the rule for the benefit of expert users, but most users are not required to understand the format of the rule. That is, a user can understand the rule's impact by analyzing what such a rule extracts. She may add negative examples (a negative example is a sentence on which the output rule should not match anything), or ask for a new rule (d). This process is repeated until the user is satisfied with the given rule (e).

[1]Our rules are generated in the Odinson rule language (Valenzuela-Escárcega et al., 2020).

[2]The Odinson wildcard, [], matches any token.

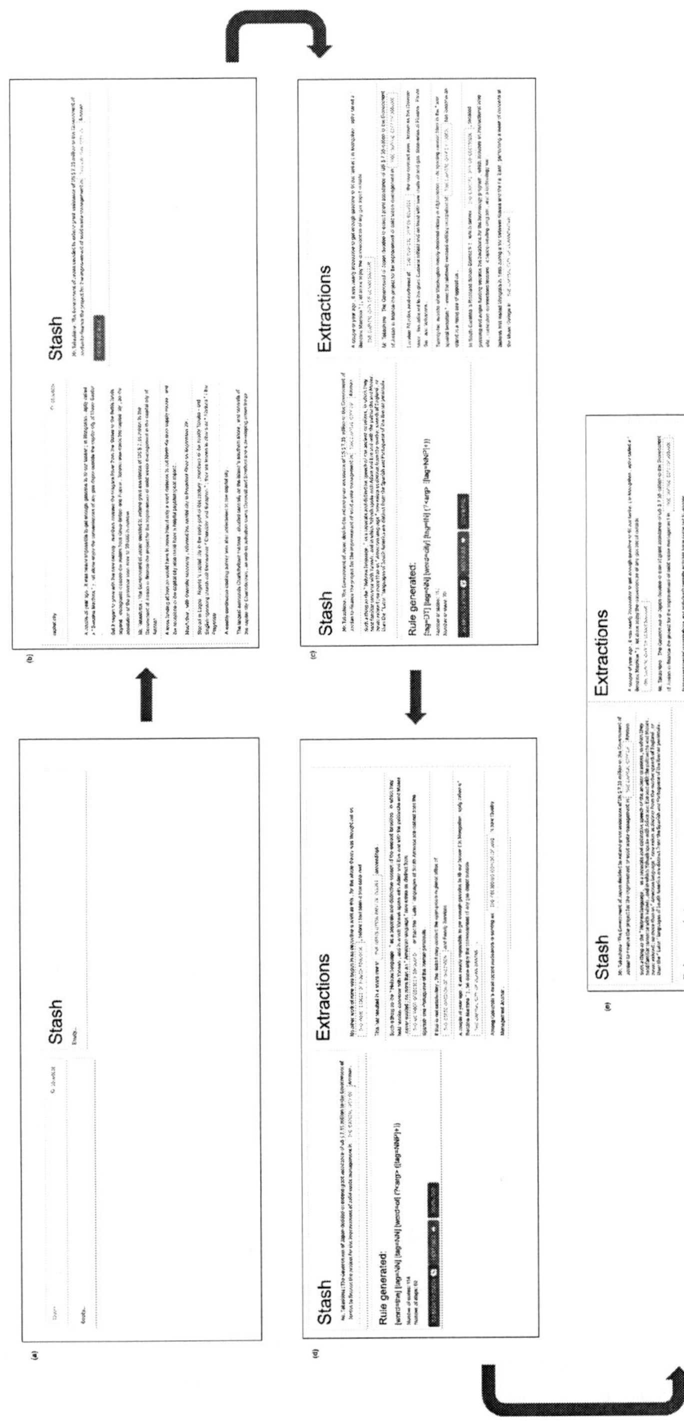

Figure 2: Walkthrough example of the user interface.

5 Evaluation

5.1 Interactive Evaluation

Even the mayor of context New Orleans entity

Figure 3: Example of a specification annotated by a user in the interactive evaluation. The entity is highlighted in orange and its context in gray.

We evaluated the performance of the system in an interactive scenario with a human in the loop. The purpose of the interactive evaluation is to quantify the performance of rules generated with the interface to extract specific entity types using a limited amount of examples. The user is tasked with using the interface to synthesize a rule to extract a specific named entity type, and then manually verify that the extractions indeed belong to the intended entity type. Given an entity type, the user queries an index of the UMBC corpus to pinpoint and select a pattern in one of the retrieved sentences. This pattern works as the user's specification, composed of the *context* and an *entity* of the relevant type (See section 3). Figure 3 depicts an example of a pattern selection.

Once the specification is selected, it is used to synthesize a candidate rule and retrieve a sample sentences with matches. We restrict the evaluation to contain *a single* specification, to emulate a one-shot learning scenario, where the model generates rules using a limited amount of information. The user inspects the rule and its matches to determine whether the candidate rule faithfully represents the original intent. If it does not, the next candidate rule is generated and the process is repeated. We encouraged users to repeat this process up to three times, but allowed them to repeat it a fourth time at their discretion.

The interactive evaluation is carried out for the following entity pairs: `CITY/CAPITAL`, `PERSON/ACTOR`, and `ORGANIZATION/ACADEMIC INSTITUTION`. Each pair represents two different levels of granularity of the same concept.

One to two users were assigned to each pair and each user was instructed to use the interface to synthesize three rules per entity type. For every rule, they retrieved and manually verified precision at 10 (P@10) and precision at 20 (P@20) on the most frequent entities in the matches from the UMBC corpus.

Table 1 contains precision at 10 and precision at 20 for each of the entity types. We can observe that using minimal supervision, i.e. using a single specification to synthesize a rule for a named entity type, the system generates rules that have high precision (P@20 $\geq$ .77) for coarse grained named entities and similar, albeit slightly lower precision (P@20 $\geq$ .63), for finer grained named entities. This is achieved with no more than three or four iterations, highlighting how domain experts can readily benefit from our proposed HMI.

Entity Type	P@10	P@20
CITY	.85	.85
CAPITAL	.83	.75
PERSON	.78	.77
ACTOR	.71	.72
ORGANIZATION	.93	.85
ACADEMIC INSTITUTION	.70	.63

Table 1: P@10 and P@20 of our rule synthesis on 6 different named entity types. `CITY`, `PERSON` and `ORGANIZATION` are coarse types. `CAPIITAL`, `ACTOR` and `ACADEMIC INSTITUTION` are fine grained types.

5.2 Non-interactive Evaluation

To facilitate a comparison with other approaches, we also include an evaluation on the TACRED dataset, a widely-used relation classification dataset (Zhang et al., 2017). In this setting, we cluster the training sentences to generate specifications. In particular, for each sentence, we compute an embedding by averaging the embeddings of the words in between the two given entities.[3] Then, we compare the similarity of two sentences by cosine similarity, and cluster similar sentences together; each cluster becomes one specification. Then, for each cluster we run our system to generate a rule, considering the words in-between the two entities as the highlighted part.

We compare our approach against several state-of-the-art approaches, as well as three baselines. Our first baseline is a traditional sequence-to-sequence approach (Sutskever et al., 2014) with transformers (Vaswani et al., 2017). We train it to decode the rule using the specification as input, akin

[3]We used GloVe (Pennington et al., 2014).

to a traditional machine translation task. Our second baseline (*Patterns*) is a rule-based system that uses the *hand-made* rules compiled for TACRED (Zhang et al., 2017). Our third baseline *No Learning* consists of directly returning a rule for trivial cases (e.g. no words or only on word in between the two entities). When there is no word, the final rule is empty. When there is one word, the final rule consists of a word, lemma, or tag constraint, depending on which will result in a shorter rule. We present our results in Table 2.

We note that both variants of our scorer (static and dynamic) perform better than the seq2seq and no-scorer baselines (34 F1 vs 28 F1). Of particular relevance for our comparison is the baseline that relies on the hand-crafted patterns for TACRED. Our contextualized weights model obtains a higher F1 score (41.4 F1 vs 36.6 F1), although at the cost of precision, but with much higher recall. Our results add evidence that it might be possible to replace the human expert with a neural expert. When comparing our contextualized-scoring approach to the supervised baselines, we note that while we do not match their performance, there are two important factors to consider. First, our proposed approach is trained on *domain agnostic* data that we automatically generated, and then applied on TACRED as is, *without fine-tuning*. On the other hand, the supervised approaches that we compare with train/fine-tune on the TACRED splits. Second, the output of our approach is a set of *human-interpretable rules*, while the output of the other approaches is a statistical model that produces only the final label. In other words, previous work is much more opaque and thus more difficult to interpret, debug, adjust, maintain, and protect from hidden biases present in the training data (e.g., Kurita et al., 2019; Sheng et al., 2019).

Model	P	R	F1
Baselines			
Seq2Seq with Transformers	53.0	19.0	28.0
Patterns	86.9	23.2	36.6
No Learning	53.0	19.0	28.0
Supervised Approaches			
Joshi et al. (2020)	70.8	70.9	70.8
Zhou and Chen (2021)	–	–	74.6
Cohen et al. (2020)	74.6	75.2	74.8
Our approach			
Static weights	54.9	24.6	34.0
Contextual weights (BERT-Tiny)	57.6	29.6	39.1
Contextual weights (BERT-Mini)	57.2	32.5	41.4
Contextual weights (BERT-Small)	57.3	32.2	41.2
Contextual weights (BERT-Medium)	55.0	31.8	40.3
Contextual weights (BERT-Base)	55.6	32.4	41.0

Table 2: Results of our rule synthesis on the testing partition of TACRED (given as precision (P), recall (R), and F1 scores), compared with 3 baselines and previous supervised approaches. We include variants of our contextualized method using different transformer backbones.

6 Conclusion and Future Work

We introduced a human-machine interface that lets users synthesize rules from natural language examples, and correct them without necessarily understanding the rule syntax. In an interactive evaluation, we showed that our method is capable to rapidly generate high-precision rules for the extraction of named entities from a single example in natural language. We also demonstrated that in a traditional, non-interactive evaluation on the TACRED dataset, our method produces rules that outperform manually-written rules, despite the fact that our rule synthesis engine is not retrained on the TACRED data.

While these initial results are exciting, there is plenty of work left to do. First, the rules generated by the system are "surface" rules, i.e., they act over sequences of tokens. Adding support for the generation of rules over syntax would allow for capturing more complicated relations and over greater distances. Second, the system is configured to generate a *single* rule that captures the whole specification, which may include multiple (positive or negative) examples. This may force the system to produce complicated rules. A better alternative would be to produce several simpler rules that together capture the whole specification. Lastly, the system generates a sequence of rule candidates that are presented to the user one-by-one, which may bias the user's perspective and impact usability. For example, the current system tends to initially propose rules that are overly general, which yield low-precision results. To better understand users' preferences (i.e., do users prefer high-precision or high-recall rules initially?) user studies must be carried out.

References

Yoshua Bengio, Jérôme Louradour, Ronan Collobert, and Jason Weston. 2009. Curriculum learning. In *Proceedings of the 26th Annual International Conference on Machine Learning*, ICML '09, page 41–48, New York, NY, USA. Association for Computing Machinery.

Amir DN Cohen, Shachar Rosenman, and Yoav Goldberg. 2020. Relation classification as two-way span-prediction. *arXiv preprint arXiv:2010.04829*.

Lushan Han, Abhay L. Kashyap, Tim Finin, James Mayfield, and Jonathan Weese. 2013. UMBC_EBIQUITY-CORE: Semantic textual similarity systems. In *Second Joint Conference on Lexical and Computational Semantics (*SEM), Volume 1: Proceedings of the Main Conference and the Shared Task: Semantic Textual Similarity*, pages 44–52, Atlanta, Georgia, USA. Association for Computational Linguistics.

Mandar Joshi, Danqi Chen, Yinhan Liu, Daniel S. Weld, Luke Zettlemoyer, and Omer Levy. 2020. SpanBERT: Improving pre-training by representing and predicting spans. *Transactions of the Association for Computational Linguistics*, 8:64–77.

Keita Kurita, Nidhi Vyas, Ayush Pareek, Alan W Black, and Yulia Tsvetkov. 2019. Measuring bias in contextualized word representations. *arXiv preprint arXiv:1906.07337*.

Ailsa H. Land and Alison G. Doig. 1960. An automatic method of solving discrete programming problems. *Econometrica*, 28(3):497–520.

Pengfei Liu, Weizhe Yuan, Jinlan Fu, Zhengbao Jiang, Hiroaki Hayashi, and Graham Neubig. 2021. Pre-train, prompt, and predict: A systematic survey of prompting methods in natural language processing. *arXiv preprint arXiv:2107.13586*.

Jeffrey Pennington, Richard Socher, and Christopher Manning. 2014. GloVe: Global vectors for word representation. In *Proceedings of the 2014 Conference on Empirical Methods in Natural Language Processing (EMNLP)*, pages 1532–1543, Doha, Qatar. Association for Computational Linguistics.

Emmanouil Antonios Platanios, Otilia Stretcu, Graham Neubig, Barnabás Póczos, and Tom M. Mitchell. 2019. Competence-based curriculum learning for neural machine translation. *CoRR*, abs/1903.09848.

Emily Sheng, Kai-Wei Chang, Prem Natarajan, and Nanyun Peng. 2019. The woman worked as a babysitter: On biases in language generation. In *Proceedings of the 2019 Conference on Empirical Methods in Natural Language Processing and the 9th International Joint Conference on Natural Language Processing (EMNLP-IJCNLP)*, pages 3398–3403.

Leslie N. Smith. 2017. Cyclical learning rates for training neural networks. In *2017 IEEE Winter Conference on Applications of Computer Vision (WACV)*, pages 464–472.

Ilya Sutskever, Oriol Vinyals, and Quoc V. Le. 2014. Sequence to sequence learning with neural networks. In *Proceedings of the 27th International Conference on Neural Information Processing Systems - Volume 2*, NIPS'14, page 3104–3112, Cambridge, MA, USA. MIT Press.

Robert Vacareanu, Marco A Valenzuela-Escarcega, George CG Barbosa, Rebecca Sharp, and Mihai Surdeanu. 2022. From examples to rules: Neural guided rule synthesis for information extraction. *arXiv preprint arXiv:2202.00475*.

Marco A Valenzuela-Escárcega, Gus Hahn-Powell, and Dane Bell. 2020. Odinson: A fast rule-based information extraction framework. In *Proceedings of the 12th Language Resources and Evaluation Conference*, pages 2183–2191.

Ashish Vaswani, Noam Shazeer, Niki Parmar, Jakob Uszkoreit, Llion Jones, Aidan N. Gomez, undefinedukasz Kaiser, and Illia Polosukhin. 2017. Attention is all you need. In *Proceedings of the 31st International Conference on Neural Information Processing Systems*, NIPS'17, page 6000–6010, Red Hook, NY, USA. Curran Associates Inc.

Yuhao Zhang, Victor Zhong, Danqi Chen, Gabor Angeli, and Christopher D. Manning. 2017. Position-aware attention and supervised data improve slot filling. In *Proceedings of the 2017 Conference on Empirical Methods in Natural Language Processing (EMNLP 2017)*, pages 35–45.

Wenxuan Zhou and Muhao Chen. 2021. An improved baseline for sentence-level relation extraction. *arXiv preprint arXiv:2102.01373*.

SETSum: Summarization and Visualization of Student Evaluations of Teaching

♠Yinuo Hu* ♠Shiyue Zhang* ♣♡Viji Sathy ♣♡A. T. Panter ♠Mohit Bansal
♠Department of Computer Science, UNC Chapel Hill
♣Department of Psychology and Neuroscience, UNC Chapel Hill
♡Office of Undergraduate Education, UNC Chapel Hill
{huyinuo, shiyue, mbansal}@cs.unc.edu;
{viji.sathy, panter}@unc.edu

Abstract

Student Evaluations of Teaching (SETs) are widely used in colleges and universities. Typically SET results are summarized for instructors in a static PDF report. The report often includes summary statistics for quantitative ratings and an unsorted list of open-ended student comments. The lack of organization and summarization of the raw comments hinders those interpreting the reports from fully utilizing informative feedback, making accurate inferences, and designing appropriate instructional improvements. In this work, we introduce a novel system, SETSum, that leverages sentiment analysis, aspect extraction, summarization, and visualization techniques to provide organized illustrations of SET findings to instructors and other reviewers. Ten university professors from diverse departments serve as evaluators of the system and all agree that SETSum help them interpret SET results more efficiently; and 6 out of 10 instructors prefer our system over the standard static PDF report (while the remaining 4 would like to have both). This demonstrates that our work holds the potential of reforming the SET reporting conventions in the future.

1 Introduction

Colleges and universities rely on student evaluations of teaching (SETs) to assess students' perceptions about their courses (Chen and Hoshower, 2003; Zabaleta, 2007). These evaluations about the course consist of both quantitative ratings using Likert-type scales and open-ended comments that describe student experiences. In many universities, SETs are a standard component of evaluations of teaching and have multiple functions. First, they help individual faculty members examine their own teaching performance in a diagnostic way so they can work to improve their approach in subsequent offerings of the course. Second, SETs allow institution leaders to review and describe the educational quality of course offerings and the performance of instructors. Third, though controversial, SET summaries often are used as part of an instructor's larger portfolio to demonstrate their teaching history during high-stakes settings. Finally, in some colleges and universities, SET summaries are released to students to help guide them with course selections. Given this wide range of uses for the SET summaries, it is important that thoughtful, accurate, and well-designed representations are provided to draw accurate inferences about teaching quality, course design, and student learning (see ethics Sec. 7 for more details).

Usually, at the end of each semester, SET results are summarized into a PDF report for instructors or other reviewers. As shown in a sample standard SET report in Fig. 5 of Appendix, quantitative ratings are summarized using basic statistics, such as mean and median, while students' comments from open-ended questions are simply listed as raw text – without adequate organization and analyses. When a college course is particularly large (e.g., with more than 100 students), the final SET report can be longer than 10 pages, which is time-consuming to read and analyze (Alhija and Fresko, 2009). In addition, instructors' or other reviewers' own cognitive biases may lead to inaccurate inferences and analyses, e.g., people tend to pay more attention to negative than positive comments (Kanouse and Hanson Jr, 1987).

Therefore, the goal of our work is to provide a new dynamic presentation of SET results to facilitate more efficient and less biased interpretations compared to the standard PDF report. After obtaining institutional SET data of four semesters from the University of North Carolina (UNC) at Chapel Hill, for demonstration we select two quantitative and two open-ended questions from the total number of questions (Sec. 3). We develop a system, SETSum, to summarize and visualize the results of these four questions. For quantitative ratings

* Equal contribution.

Proceedings of the 2022 Conference of the North American Chapter of the Association for Computational Linguistics: Human Language Technologies: System Demonstrations, pages 71 - 89
July 10-15, 2022 ©2022 Association for Computational Linguistics

(Sec. 4.1), we visualize two statistics: *response rate* and *sentiment distribution*. For open-ended comments (Sec. 4.2), we develop a sentiment analysis model to predict whether each comment sentence is positive or negative. We use an aspect extraction approach to help instructors quickly know the popularly discussed topics by students, e.g., assignment, and the corresponding topic sentiments. Finally, we propose an unsupervised extractive summarization method that extracts top sentences with high centrality, low redundancy, and balanced sentiments as a summary of each aspect.

Automatic evaluations (Sec. 5.1) demonstrate that our sentiment prediction and aspect extraction modules achieve good accuracy, and our summarization method produces more diverse and less biased summaries than simply picking top central sentences. More critically, the effectiveness of SETSUM should be judged by its main users – instructors. Thus, we begin by conducting human evaluations (Sec. 5.2) with 10 professors from 8 different academic departments at UNC. Note that SETSUM is continuously under development, and our human evaluations were conducted on our very first version: SETSUM V1.0. After evaluating the two SET presentation approaches, instructors are asked to complete a survey comparing the usefulness of SETSUM to the standard SET report. According to their responses, most of the new features introduced on SETSUM are perceived as *useful* to *very useful* by most instructors (on average, 8.8 out of 10), compared to the standard report. All 10 instructors agree that SETSUM helps them interpret their ratings and comments more efficiently; while 4 out of 10 think the new system also supports less biased interpretations. Finally, 6 of 10 favor SETSUM more than the standard approach; the remaining 4 think both reports could be helpful. Overall, for our first evaluation, instructors hold a *positive* attitude towards SETSUM and offer valuable and constructive suggestions to us.

Lastly, in Sec. 7, we discuss if machine-involved representations of SETs may introduce new errors or bias and if so, what improvement needs to be made before the "demonstration" can transition to an "application". Our system aims to provide accurate, efficient, and visualized SET results to instructors or other reviewers. It does not directly make any value judgments or evaluations about the instructor's skills, the course design, or the amount of student learning during the term.

To the best of our knowledge, despite its widespread use, we are among the few researchers to develop a pilot system that presents student-reported evaluations of teaching by using natural language processing (NLP) techniques. In addition, we are the first to apply the system for a SET instrument and evaluate it using actual SET data from a large public university. Though more development work is in progress, our results demonstrate that our approach is promising to reform the SET report conventions in the future. Our SETSUM V1.1 website requires credentials to login, please contact us for an access to the website. We provide a YouTube video to walk you through SETSUM V1.1. Our code is hosted at SETSum Github Repo.

2 Background & Related Work

As mentioned, SETs are widely used in higher education (Chen and Hoshower, 2003; Zabaleta, 2007). SET studies have shown that they can capture students' opinions about instruction (Balam and Shannon, 2010), enhance course design, can be used as a tool for assessing teaching performance (Penny and Coe, 2004; Chen and Hoshower, 2003), and reflect institutional accountability about teaching (Spooren et al., 2013). Many instructors view SETs as valuable feedback to improve their teaching quality (Griffin, 2001; Kulik, 2001). Many studies focus on instrument design (i.e., which questions to ask), reliability and validity of SET results (i.e., are the scores consistent across contexts; are scores related to other key constructs), and potential confounding variables that affect SETs (e.g., do scores differ by discipline, instructor race/ethnicity and gender, student grade) (Simpson and Siguaw, 2000; Spooren et al., 2013).

Typical SET instruments include quantitative Likert-scale ratings. They are supplemented by open-ended comments (Stupans et al., 2016; Marshall, 2021). Therefore, compared to quantitative ratings, open-ended comments are often under-analyzed or ignored completely due to labor required to provide an adequate summary (Alhija and Fresko, 2009; Hujala et al., 2020), raising the need for contemporary methods in automated text analysis. Recent works start to analyze student comments via text mining and machine learning methods such as sentiment analysis (Wen et al., 2014; Azab et al., 2016; Cunningham-Nelson et al., 2018; Baddam et al., 2019; Sengkey et al., 2019; Hew et al., 2020), and identify *topics*, *themes*, or

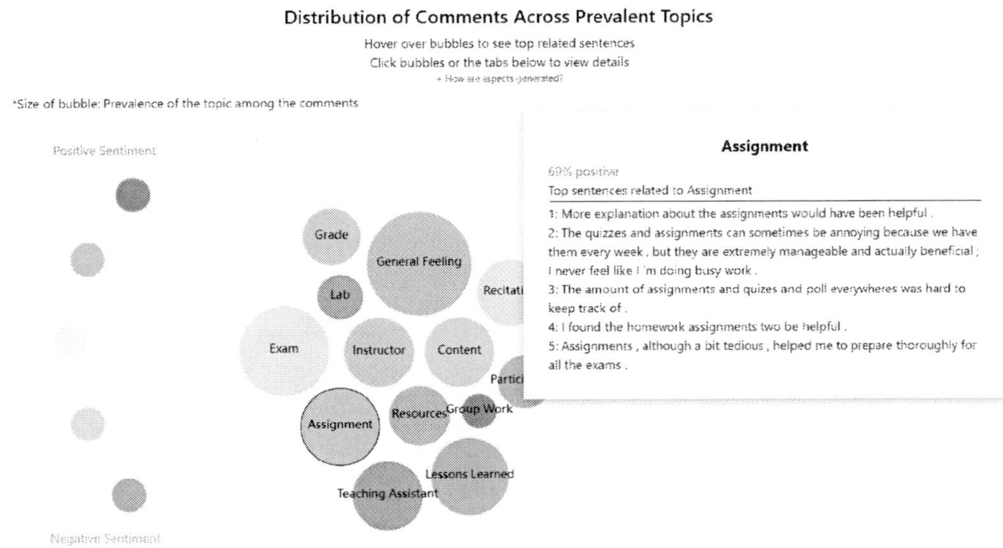

Figure 1: The distribution of comments across prevalent topics (aspects). On the left, it shows the aspect bubble chart, and on the right, it shows the summary of the "assignment" aspect.

suggestions from student comments (Ramesh et al., 2014; Stupans et al., 2016; Gottipati et al., 2018; Unankard and Nadee, 2019; Hynninen et al., 2019). The common goal of these works is to answer some research questions (e.g., what are sentiment differences across courses and students). In contrast, we provide a demonstration tool of SET results to help instructors gain insights on their own and to allow others have access to organized summaries.

The most relevant works to ours are SUFAT (Pyasi et al., 2018) and Palaute (Grönberg et al., 2021) – two analytic tools for student comments. They both support sentiment analysis and LDA topic models (Blei et al., 2003), while we use more advanced RoBERTa-based sentiment analysis and weakly-supervised aspect extraction models. SUFAT requires users to install the tool and load SET files locally, while our online website directly reads the data from the SET instrument. More importantly, none of them conducts human evaluations, which makes it unclear if their tools are useful from the actual users' perspectives. Therefore, we develop the first demonstration system that uses an actual university SET instrument and is evaluated by university instructors who are interpreting their own evaluations.

3 SET Data

We use Student Evaluations of Teaching (SETs) data of over four academic terms (Fall 2017, Spring 2018, Fall 2018, Spring 2019) collected at UNC Chapel Hill. We utilize "semester + course number" as the specific identity of each course. We assume each course has just one instructor.[1] In total, there are about 5.6K courses and 298K SETs. Each SET is an evaluation questionnaire assigned to a student for a specific course they enrolled in, including both quantitative and open-ended questions.

UNC's SET instrument includes a series of evaluation questions assessing different aspects of the course and instructor. For demonstration, we select four representative questions – two quantitative and two open-ended items. For quantitative items, we choose *Overall, this course was excellent (Course Rate)* and *Overall, this instructor was an effective teacher (Instructor Rate)*, showing students' overall ratings on the course and instructor performance. Both items are based on a 5-point Likert scale (1 = Strongly Disagree to 5 = Strongly Agree). For open-ended items, we choose *Comments on overall assessment of this course (Course Comments)* and *Comments on overall assessment of this instructor (Instructor Comments)*. Our system can be easily extended to the full set of SET questions.

Because completing the SET form is not mandatory, the average response rates of the two quantitative items we choose are 46% and 43% respectively, and even lower response rates are observed for the two open-ended items: 17% and 16%, respectively.

[1] This is not always true, and we will deal with co-teaching situations in the next version of our system.

4 System Description

After logging in, instructors can select to display their SET results of which semester and which course. The dashboard shows two main sections: *Rating Analysis* and *Comment Analysis*. See screenshots of our demo in Fig. 6 (SETSUM V1.0) and Fig. 7 (SETSUM V1.1) in Appendix.

4.1 Rating Analysis

For each of the two quantitative questions, we show the following statistics.

Response Rate. Since students do not always respond to every SET question, knowing how many students responded is critical for interpreting the generalizability and representativeness of the results. The standard report (Fig. 5) provides the number of responses for each question. To make this information stand out, we use a circular packing chart to describe the proportion of students who answered the question in comparison to the total enrollment of the course (Fig. 2).

Sentiment Distribution. The standard SET report summarizes quantitative ratings by mean, median, standard deviation, and percentages of the 5 rating options. Instead, in SETSUM V1.0, we simplify ratings to be either *positive* (4 and 5) or *negative* (3 or lower). We show the positive vs. negative ratings via a pie chart (Fig. 3 in Appendix). However, after conducting human evaluations on SETSUM V1.0, we received feedback from instructors preferring the original 5-point scale distribution. Thus, in SETSUM V1.1, we include a detailed breakdown of all scores.

4.2 Comment Analysis

For open-ended questions, besides the option to view all raw comments as the standard report (by clicking the "View Raw Comments" button in SETSUM V1.0 or the "Table View" button in SETSUM V1.1), we provide the following new features.

4.2.1 Basic Statistics

We present the **Response Rate** of open-ended questions also by a circular packing chart. Student comments are raw texts without sentiment labels. Therefore, we develop a sentiment analysis model (Sec. 4.2.2) and get the sentiment of each comment sentence. Then, we display the **Sentiment Distribution** (positive vs. negative ratio) via a pie chart for instructors to acquire an overview of students' sentiments expressed in comments.

4.2.2 Sentiment Analysis

As mentioned in Sec. 2, many existing works have conducted sentiment analysis on SET data (Wen et al., 2014; Azab et al., 2016; Baddam et al., 2019). In UNC's SET instrument, no sentiment labels are explicitly related to student comments. To train a sentiment analysis model, we pair *Course Comments* with the *Course Rate* since they are both overall assessment of the course. Similarly, we pair *Instructor Comments* with *Instructor Rate*.

We want to get sentence-level sentiments to compute the overall sentiment of each aspect (Sec. 4.2.3) and conduct summarization (Sec. 4.2.4). However, ratings are comment-level sentences. Thus, we first train a comment-level sentiment analysis model, and then we use it to predict the sentiments of each comment sentence.

4.2.3 Aspect Extraction

Students usually comment on some common *aspects* of the course, e.g., grade, assignment. Previous works resort to LDA (Blei et al., 2003) to learn *topics* from student comments (Ramesh et al., 2014; Pyasi et al., 2018; Grönberg et al., 2021). We argue that each topic learned from LDA is a set of words that is hard to be assigned a post hoc name, and topics sometimes lack distinctions (Ramesh et al., 2014). Therefore, we apply a weakly-supervised aspect extraction model, MATE (Angelidis and Lapata, 2018), that can extract aspects from comments using a set of pre-defined aspects.

MATE. *Multi Seed Aspect Extractor* (MATE) (Angelidis and Lapata, 2018) is derived from *Aspect-Based Autoencoder* (ABAE) (He et al., 2017). ABAE learns a sentence-level aspect predictor without supervision by reconstructing the sentence embedding as a linear combination of aspect embeddings. Assume $\mathbf{v}_s$ is the sentence embedding and $\mathbf{A}$ is a matrix of aspect embeddings, ABAE first predicts aspects: $\mathbf{p}_s^{aspect} = softmax(\mathbf{W}\mathbf{v}_s + \mathbf{b})$, and then reconstructs the sentence vector: $\mathbf{r}_s = \mathbf{A}^\top \mathbf{p}_s^{aspect}$. The objective is a max-margin loss using random sentences n_i as negative examples:

$$\mathcal{L} = \sum_s \sum_i max(0, 1 - \mathbf{r}_s \mathbf{v}_s + \mathbf{r}_s \mathbf{v}_{n_i})$$

Similar to LDA, ABAE has to interpret the learned aspects post hoc. To address this, MATE predefines a set of aspects by humans, and each aspect is given a set of *seed words*. Concatenating seed word embeddings together forms an aspect seed matrix $\mathbf{A}_i$, and the final aspect embedding matrix $\mathbf{A} = [\mathbf{A}_1^\top \mathbf{z}_1, ..., \mathbf{A}_K^\top \mathbf{z}_K]$, where $\mathbf{z}_i$ is a weight vector of seed words.

Aspect Annotation. To pre-label aspects of student comments and get seed words for each aspect, we randomly sample 100 comments for each of the two open-ended questions from the entire corpus and split them into sentences. Two human annotators (two authors) work together, attribute one or more aspects to each sentence, and label the corresponding aspect sentiments (positive or negative). Table 3 in Appendix shows two examples. In the end, we obtain 14 and 10 aspects of comments on course and instructor, respectively, and their terminology is defined in Table 5, 6 in Appendix. With the annotations, we calculate *clarity* scores (Cronen-Townsend et al., 2002) of each word w.r.t. each aspect (see details in Appendix A). The higher the clarity score, the more likely the word will appear in sentences of a specific aspect. We manually select 5 top-scored words for each aspect while removing noise (stopwords, names). Their scores are re-normalized to add up to 1. Table 4 shows the 5 seed words (plus weights) for each aspect.

Visualization. After training the MATE model, we predict the aspects of each comment sentence. We select all aspects that have $p_s^{aspect} > 0.4$. The threshold (0.4) is tuned on the subset with aspect annotations. Then, for each open-ended question of each course, we visualize its aspect distribution via a bubble chart (Fig. 1). Bubble size represents the number of sentences of this aspect. While bubble color denotes the aspect sentiment – the average of sentence-level sentiments, we chose accessible color palette (the more blue the more positive, the more yellow the more negative).

4.2.4 Extractive Summarization

After clustering comments by aspects, we want to provide a summary of each aspect. We first obtain the "centrality" of each sentence and then propose a method to extract summaries with high centrality, low redundancy, and balanced sentiments.

LexRank. For all the comment sentences under a certain aspect, we use LexRank (Erkan and Radev, 2004) to get the graph-based "centrality" of each sentence, where we use the cosine similarity of sentence embeddings from Sentence-BERT (Reimers and Gurevych, 2019). Intuitively, if a sentence is similar to many other sentences, it will be close to the "center" of the graph and thus it is prominent.

Algorithm 1: Summarization

```
Input: S^a, K
Output: S'
S' ← ∅, S'_a ← S_a, k ← 1;
while k ≤ K do
    s ← argmax_{s∈S'_a} J(s, S', S_a);
    S' ← S' ∪ {s};
    S'_a ← S'_a − {s};
    k ← k + 1
end
```

Sentence Extraction Algorithm. Naively, we could extract the top central sentences as the summary. However, such summary sometimes includes redundant information and tends to only select positive sentences as they are more common. Inspired by Hsu and Tan (2021), we propose a greedy sentence extraction algorithm that optimizes three objectives on sentence selection: (1) maximizes centrality; (2) maximizes the difference between the sentence and other sentences extracted from previous steps; (3) minimizes the difference between the summary sentiment and the overall sentiment of the aspect. Algorithm 1 demonstrates our unsupervised extractive summarization algorithm, in which S_a represents all sentences under an aspect a, K is the number of sentences we want to extract (K=5), and S' is the target summary. Our learning objective (we want to maximize it) at each extraction step is written as:

$$\begin{aligned} J(s, S', S_a) = &\ \text{centrality}_s - \text{cosine\_sim}(s, S') \\ &- \text{senti\_diff}(S' \cup \{s\}, S_a) \end{aligned}$$

Essentially, we want to extract a summary with high centrality, low redundancy, and a balanced sentiment. centrality_s is the centrality of sentence s. Following Hsu and Tan (2021), we define $\text{cosine\_sim}(s, S')$ as follows:

$$\text{cosine\_sim}(s, S') = \max_{s' \in S'} \text{cosine}(v_s, v_{s'})$$

where v_s and $v_{s'}$ are sentence embeddings from Sentence-BERT (Reimers and Gurevych, 2019). And we define $\text{senti\_diff}(S' \cup \{s\}, S_a)$, as the following:

$$\text{senti\_diff} = \left| \frac{\sum_{s' \in S' \cup \{s\}} p(s')}{|S' \cup \{s\}|} - \frac{\sum_{s' \in S_a} p(s')}{|S_a|} \right|$$

where p is the probability of positive sentiment predicted by our sentiment analysis model.

Visualization. Hovering any bubble in the aspect bubble chart will display its summary on the right (Fig. 1). Clicking on the aspect tab will display listed summary sentences within their the original comments to provide contextual information. A table of all sentences is on the bottom.

5 Evaluation & Results

5.1 Automatic Evaluation

Sentiment Analysis. We train two comment-level sentiment analysis models for *Course Comments* and *Instructor Comments* respectively. We split our data into training (90%) and development (10%) sets, and about 6.3K and 5.8K examples are in Course and Instructor development sets respectively. We first report comment-level sentiment prediction performance on the dev sets. Second, we use the comment-level sentiment analysis models to predict sentence-level sentiments during inference. To evaluate this, we use our aspect annotation data (Table 3 in Appendix), and we only use sentences with just one sentiment (i.e., all aspects are positive or negative), resulting in 202 and 230 testing examples for Course and Instructor. We report micro F1 (=accuracy) and macro F1. Table 1 shows the results. It can be seen that our models achieve reasonably good sentiment prediction performance, though they perform worse on predicting sentence-level sentiments than the comment level.

Aspect Extraction. Similarly, we also train two aspect extraction models for *Course Comments* and *Instructor Comments* separately. We evaluate their performance by comparing to human annotated aspects using F1 score. In total, we have 213 and 234 testing examples for course and instructor models, and the average number of aspects is 1.38 and 1.31, respectively. We achieve F1 score of 48.6 for the course model and 48.9 for the instructor model, which are similar to the results of the MATE paper (Angelidis and Lapata, 2018). We also explore another approach by treating aspect extraction as a multi-label aspect classification task. We use half of the annotated data to finetune a RoBERTa-base (Liu et al., 2019) model and test on the other half annotated aspects. Our experiment shows improved F1 scores of 62.6 for the course model and 64.9 for the instructor model. We plan to combine RoBERTa and MATE to deploy a weakly-supervised RoBERTa-based MATE in our next version of website.

Sentiment Analysis	Course	Instructor
Comment-level micro F1	0.87	0.94
Comment-level macro F1	0.83	0.86
Sentence-level micro F1	0.83	0.90
Sentence-level macro F1	0.84	0.85

Table 1: Sentiment analysis results.

Summarization	Course		Instructor	
	Base.	Ours	Base.	Ours
Centrality↑	**1.13**	1.09	**1.14**	1.10
Redundancy↓	0.05	**0.03**	0.05	**0.02**
Sentiment Diff↓	0.41	**0.34**	0.43	**0.36**

Table 2: Summarization results.

Summarization. Due to the lack of gold summaries, we use three metrics (*Centrality*, *Redundancy*, and *Sentiment Difference*) to evaluate our summarization approach and compare it to the baseline of extracting the top 5 central sentences. Please refer to Appendix C for detailed definitions of these three metircs. We randomly sampled 100 courses as the testing set to report the performance. Table 2 shows the results. As expected, our method leads to lower redundancy and sentiment difference than the baseline, though it scarifies some centrality.

5.2 Human Evaluation

It is critical to evaluate how our demonstration system is perceived by its primary users: instructors.

5.2.1 Evaluation Setup

Design a Survey. We design an evaluation survey using Qualtrics. Our complete survey can be found at SETSum Github Repo. In the survey, we first introduce the background and purpose. We define the standard PDF report *Usual Approach* and our SETSUM V1.0 as *Comparison Approach*, and then we ask instructors to compare the two approaches. The main survey body contains 5 parts of questions:

(1) *Rate the Usual Approach*: Without comparing to SETSUM, we ask how they rate the usefulness of standard SET reports in a 5-point scale: not at all, slightly, moderately, very, or extremely useful;

(2) *Rate* SETSUM *(Rating Analysis)*: Compared to the usual approach, instructors rate our new features of summarizing ratings in a slightly different 5-point scale: not at all useful, not useful, equally useful, useful, or very useful;

(3) *Rate* SETSUM *(Comments Analysis)*: Compared to the usual approach, we ask how useful each of our new features of summarizing comments is (using the same response anchors as (2)).

(4) *Rate the overall experience with* SETSUM: We ask if our website helps them interpret SET results more efficiently and/or with less bias (definitely not, probably not, might or might not, probably yes, definitely yes) as well as if they prefer the standard SET report or our website or both.

(5) *Comments*: Instructors may leave additional comments on the website under development.

Invite Instructors. We invited 15 professors at UNC, who taught large introductory courses within the studied period (4 semesters). We estimated the survey to take 20-30 minutes, and each participant was offered a $25 gift card to a campus coffee shop. In the end, 10 instructors from 8 different departments completed the survey successfully.

5.2.2 Results Analysis

Fig. 4 shows the survey results, and the Qualtrics report can be found at SETSum Github Repo. Here, we summarize some main takeaways.

Instructors have positive opinions about the standard SET report. 8 out of 10 (and 6 out of 10) instructors think the PDF report is *moderately to extremely useful* in summarizing students' ratings (and comments), respectively. This demonstrates the well-perceived usefulness of existing SET reports by instructors, though they are less satisfied with the comment summarization.

New features introduced on SETSUM are perceived to be useful or very useful. On average, for rating analysis, 7 out of 10 instructors think each of the 2 new features (response rate and sentiment distribution) is *useful* or *very useful*, and for comments analysis, 8.8 out of 10 instructors on avg. think each of the 5 new features (response rate, sentiment distribution, topic bubbles, summary sentences, showing original comments for each summary sentence) is *useful* or *very useful*, while fewer instructors (5.5 out of 10 on avg.) think the scatter plot[2] and the table showing all comment sentences are *useful* or *very useful*. Overall, most instructors perceive our SETSUM as being useful.

SETSUM helps all instructors interpret SET results more efficiently, and it helps some instructors interpret SET results with less bias. All instructors agree that SETSUM helps them interpret SETs *more efficiently* (i.e., probably to definitely yes). 4 out of 10 instructors think it helps them understand SETs *with less bias*.

Instructors prefer SETSUM than the standard report or would like to have both. Lastly, 6 out of 10 instructors prefer SETSUM compared to the usual approach, while 4 instructors would like to have both approaches.

Constructive suggestions. We identify the following suggestions from instructors' comments for improving our future version: (1) The accuracy of the sentiment analysis and aspect extraction models can still be improved. (2) Many instructors prefer the complete display of ratings in the 5-point scale, rather than presenting only a positive v.s. negative ratio. (3) Instructors without a computer science background had difficulty understanding concepts like "centrality". So far, we addressed (2) and (3) in SETSUM V1.1 by providing the 5-point scale rating distribution and adding detailed explanations for each Machine Learning related modules.

Overall, instructors show a very positive attitude towards our SETSUM demonstration system and provided important suggestions and direction for our future work.

6 Conclusion

In this work, we propose SETSUM, a system to summarize and visualize results from student evaluations of teaching. We integrate NLP, statistical, visualization, and web service techniques. We are among the few researchers to build a tool for instructor use and are the first to evaluate the tool by university professors. Our results demonstrate that our system is promising at improving the SET report paradigm and helps instructors gain insights from their SETs more efficiently. In the future, we will keep improving the sentiment analysis and aspect extraction models to provide more accurate summarization of SET results. The instructor evaluation offered key recommendations for the next iterations of the system. We will incorporate more functions to our system, including allowing instructors to compare different courses and track their own teaching history of their courses as well as developing a separate administrator dashboard to identify themes across academic courses, departments, and programs.

[2]We had a scatter plot showing all comment sentences in SETSUM V1.0, which was removed from SETSUM V1.1.

7 Ethical Considerations

As mentioned earlier, SETs have multiple functions such as (1) faculty members examining their teaching performance in a diagnostic way, (2) allowing institution leaders to review and describe the quality of course offerings, (3) part of an instructor's larger portfolio to demonstrate their teaching history during high-stakes settings, and (4) summaries being released to students to guide them with course selections. Given this wide range of uses for the SET summaries, our work's purpose is to take initial steps towards developing thoughtful, accurate, and well-designed representations that can be provided to draw accurate inferences about teaching quality, course design, and student learning. However, it is also critical to examine all aspects of SETs through an ethical lens. Errors in NLP-based analysis could lead to misinterpretation and inaccurate judgments in high-stakes settings. Therefore in the following, we discuss how each module of our SETSum website affects the interpretation of SET results.

For quantitative items, we provide visualizations of two statistics that are directly computed from SET data. Therefore, no errors or biases should be introduced compared to the standard PDF report. In fact, some instructors who participated in our evaluations say that the *response rate* feature for each individual question helps them understand the results with less bias.

For open-ended items, to obtain their sentiment distributions, we develop sentiment analysis models to obtain sentence-level sentiments. Though we obtain good sentiment prediction performance (Table 1), errors are inevitable. We use these features to demonstrate the relative number of positive to negative comments (ratio). In general, unless very few students evaluate a course (low response rate for comments), the system can still convey the information fairly well. Another important feature that we develop as part of this system is to group comment sentences by aspects. Although we achieve similar aspect prediction F1 scores consistent with past research, we find that the results are not precise enough yet for widespread use. Our human evaluators notice that some sentences from the open-ended comments are inaccurately clustered. Therefore, in future iterations of this system, we believe it is very important to develop a more accurate aspect extraction model. The final important feature is the unsupervised extraction summarization module. We choose an extraction method because it does not suffer from faithfulness (not staying true to the source) issues as abstractive methods (Cao et al., 2018). Meanwhile, our algorithm extracts summaries with more balanced sentiments (Table 2). Nonetheless, we hope to find a summarization approach that aligns more closely with the sentiments underlying the students' comments.

Though instructors express positive attitudes towards our system and 4 instructors think it help them understand SETs with less bias, we believe that additional thorough evaluations need to be conducted in the future. Outside of SETs, our work recognizes the different ways, reporters, and methods that could be used to assess teaching effectiveness, including but not limited to peer reports, analysis of classroom sound, student learning, and an instructor's own teaching portfolio.

Finally, at this time our system is designed to be used and reviewed by instructors or other reviewers, and it *does not* directly make any broad judgments or decisions (e.g., whether the instructor is qualified for promotion). The primary end-users of the system should be instructors who wish to analyze their SET findings more thoroughly and acquire the main takeaways more efficiently. Other reviewers and administrators can use the system to view the SET findings in a broader scope, such as reading the report summary per department or per division. Overall, the goal of SETSUM is to help instructors and other reviewers to understand more of students' needs and make improvements to future course design.

Acknowledgments

We thank the reviewers for their helpful comments. We thank the UNC instructors who participated in our human evaluations. We would also like to thank Heather Thompson from the Office of Undergraduate Curricula for providing the data and Rob Ricks from the Office of Institutional Research and Assessment for additional data preparation activities. This work was supported by NSF-CAREER Award 1846185, NSF-AI Engage Institute DRL-2112635, a Bloomberg Data Science Ph.D. Fellowship, and the Howard Hughes Medical Institute Inclusive Excellence 3 Grant.

References

Fadia Nasser-Abu Alhija and Barbara Fresko. 2009. Student evaluation of instruction: What can be learned from students' written comments? *Studies in Educational evaluation*, 35(1):37–44.

Stefanos Angelidis and Mirella Lapata. 2018. Summarizing opinions: Aspect extraction meets sentiment prediction and they are both weakly supervised. In *Proceedings of the 2018 Conference on Empirical Methods in Natural Language Processing*, pages 3675–3686, Brussels, Belgium. Association for Computational Linguistics.

Mahmoud Azab, Rada Mihalcea, and Jacob Abernethy. 2016. Analysing ratemyprofessors evaluations across institutions, disciplines, and cultures: The tell-tale signs of a good professor. In *International Conference on Social Informatics*, pages 438–453. Springer.

Swathi Baddam, Prasad Bingi, and Syed Shuva. 2019. Student evaluation of teaching in business education: Discovering student sentiments using text mining techniques. *e-Journal of Business Education and Scholarship of Teaching*, 13(3):1–13.

Esenc M Balam and David M Shannon. 2010. Student ratings of college teaching: A comparison of faculty and their students. *Assessment & Evaluation in Higher Education*, 35(2):209–221.

David M Blei, Andrew Y Ng, and Michael I Jordan. 2003. Latent dirichlet allocation. *Journal of machine Learning research*, 3(Jan):993–1022.

Ziqiang Cao, Furu Wei, Wenjie Li, and Sujian Li. 2018. Faithful to the original: Fact aware neural abstractive summarization. In *Proceedings of the AAAI Conference on Artificial Intelligence*, volume 32.

Yining Chen and Leon B Hoshower. 2003. Student evaluation of teaching effectiveness: An assessment of student perception and motivation. *Assessment & evaluation in higher education*, 28(1):71–88.

Steve Cronen-Townsend, Yun Zhou, and W Bruce Croft. 2002. Predicting query performance. In *Proceedings of the 25th annual international ACM SIGIR conference on Research and development in information retrieval*, pages 299–306.

Sam Cunningham-Nelson, Mahsa Baktashmotlagh, and Wageeh Boles. 2018. Visually exploring sentiment and keywords for analysing student satisfaction data. *Proceedings of the 29th Australasian Association of Engineering Education (AAEE 2018)*, pages 1–7.

Günes Erkan and Dragomir R Radev. 2004. Lexrank: Graph-based lexical centrality as salience in text summarization. *Journal of artificial intelligence research*, 22:457–479.

Swapna Gottipati, Venky Shankararaman, and Jeff Rongsheng Lin. 2018. Text analytics approach to extract course improvement suggestions from students' feedback. *Research and Practice in Technology Enhanced Learning*, 13(1):1–19.

Bryan W Griffin. 2001. Instructor reputation and student ratings of instruction. *Contemporary educational psychology*, 26(4):534–552.

Niku Grönberg, Antti Knutas, Timo Hynninen, and Maija Hujala. 2021. Palaute: An online text mining tool for analyzing written student course feedback. *IEEE Access*, 9:134518–134529.

Ruidan He, Wee Sun Lee, Hwee Tou Ng, and Daniel Dahlmeier. 2017. An unsupervised neural attention model for aspect extraction. In *Proceedings of the 55th Annual Meeting of the Association for Computational Linguistics (Volume 1: Long Papers)*, pages 388–397.

Khe Foon Hew, Xiang Hu, Chen Qiao, and Ying Tang. 2020. What predicts student satisfaction with moocs: A gradient boosting trees supervised machine learning and sentiment analysis approach. *Computers & Education*, 145:103724.

Chao-Chun Hsu and Chenhao Tan. 2021. Decision-focused summarization. In *Proceedings of the 2021 Conference on Empirical Methods in Natural Language Processing*, pages 117–132.

Maija Hujala, Antti Knutas, Timo Hynninen, and Heli Arminen. 2020. Improving the quality of teaching by utilising written student feedback: A streamlined process. *Computers & Education*, 157:103965.

Timo Hynninen, Antti Knutas, Maija Hujala, and Heli Arminen. 2019. Distinguishing the themes emerging from masses of open student feedback. In *2019 42nd International Convention on Information and Communication Technology, Electronics and Microelectronics (MIPRO)*, pages 557–561. IEEE.

David E Kanouse and L Reid Hanson Jr. 1987. Negativity in evaluations. In *Preparation of this paper grew out of a workshop on attribution theory held at University of California, Los Angeles, Aug 1969.* Lawrence Erlbaum Associates, Inc.

Diederik P Kingma and Jimmy Ba. 2015. Adam: A method for stochastic optimization. In *ICLR (Poster)*.

James A Kulik. 2001. Student ratings: Validity, utility, and controversy. *New directions for institutional research*, 2001(109):9–25.

Yinhan Liu, Myle Ott, Naman Goyal, Jingfei Du, Mandar Joshi, Danqi Chen, Omer Levy, Mike Lewis, Luke Zettlemoyer, and Veselin Stoyanov. 2019. Roberta: A robustly optimized bert pretraining approach. *arXiv preprint arXiv:1907.11692*.

Ilya Loshchilov and Frank Hutter. 2018. Decoupled weight decay regularization. In *International Conference on Learning Representations*.

Pablo Marshall. 2021. Contribution of open-ended questions in student evaluation of teaching. *Higher Education Research & Development*, pages 1–14.

Jeffrey Pennington, Richard Socher, and Christopher D Manning. 2014. Glove: Global vectors for word representation. In *Proceedings of the 2014 conference on empirical methods in natural language processing (EMNLP)*, pages 1532–1543.

Angela R Penny and Robert Coe. 2004. Effectiveness of consultation on student ratings feedback: A meta-analysis. *Review of educational research*, 74(2):215–253.

Siddhant Pyasi, Swapna Gottipati, and Venky Shankararaman. 2018. Sufat-an analytics tool for gaining insights from student feedback comments. In *2018 IEEE Frontiers in Education Conference (FIE)*, pages 1–9. IEEE.

Arti Ramesh, Dan Goldwasser, Bert Huang, Hal Daumé III, and Lise Getoor. 2014. Understanding mooc discussion forums using seeded lda. In *Proceedings of the ninth workshop on innovative use of NLP for building educational applications*, pages 28–33.

Nils Reimers and Iryna Gurevych. 2019. Sentence-bert: Sentence embeddings using siamese bert-networks. In *Proceedings of the 2019 Conference on Empirical Methods in Natural Language Processing and the 9th International Joint Conference on Natural Language Processing (EMNLP-IJCNLP)*, pages 3982–3992.

Daniel Febrian Sengkey, Agustinus Jacobus, and Fabian Johanes Manoppo. 2019. Implementing support vector machine sentiment analysis to students' opinion toward lecturer in an indonesian public university. *Journal of Sustainable Engineering: Proceedings Series*, 1(2):194–198.

Penny M Simpson and Judy A Siguaw. 2000. Student evaluations of teaching: An exploratory study of the faculty response. *Journal of Marketing Education*, 22(3):199–213.

Pieter Spooren, Bert Brockx, and Dimitri Mortelmans. 2013. On the validity of student evaluation of teaching: The state of the art. *Review of Educational Research*, 83(4):598–642.

Ieva Stupans, Therese McGuren, and Anna Marie Babey. 2016. Student evaluation of teaching: A study exploring student rating instrument free-form text comments. *Innovative Higher Education*, 41(1):33–42.

Sayan Unankard and Wanvimol Nadee. 2019. Topic detection for online course feedback using lda. In *International Symposium on Emerging Technologies for Education*, pages 133–142. Springer.

Miaomiao Wen, Diyi Yang, and Carolyn Rose. 2014. Sentiment analysis in mooc discussion forums: What does it tell us? In *Educational data mining 2014*.

Thomas Wolf, Lysandre Debut, Victor Sanh, Julien Chaumond, Clement Delangue, Anthony Moi, Pierric Cistac, Tim Rault, Remi Louf, Morgan Funtowicz, Joe Davison, Sam Shleifer, Patrick von Platen,

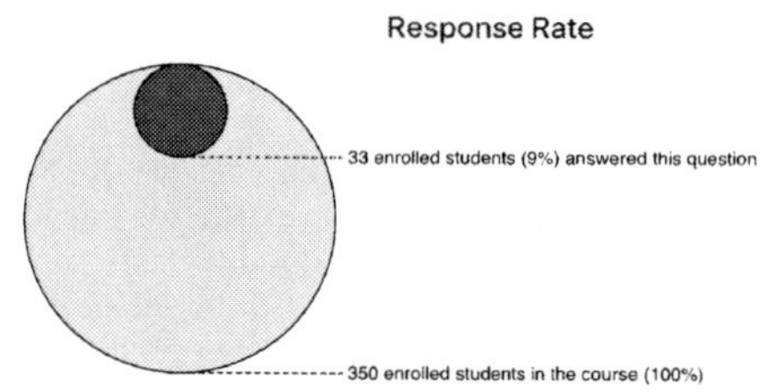

Figure 2: A circular packing chart describes the response rate.

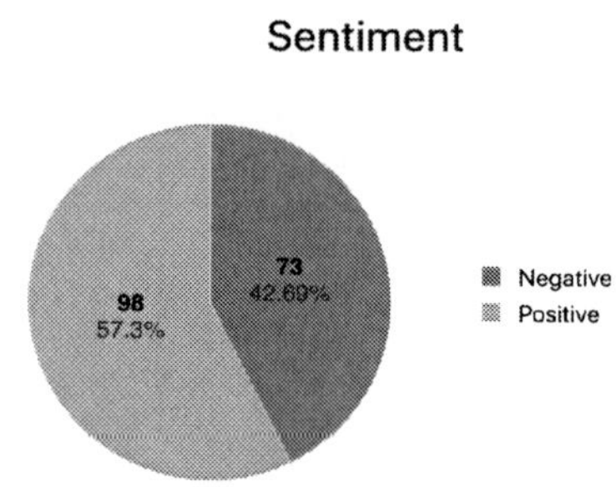

Figure 3: A pie chart describes the sentiment distribution.

Clara Ma, Yacine Jernite, Julien Plu, Canwen Xu, Teven Le Scao, Sylvain Gugger, Mariama Drame, Quentin Lhoest, and Alexander Rush. 2020. Transformers: State-of-the-art natural language processing. In *Proceedings of the 2020 Conference on Empirical Methods in Natural Language Processing: System Demonstrations*, pages 38–45, Online. Association for Computational Linguistics.

Francisco Zabaleta. 2007. The use and misuse of student evaluations of teaching. *Teaching in higher education*, 12(1):55–76.

Appendix

A Clarity Score

To identify seed words for each aspect. We compute the clarity score (Cronen-Townsend et al., 2002; Angelidis and Lapata, 2018) of each word with respect to each aspect. The score measures how likely it is to observe word w in comments of aspect a: $score_a(w) = t_a(w) log \frac{t_a(w)}{t(w)}$, where $t_a(w)$ is the tf-idf score of w in comments of aspect a and $t(w)$ is that in all comments.

B Implementation Details

Sentiment Analysis. We finetuned a RoBERT-large model (Liu et al., 2019) using HuggingFace's Transformers (Wolf et al., 2020) for 5 epochs and chose the best performed checkpoint on the development set. We used the AdamW optimizer

(Loshchilov and Hutter, 2018) with learning rate 1e-5 and batch size 16.

Aspect Extraction. We used NLTK to conduct sentence and word segmentation. We initialized the MATE model using GloVe embeddings (Pennington et al., 2014). During the training, the word embeddings, seed word matrices, and seed weight vectors were fixed and we trained the model for 10 epochs using Adam optimizer (Kingma and Ba, 2015) with learning rate 10^{-1} and batch size 50. We also experimented the multi-label classification approach by finetuning a RoBERTa-base model (Liu et al., 2019) for 10 epochs using AdamW optimizer (Loshchilov and Hutter, 2018) with learning rate 2e-5 and batch size 16.

Website. We developed the website using the React framework for the front-end interface. For the back-end, we set up a database with Firebase and created a RESTful API with Firebase Cloud Functions. Our website is deployed to Netlify.com for an online demonstration.

C Summarization Evaluation Metrics

We define the *Centrality* metric as the average centrality of summary sentences. The higher the metric is, the better. Assume the summary to evaluate is S'.

$$\text{Centrality}(S') = \frac{\sum_{s \in S'} \text{centrality}_s}{|S'|}$$

We compute the information *Redundancy* within a summary S' by taking the average of cosine similarity among sentences. We use sentence embeddings from Sentence-BERT (Reimers and Gurevych, 2019) to compute cosine similarities. The lower the metric is, the better.

$$\text{Redun}(S') = \frac{\sum_{s \in S'} \max_{s' \in S' - \{s\}} \text{cosine}(v_s, v_{s'})}{|S'|}$$

We first compute the average sentiments for the summary S' and all sentences under the aspect S_a, respectively. Then, we take their absolute difference as the final score of *Sentiment Difference*. The lower the metric is, the better.

$$\text{Senti\_diff} = \left|\frac{\sum_{s \in S'} p(s)}{|S'|} - \frac{\sum_{s \in S_a} p(s)}{|S_a|}\right|$$

where p is the probability of positive sentiment predicted by our sentiment analysis model.

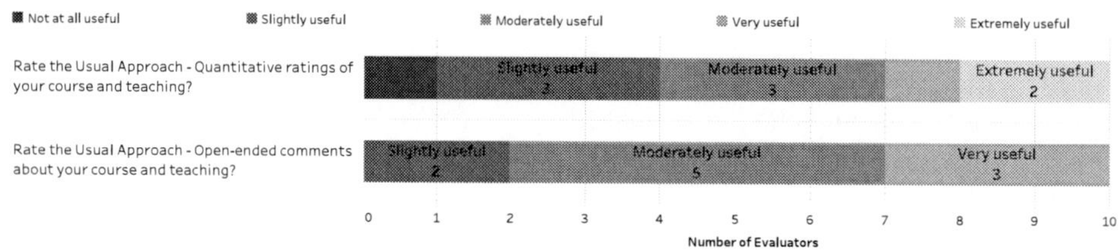

(a) *How useful is the **Usual Approach** in summarizing students' quantitative ratings and open-ended comments of your course and teaching?*

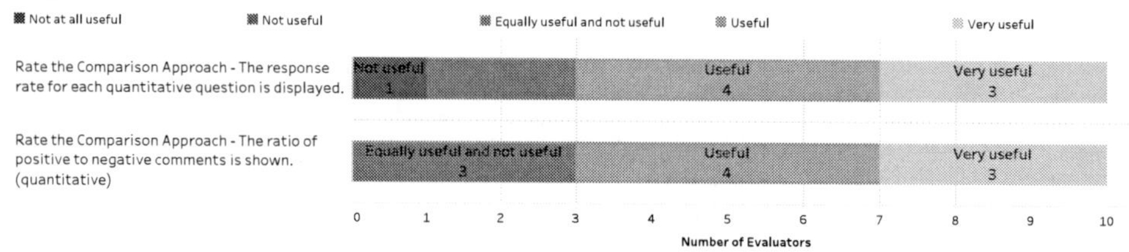

(b) *How useful is the **Comparison Approach** in summarizing students' quantitative comments about your course and teaching?*

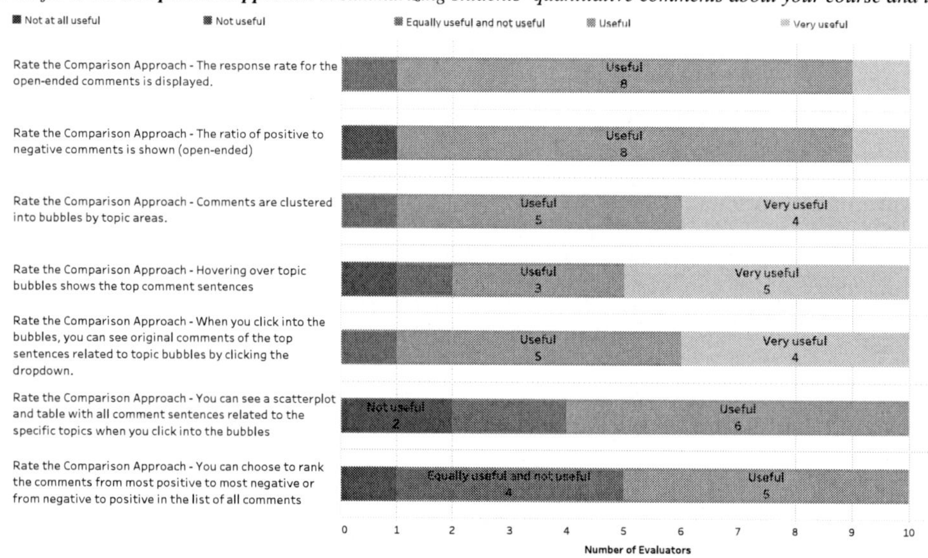

(c) *How useful is the **Comparison Approach** in summarizing students' open-ended comments about your course and teaching?*

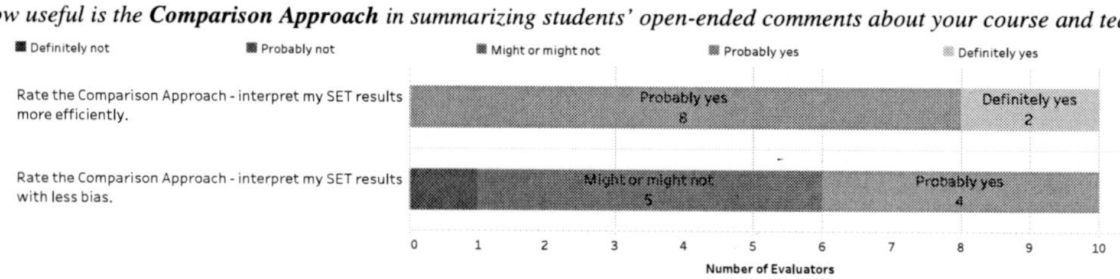

(d) *Overall, how useful is the **Comparison Approach** in summarizing students' opinions about your course and teaching?*

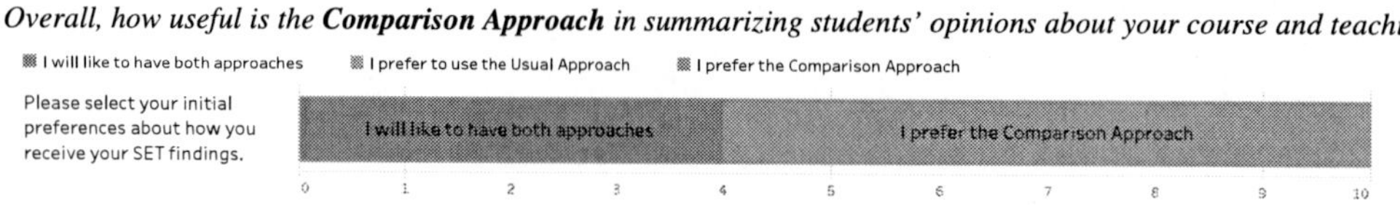

(e) *Overall, please select your initial preference about how you receive your SET findings.*

Figure 4: Results of human evaluation comparing the standard SET report (the Usual Approach) and the SETSUM v1.0 website (the Comparison Approach).

SET Question	Comment Sentence	(Aspect, Sentiment)
Comments on overall assessment of this course	Because, even though the lecture was fine the exams were brutal or was just wrong because of the answer key being wrong.	(content, positive); (exam, negative)
Comments on overall assessment of this instructor	The instructor was clear at explaining information and fairly evaluating all assignments.	(delivery, positive); (grade, positive)

Table 3: Two examples of Aspect Annotation.

University of North Carolina at Chapel Hill, [College]

Student Evaluation of Teaching, [TERM]
[NAME], [COURSE]

Raters	Students
Responded	120
Invited	169
Response Ratio	71.0%

Overall

	Mean	Median	SD	N	Strongly Disagree	Disagree	Neutral	Agree	Strongly Agree
1. Overall, this course was excellent.	4.09	4.00	0.97	120	3.3 %	3.3 %	12.5 %	42.5 %	38.3 %
2. Overall, this instructor was an effective teacher.	4.52	5.00	0.78	117	1.7 %	1.7 %	2.6 %	30.8 %	63.2 %

Comments on Overall Assessment of This Course.

Comments
I did not think I would take what I learned from this class and be able to apply it to any of my other studies or interests in school/life/career, but I am very surprised and happy that I've learned so much and feel way more comfortable and proficient with numbers and data. These are important skills that I am happy to have now.
Dr. [NAME] cares so much about her students and at it made students want to learn more in the course.
I think it could have been structured better. We spent so much time on the relatively easy stuff in the beginning and then spent hardly any time working through the harder topics in the end.
Ms. [NAME] is a great instructor. She really loves what she is teaching, and tries to create a close community between the students.
Everything was great about this course, however I felt very overwhelmed by the group project at the end of the semester and felt like it had been thrown in as an afterthought. If we would have been given more time to complete it, it wouldn't have been as bad. Given the timing in the semester was at the very end and my motivation was already lacking, the project just seemed like a little too much in a short span of time.
I really felt seen and heard by Dr. [NAME]. I appreciate the format of the class and the personalized feed back she gave me at office hours. I like how she encouraged us to share events on campus that are going on, and how she shared about her life as well.
This course, while very challenging, was taught well. While i think the flipped classroom technique is not the most beneficial, Dr. [NAME] was really passionate about the class and tried to make information understood by all.

Comments on Overall Assessment of This Instructor.

Comments
Dr. [NAME] is obviously very passionate about her work and it shows every day. She does all that she can to cater to the needs of her students individually and as a whole. She goes out of her way to provide ample resources to everyone to make sure we all learn course materials to the best of our ability. I specifically appreciated the videos she provided and the notes and tables. I don't believe there is anything I would change as everything worked ideally for me.
She did an excellent job. You can see how passionate she is about the subject which made it more entertaining in class
I think she is an intelligent woman who clearly cares a great deal about her students, but I think she made the course too complicated. There were too many resources, and I didn't find the assignments to be a great help. I also found that "review" before exams was a waste of time and didn't help me at all.
Professor [NAME] was incredible. She worked hard to help her students succeed, and took into account our opinions as students in order to better design the course. Professor [NAME] made herself available to help her students, and showed interest in our success in the class, as well as outside of the class.
I enjoyed the polleverywhere questions we did in class; although I would like to see more questions similar to exam questions.
One of the best instructors I have had at UN
One of the best professors I have had at UNC. She was very understanding and so excited to share her knowledge with us. The videos were so so helpful — I knew/understand almost everything we did in class because of watching the videos beforehand.

[COURSE] - [NAME] - Report Issue Date [DATE] 1

Figure 5: The standard PDF SET report.

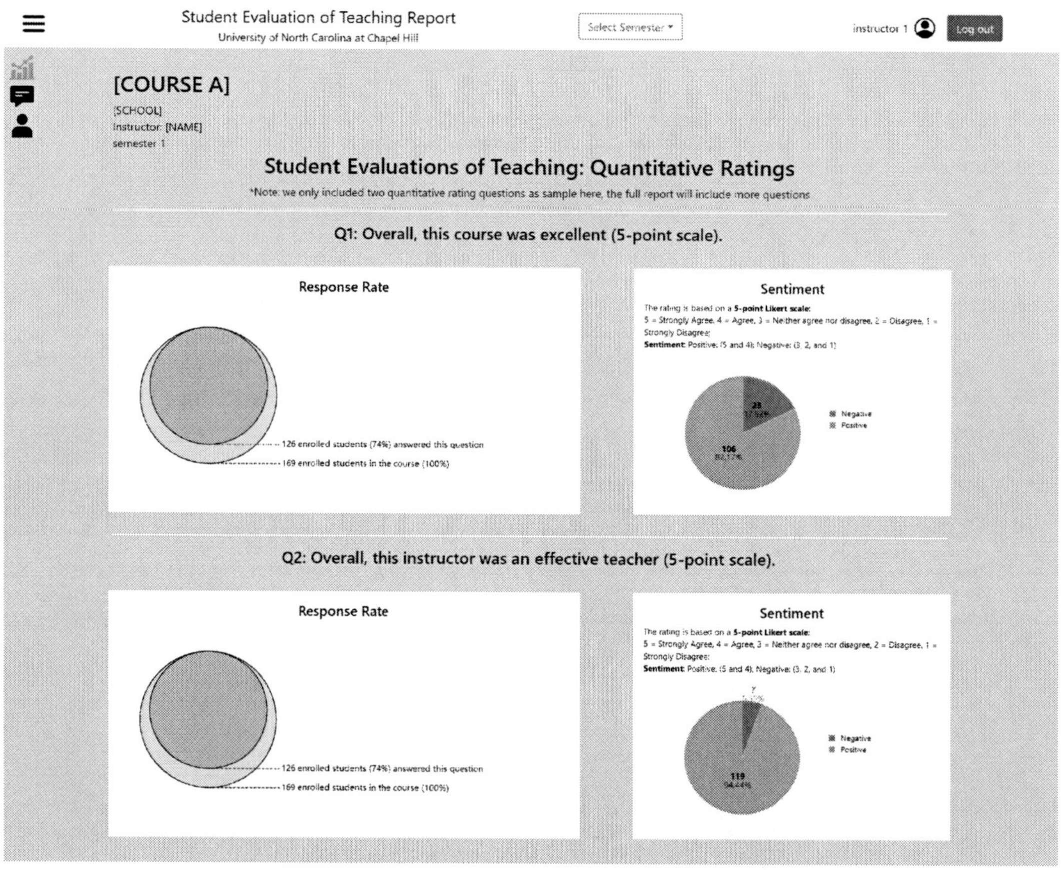

(a) A page shows the Rating Analysis (Quantitative Questions) part.

Figure 6: Screenshots of SETSUM v1.0 (Part1, see Part2 in the next page).

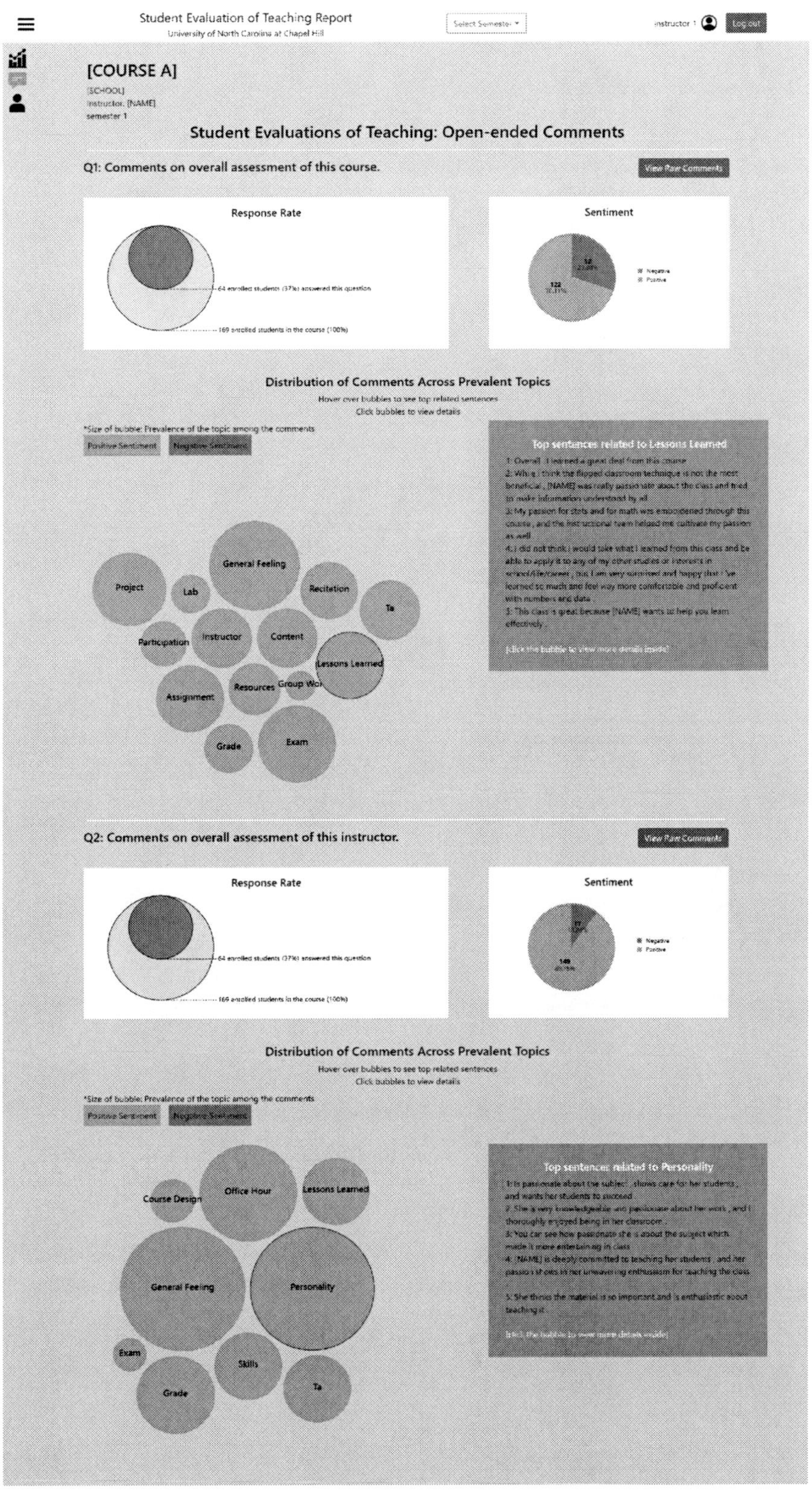

(b) A page shows the Comments Analysis (Open-ended Questions) part.

Figure 6: Screenshots of SETSUM v1.0 (Part2).

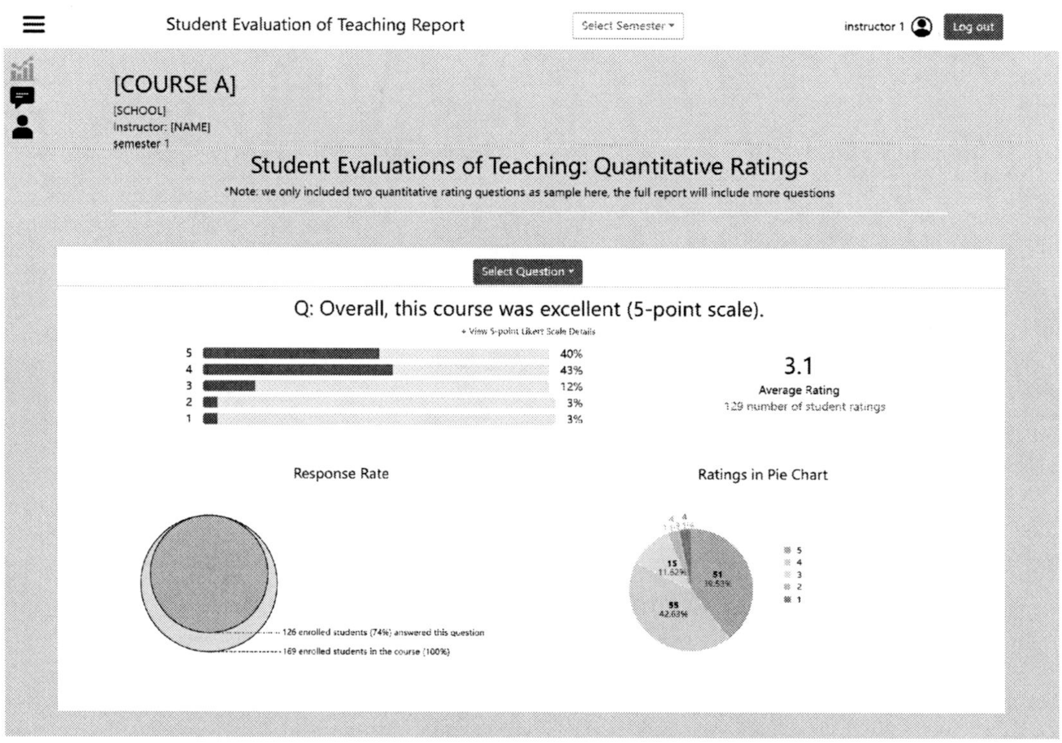

(a) A page shows the Rating Analysis (Quantitative Questions) part.

Figure 7: Screenshots of SETSUM v1.1 (Part1, see Part2 in the next page).

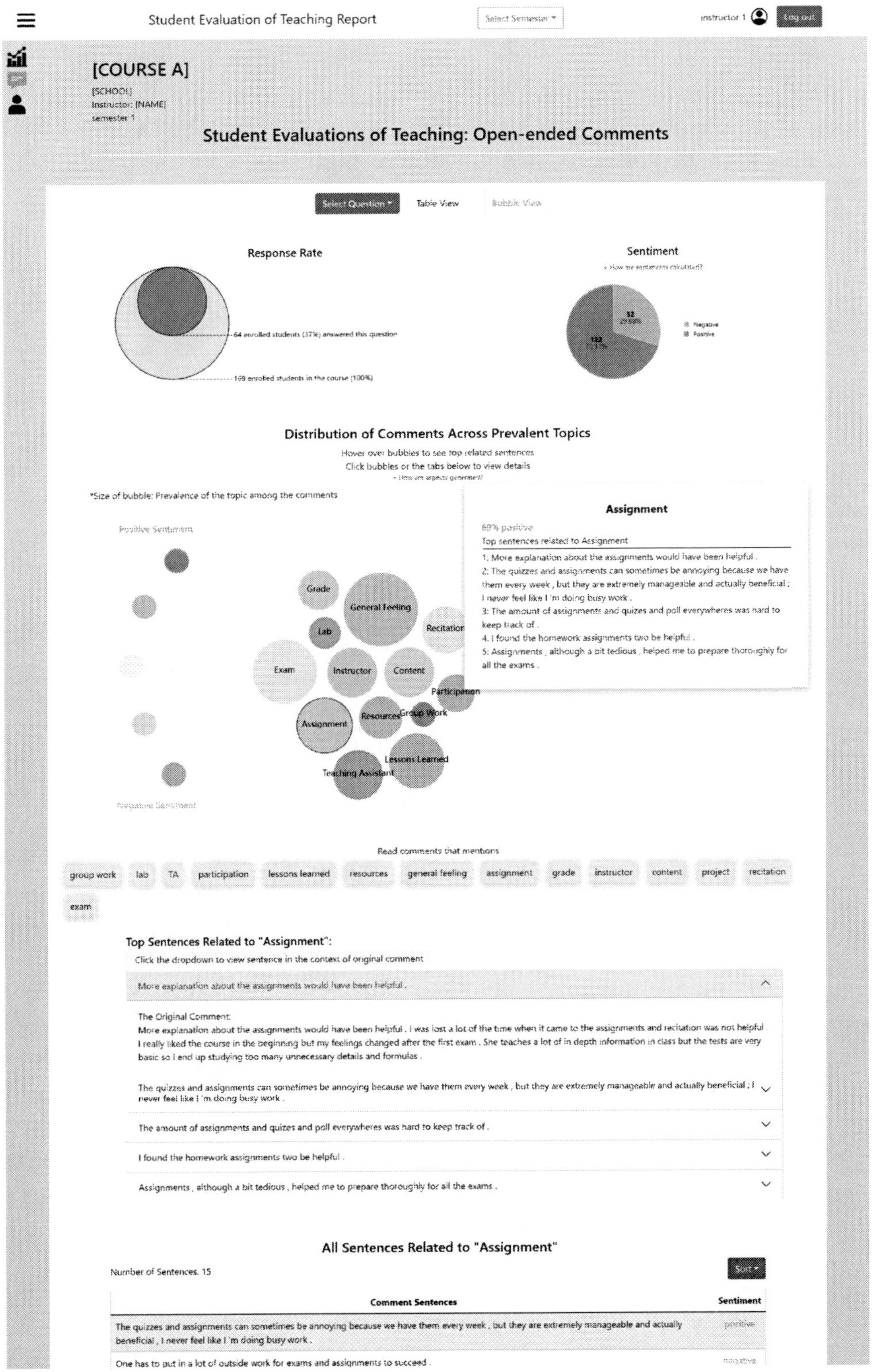

(b) A page shows the Comments Analysis (Open-ended Questions) part.

Figure 7: Screenshots of SETSUM v1.1 (Part2).

Aspect	Top words (normalized weight)
assignment	assignment (0.33), homework (0.31), concept (0.17), reading (0.13), exercise (0.07)
content	material (0.42), lecture (0.17), reading (0.15), subject (0.13), content (0.13)
course design	syllabus (0.21), requirement (0.20), communicated (0.20), wish (0.20), discussion (0.19)
exam	exam (0.31), test (0.24), question (0.20), answer (0.13), problem (0.13),
general feeling	course (0.33), enjoyed (0.25), favorite (0.19), challenging (0.12), hard (0.11)
grade	grading (0.39), feedback (0.19), harsh (0.16), midterm (0.16), easy (0.11)
group work	group (0.30), project (0.24), recitation (0.20), work (0.06), team (0.20)
instructor	professor (0.50), instructor (0.21), passionate (0.11), teach (0.11), condescending (0.06)
lab	lab (0.32), hand (0.20), report(0.20), grading (0.10), experiment (0.18)
lessons learned	learned (0.23), real (0.22), life (0.22), skill (0.19), understanding (0.14)
participation	discussion(0.30), speak(0.23), comfortable (0.18), participation (0.16), stressful (0.13)
project	project (0.30), instance (0.23), expectation (0.18), clearly (0.16), explained (0.13)
recitation	recitation (0.57), content (0.18), project (0.10), review (0.09), group (0.05)
resources	peer (0.20), mentor (0.20), book (0.20), software (0.20), reference (0.20)
teaching assistant (TA)	TA (0.42), job (0.20), helping (0.12), explained (0.06). available (0.20)

(a) Highest ranked words list for each aspect of *Comments on overall assessment of this course.*

Aspect	Top words (normalized weight)
course design	lecture (0.28), assignment (0.21), topic (0.18), activity (0.17), structured (0.17)
delivery	engaged (0.26), clear (0.22), lecture (0.22), example (0.16), explain (0.14)
exam	unfair (0.25), fair (0.25), exam (0.23), guide (0.20), question (0.08)
general feeling	professor (0.37), great (0.27), instructor (0.25), bad (0.05), overall (0.05)
grade	grade (0.36), passing (0.20), average (0.20), exam (0.13), comment (0.11)
lessons learned	conceptual (0.27), intellectual (0.27), learned (0.20), knowledge (0.16), understanding (0.11)
office hour	office (0.38), hour (0.38), time (0.09), comment (0.08), meet (0.08)
personality	enthusiastic (0.30), passionate (0.22), person (0.19), care (0.18), funny (0.12)
recitation	recitation (0.26), time (0.14), project (0.20), group (0.20), organized (0.20)
skills	knowledgeable (0.40), experience (0.26), information (0.14), quality (0.10), deep (0.10)
teaching assistant (TA)	TA (0.41), interactive (0.15), supportive (0.15), constructive (0.15), feedback (0.15)

(b) Highest ranked words list for each aspect of *Comments on overall assessment of this instructor.*

Table 4: Highest ranked words and normalized weight for each aspect.

Terminology	Description	Example
general feeling	General high-level comments or overall feelings about the course	The course is really interesting for me as a CS major and I learned a lot form it.
instructor	Any comments towards the instructor	Professor [NAME] is a joy, and is incredibly understanding, passionate, and enjoyable to simply listen to in class!
teaching assistant (TA)	Any comments related to TA	Resources are always available, the instructors and TAs were easily accessible and always friendly, the material was challenging, and examples were always fun and engaging.
lab	Any comments related to lab	I thought this course was very engaging and I liked that it was very hands on, like a lab should be.
recitation	Any comments related to recitation	This recitation was a bit odd.
course design	Any comments on the organization and structure of the course	I thought this course was excellently structured and formatted.
assignment	Any comments related to homework/assignments	The assignment is really, really well designed that it builds upon each other from assignment 2 through assignment 9 and it helped me exercise various topics/concepts that I learned from class.
exam	Any comments related to exam/test	This class is extremely hard and the second test is expected to be failed by most students, which is ridiculous.
content	Any comments related to course materials or specific contents of the course	The material was very useful for our course although the professors could have made a better connection with the techniques learned in the lab.
participation	Talk about the participation / attendance / engagement / discussion	Needs more class participation and discussion.
grade	Comments on the grading of the course	Harsh grading on lab reports.
group work	Any comments related to group work	All of the recitations consisted of group work towards a final project, though the early recitations seemed largely irrelevant to the project.
resources	Resources provided by course such as readings, textbooks, peer tutors etc.	I did however get all the help I needed from the peer mentors.
lessons learned	Learning outcomes or skills acquired from the course	The professor is really good, I learned a lot of interesting and classic dramas this semester.

Table 5: Aspect Annotation Terminology for *Comments on overall assessment of this course.*

Terminology	Description	Example
general feeling	General high-level comments or overall feelings about the instructor	Awesome Professor.
teaching assistant (TA)	Any comments related to TA	One of the best TAs I have had so far at UNC
recitation	Any comments related to recitation	Recitation felt like a waste of time.
office hour	Any comments related to office hour	She was great during her office hours and was always concerned that we understood the material.
personality	Describe personality of the instructor	She cares a lot about the subject material and her students.
skills	Describe the skill sets or experiences of the instructor	The instructor had a deep understanding of the course material and provided many real world examples built from her own experience and previous work.
grade	Comments on the grading style	The instructor was clear at explaining information and fairly evaluating all assignments.
delivery	How the instructor delivers the information and explains concepts	I really enjoyed her teaching style, she helped us through tough topics by breaking them down into more digestible chunks and was really positive overall, which helped for class moral.
course design	Comments on the organization and structure of the course	I didn't really get to know the TA because we didn't have a lot of recitations.
lessons learned	Learning outcomes or skills acquired from the course	I now have a greater understanding of the German language and of Swiss;German literature and culture.

Table 6: Aspect Annotation Terminology for *Comments on overall assessment of this instructor.*

Towards Open-Domain Topic Classification

Hantian Ding[1], **Jinrui Yang**[1,2], **Yuqian Deng**[1], **Hongming Zhang**[1], **Dan Roth**[1]
[1]University of Pennsylvania, [2]University of Melbourne
{hantian2, jinruiy, yuqiand, hzhangal, danroth}@seas.upenn.edu

Abstract

We introduce an open-domain topic classification system that accepts user-defined taxonomy in real time. Users will be able to classify a text snippet with respect to any candidate labels they want, and get instant response from our web interface. To obtain such flexibility, we build the backend model in a zero-shot way. By training on a new dataset constructed from Wikipedia, our label-aware text classifier can effectively utilize implicit knowledge in the pretrained language model to handle labels it has never seen before. We evaluate our model across four datasets from various domains with different label sets. Experiments show that the model significantly improves over existing zero-shot baselines in open-domain scenarios, and performs competitively with weakly-supervised models trained on in-domain data.[1][2]

1 Introduction

Text classification is a fundamental natural language processing problem, with one of its major applications in topic labeling (Lang, 1995; Wang and Manning, 2012). Over the past decades, supervised classification models have achieved great success in closed-domain tasks with large-scale annotated datasets (Zhang et al., 2015; Tang et al., 2015; Yang et al., 2016). However, they are no longer effective in open-domain scenarios where the taxonomy is unbounded. Retraining the model for every new label set often incurs prohibitively high cost in the sense of both annotation and computation. By contrast, having one classifier that is flexible with unlimited labels can save such tremendous efforts while keeping the solution simple. Therefore, in this work, we build a system for open-domain topic classification that can classify a given text snippet into any categories defined by users.

At the core of our system is a zero-shot text classification model. While supervised models are typically insensitive to class names, a zero-shot model is usually label-aware, meaning that it can understand label semantics directly from the name or definition of the label, without accessing any annotated examples. Our model **TE-Wiki** combines a **T**extual **E**ntailment (TE) formulation with Wikipedia finetuning. Specifically, we construct a new dataset that contains three million article-category pairs from Wikipedia's subcategory graph, and finetune a pretrained language model (e.g. BERT) to predict the entailment relations between articles and their associated categories. We simulate the diversity in open-domain classification with the wide coverage of Wikipedia, while preserving label-awareness through an entailment framework.

In our benchmarking experiments, **TE-Wiki** outperforms all previous zero-shot methods on four benchmarks from different domains. It also shows competitive performance against weakly-supervised models trained on in-domain data. By learning from Wikipedia, our method does not require any data that is specifically collected from the evaluation domains. On the other hand, since our model is label-aware, it can flexibly classify text pieces into any labels outside Wikipedia.

Finally, we compare our system against humans for further insights. We show that even humans are sometimes confused by ambiguous labels through a crowdsourcing study, which explains the performance gap between open-domain and supervised classification. The gap is reduced significantly when label meanings are clear and well aligned with the semantics of text. We also use an example to illustrate the negative effect of a bad label name. Through the analysis, we demonstrate the importance of choosing proper label names in open-domain classification.

[1]Interactive online demo at https://cogcomp.seas.upenn.edu/page/demo_view/ZeroShotTC

[2]Code and data available at http://cogcomp.org/page/publication_view/980

Proceedings of the 2022 Conference of the North American Chapter of the Association for Computational Linguistics: Human Language Technologies: System Demonstrations, pages 90 - 98
July 10-15, 2022

Figure 1: An overview of our open-domain topic classification system. Users can choose multiple models (*top*), and define their own text input and candidate labels (*middle*). Prediction results from different models are displayed in the bar chart and the table (*bottom*).

2 Related Work

Open-domain zero-shot text classification was first studied in the NLP domain in (Chang et al., 2008) (under the name "dataless classification") as a method that classifies solely based on a general knowledge source and does not require any in-domain data, whether labeled or not. It was proposed to embed both the text and labels into the same semantic space, via Explicit Semantic Analysis, or ESA (Gabrilovich and Markovitch, 2007), and pick the label with the highest relevance score. This idea was further extended to hierarchical (Song and Roth, 2014) and cross-lingual (Song et al., 2016) text classification. Later on, (Yin et al., 2019) called this protocol "label fully unseen" and proposed an entailment approach to transfer knowledge from textual entailment to text classification. It formulates an n-class classification problem as n binary entailment problems by converting labels into hypotheses and the text into the premise, and selects the premise-hypothesis pair with highest entailment score. More recently, another concurrent work (Chu et al., 2021) proposed to explore resources from Wikipedia for zero-shot text classification, but with a different formulation.

There are many other methods that also require less labeling than supervised classification, though in slightly different settings. For example, previous works have explored to generalize from a set of known classes (with annotation) to unknown classes (without annotation) using word embeddings of label names (Pushp and Srivastava, 2017; Xia et al., 2018; Liu et al., 2019), class correlation on knowledge graphs (Rios and Kavuluru, 2018; Zhang et al., 2019), or joint embeddings of documents and labels (Nam et al., 2016). Besides, Weakly supervised approaches (Mekala and Shang, 2020; Meng et al., 2020) learn from an unlabeled, but in-domain training set. Given a set of predefined labels, a label-aware knowledge mining step is first applied to find class-specific indicators from the corpus, followed by another self training step to further enhance the model by propagating the knowledge to the whole corpus. However, none of these approaches are suitable for building an open-domain classification system. They either require domain-specific annotation or knowing test labels beforehand.

3 System Description

We present details about our open-domain topic classification system, starting with an overview of our web interface, followed by the backend model.

3.1 User Interface

Figure 1 is a snapshot of our online demo. The system is supported by multiple backend models for test and comparison. Among them, "Bert-Wiki", corresponding to **TE-Wiki** in this paper, is the best-performing one in our evaluation. After selecting the model(s), users can create their own taxonomy in the "Labels" column, and input the text snippet.

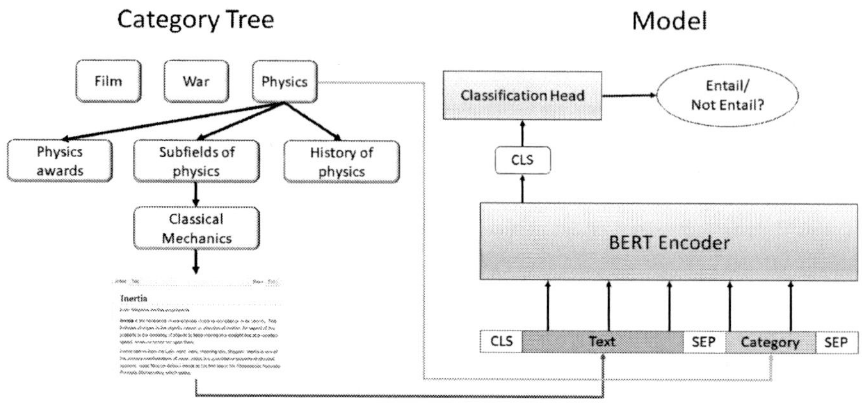

Figure 2: An overview of our proposed **TE-Wiki**. *Left*: the data collection process. For each of the top-level categories, we run DFS to find its descendant categories as well as their member articles. These articles are paired with the root category for model input. *Right*: the model architecture. We use BERT for sequence classification. The article text is concatenated with the category name to feed into a BERT encoder. The classification head takes the output embedding of the "[CLS]" token to classify the input text-category pair.

The system will then classify the text with the user-defined taxonomy. Results are presented in two formats: a bar chart and a ranking table. The table on the right provides a clear view of rankings by each model, while the bar chart on the left is useful to compare the scale of the scores from different models for different labels. These scores, ranging from 0 to 1, are probabilities of the label being relevant to the text, which we will explain further in the next section.

Consider the example in Figure 1. The input text is most relevant to *lifestyle*, somewhat relevant to *technology*, and irrelevant to *children*, which aligns with the prediction of our "Bert-Wiki" model.

3.2 TE-Wiki

We now describe our best performing model **TE-Wiki**. Previous work (Yin et al., 2019) has demonstrated that an n-way classification problem can be converted into n binary entailment problems. Specifically, we can use the text as the premise, and candidate labels as the hypotheses, to generate n statements "[Text] **Entails** [Label$_i$]" for $i \in [n]$. The motivation is that classification is essentially a special kind of entailment. Suppose we want to classify a document into 3 classes: *politics*, *business*, *sports*. We can ask three binary questions: "Is it about politics?", "Is it about business?", "Is it about sports?". By doing so, the model is no longer constrained to a fixed label set, as we can always ask more questions to handle new labels.

With the above framework, it is straightforward to train a model on an entailment dataset (e.g. MNLI (Williams et al., 2018), FEVER (Thorne et al., 2018), RTE (Dagan et al., 2005; Wang et al., 2019).) and use it for classification. However, this may not be the optimal choice as topic classification only focuses on high-level concepts, while textual entailment has a much wider scope and involves many other aspects (e.g., see (Dagan et al., 2013)). Therefore, we propose to construct a new dataset from Wikipedia with articles as premises, and categories as hypotheses. Our desired training pair should meet the following two criteria:

1. The hypothesis is consistent with the premise, i.e. the categorization is correct.
2. The hypothesis should be abstract and concise to reflect the high-level idea of the premise, rather than focus on certain details.

Directly using all the categories associated with an article satisfies the first criterion, but fails with the second, as some of them do not represent the article well. For example, the page *Bill Gates* is assigned *Category:Cornell family*, which is correct about the person but probably not a suitable label for the whole article. To resolve the issue, we instead use higher-level categories on Wikipedia's subcategory graph to yield better hypotheses.

The overview of **TE-Wiki** is illustrated in Figure 2. Specifically, we start with a set of 700 top-level categories from Wikipedia's overview page[3] as roots. For each of them, we run a depth-first search (DFS) to find its subcategories. In our experiment, we set the max depth to 2 to ensure the subcategories found are strongly affiliated with the

[3] https://en.wikipedia.org/wiki/Wikipedia:Contents/Categories

Algorithm 1: Collect training data

Input : Top-level category set S,
Wikipedia subcategory graph $\mathcal{G}$,
max search depth $r = 2$;
Initialize $d(x, c) = \infty$ for any article $x \in X$ and $c \in S$. $M = \{\}$;
for c in S **do**
  T = DFS$(c, \mathcal{G}, r)$;
  for t in T.nodes **do**
    for x in t.articles **do**
      $d(x, c) = \min\{d(x, c), 1 + \text{depth}(t)\}$;
    end
  end
end
for x in X **do**
  if $\min_{c \in S} d(x, c) < \infty$ **then**
    $P = \text{argmin}_{c \in S} d(x, c)$;
    for c in P **do**
      Add $(x, c, 1)$ to M;
    end
    Sample c' from $S - P$;
    Add $(x, c', -1)$ to M;
  end
end
Output : M

root. We collect all member articles of categories in the DFS tree, including both leaves and internal nodes, and pair them with the root to construct positive examples. In case an article can be reached from multiple root categories, we only pair it with the root(s) that has the smallest tree distance to the article to ensure supervision quality. Then for each article, we randomly choose a different category to construct a negative example. While we have tried more sophisticated negative sampling strategies with the aim to confuse the model, none of them makes a significant improvement. Thus, we keep to this simple version. The final training set $D = \{(x_i, c_i, p_i)_{i=1}^{n}\}$ consists of 3-tuples such that x_i is a Wikipedia article, c_i is the corresponding high-level category name, and $p_i \in \{+1, -1\}$ is the label. The procedure for constructing the training set is summarized in Algorithm 1.

We then fine-tune the pre-trained BERT model (Devlin et al., 2019) with the collected dataset. Given a tuple (x_i, c_i, p_i), the concatenation of x_i and c_i is passed to a BERT encoder, followed by a classification head to predict whether the article x_i belongs to the category c_i. During test, (i) for the single-labeled case, we pick the label with the highest predicted probability, (ii) for the multi-labeled case, we pick all labels predicted as positive (i.e. probability > 0.5). We do not use any hypothesis template to convert label names into sentences as in (Yin et al., 2019), for consistency with training.

Dataset	#Classes	#samples
Yahoo (Zhang et al., 2015)	10	100,000
Situation (Mayhew et al., 2019)	12	3525
AG News (Zhang et al., 2015)	4	7,600
DBPedia (Lehmann et al., 2015)	14	70,000

Table 1: Dataset Statistics.

4 Evaluation

We evaluate all the backend models of our system on four classification benchmarks to compare their performance. We also compare them against weakly-supervised and supervised models to quantify how much we can achieve without any domain-specific training data.

4.1 Experiment setup

Datasets: We summarize all test datasets in Table 1. For *Yahoo! Answers*, we use the reorganized train/test split by (Yin et al., 2019). All datasets are in English. Among the four, *Situation Typing* is a multi-labeled dataset with imbalanced classes, for which we report the weighted average of per-class F1 score. We refer readers to (Yin et al., 2019) for the class distribution statistics. The other three are single-labeled and class-balanced, and we report the classification accuracy.
Models: Apart from **TE-Wiki**, we run five zero-shot models for open-domain evaluation, as well as a weakly-supervised and a supervised model for close-domain comparison.

- **Word2Vec** (Mikolov et al., 2013): To measure cosine similarity between the embedding vectors of text and label.
- **ESA** (Chang et al., 2008): Same as above, except using embeddings in Wikipedia title space
- **TE-MNLI, TE-FEVER, TE-RTE** (Yin et al., 2019): Textual entailment models by finetuning BERT on MNLI, FEVER, and RTE respectively.[4]
- **LOTClass** (Meng et al., 2020): A weakly-supervised method that learns label information from unlabeled, but in-domain training data.
- **BERT** (Devlin et al., 2019): We finetune a supervised BERT on training data for each dataset.

Implementation: We finetune the bert-base-uncased model on the Wikipedia article-category dataset to train **TE-Wiki**. We removed 26 categories whose name starts with "List of" from the 700 top-level categories, resulting in 674 categories

[4]In experiments, we always use bert-base-uncased.

Supervision Type	Methods	Yahoo	Situation	AG News	DBPedia
Zero-shot	Word2Vec (Mikolov et al., 2013)	35.7	15.6	71.1	69.7
	ESA (Chang et al., 2008)	40.4	30.2	71.1	64.7
	TE-MNLI (Yin et al., 2019)	37.9	15.4	68.8	55.3
	TE-FEVER (Yin et al., 2019)	40.1	21.0	78.0	73.0
	TE-RTE (Yin et al., 2019)	43.8	37.2	60.5	65.9
	TE-Wiki	**57.3**	**41.7**	**79.6**	**90.2**
Weakly-supervised	LOTClass (Meng et al., 2020)	54.7	N/A	86.4	91.1
Supervised	BERT (Devlin et al., 2019)	75.3	58.0	94.4	99.3

Table 2: Test results of all methods on four datasets. Compared with Word2Vec and ESA, ESA-WikiCate is overall the best among the three embedding-based methods. TE-WikiCate outperforms all other zero-shot methods across all four datasets, and performs competitively against the weakly-supervised LOTClass.

as hypotheses and 1,367,784 articles as premises. The final training set contains 3,387,028 article-category pairs. We set the max sequence length to be 128 tokens and the training batch size to be 64. The model is optimized with AdamW (Loshchilov and Hutter, 2019) with initial learning rate as 5e-5. Since we do not have a development set in the zero-shot setting, we train the model for 1500 steps to prevent overfitting. For all zero-shot methods, we train once and evaluate the model on all test datasets. For supervised and weakly-supervised methods, we train a different model for each different dataset.

4.2 Result Analysis

The main results are presented in Table 2. We observe that **TE-Wiki** performs the best among all zero-shot methods on all four datasets with different labels and from different domains, demonstrating its effectiveness as an open-domain classifier. It also performs closely with the weakly-supervised **LOTClass** which is trained on in-domain data with known taxonomy, showing that an open-domain zero-shot model can achieve similar accuracy as those domain-specific classifiers. In particular, **TE-Wiki** outperforms **LOTClass** on *Yahoo*, whose training set contains quite a few ambiguous examples. These examples can have negative impact on self-training. On the other hand, our zero-shot model does not rely on any domain-specific data, making it more robust against imperfect data.

It is possible that some of the testing labels also appear in the Wikipedia categories used for training.[5] To ensure the quality and fairness of our zero-shot evaluation, we remove the overlapping categories from Wikipedia training data, and retrain the **TE-Wiki** model for each test set. Specifically, we normalize labels and categories by their lower-cased, lemmatized names, and perform a token-based matching. We report in Table 3 the performance before and after deduplication. We find that deduplication has little or even positive influence on performance, which shows that **TE-Wiki** does not rely on seeing test labels during training. In particular, the performance on *Yahoo* gets improved with deduplication. We suspect that exact match between training and testing labels can lead to overfitting, since the same label may have different meanings under different context. Notice that this study is only for justifying our zero-shot evaluation. For real-word applications, excluding overlapping categories is neither necessary nor feasible as users do not know the test labels beforehand in zero-shot scenarios.

4.3 Early stopping and knowledge transfer

To study the convergence of our model, we sample a small dev set of 1000 examples from *Yahoo*'s original validation set. During training, we find that with 25 steps the **TE-Wiki** model already achieves a reasonably good performance on the dev set. Further training for longer steps yields some, but not significant gains. Since the model has only seen $25 \times 64 = 1600$ examples at that point, there is little chance for the model to acquire label specific knowledge with such a small amount of data. Hence, we believe that during the early steps, the model actually learns *"what topic classification is about"*, while the knowledge specific to different labels has already been implicitly stored in the pretrained BERT encoder. The category prediction task takes a minor role in transferring world knowledge. Rather, it teaches the model how to use existing knowledge to make a good inference.

5 Importance of label names

Since zero-shot classifiers understand a label by its name, the quality of label names can be a important performance bottleneck in designing open-domain text classification systems. To study this, We con-

[5]Throughout this subsection, we use the word "category" for the training set and "label" for the testing sets.

	Yahoo	Situation	AG News	DBPedia
TE-Wiki	57.3	41.7	79.6	90.2
- Overlapping categories	59.4(+2.1)	38.8(-2.9)	79.7(+0.1)	88.9(-1.3)
Removed training categories	15	2	4	10
Overlapping test examples (%)	100.0	24.0	100.0	50.0

Table 3: Performance before and after removing the overlapping categories, as well as their difference. We also show the number of removed categories, and the percentage of test documents that belong to the overlapping labels.

	TE-Wiki	Human	Supervised
Yahoo	58.9	64.8	77.4
Yahoo-5	82.1(+23.2)	88.1(+23.3)	89.4(+12.0)
AG News	79.0	80.2	94.7
AG News-5	86.4(+7.4)	90.8(+10.6)	96.4(+1.7)

Table 4: Classification accuracy on crowdsourcing datasets. Yahoo-5 and AG News-5 count only examples for which all five workers choose the same label.

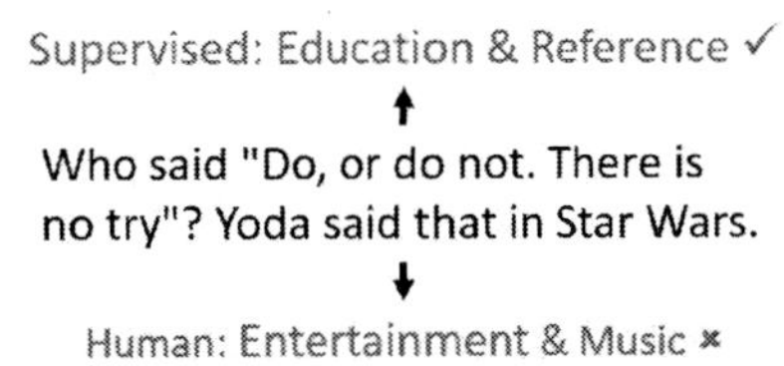

Figure 3: An example with a bad label name. Annotators are confused by the word "Reference".

duct crowdsourcing surveys on subsets of *Yahoo* and *AG News*. For each dataset, we randomly sample 1,000 documents while preserving class balance. Every document is independently annotated by five workers. In the survey question, we only provide the document to be classified and names of candidate labels, without giving workers examples for each class. We consider an example to be correctly classified by humans only if at least three workers choose the gold label. Details about the survey are in Appendix.

We summarize the results in Table 4. Row 1&3 are classification accuracy on the whole crowdsourcing datasets, and row 2&4 are on subsets of examples where all 5 workers choose the same label. We observe that when including all examples, both **TE-Wiki** and humans perform much worse than the supervised method. The supervised approach has the advantage that it learns data-specific features to resolve ambiguity among different classes. On the other hand, humans only make judgements based on their understanding of the labels and a stand-alone test document, and so does our zero-shot algorithm. Ideally, this task should not be difficult for humans as long as the labels properly describe the text topics. However, in some cases the labels could be ambiguous and confusing. Figure 3 shows an example of a bad label name leading to a mistake. The word "Reference" in the correct label actually means "quoting other people's words". However, it is hard for an ordinary person to understand the meaning without any example as illustration. 4 out of 5 annotators instead chose "Entertainment & Music" due to the movie "Star Wars". By contrast, the supervised model has no difficulty in making the correct decision because it has seen plenty of quotation examples during training and can easily capture the useful pattern like "Who said XXX". The main reason for humans' confusion here is that the label name does not directly reflect the semantics of the text. A better description of the class should be provided for classification without examples.

We also calculate the accuracy on examples where all 5 workers agree, as in row 2&4 in Table 4. We believe the high inter-annotator agreement here indicates a better alignment between the semantics of text and label. We find a significant improvement of human performance on these less ambiguous cases. The same happens to our zero-shot model, but the supervised method benefits much less. Consequently, the performance gap between humans and the supervised model is also getting closer, which demonstrates that ambiguous labels have a strongly negative impact on classification. Therefore, we believe picking good labels is crucial for open-domain topic classification.

6 Conclusion

We introduce a system for open-domain topic classification. The system allows users to define customized taxonomy and classify text with respect to that taxonomy at real time, without changing the underlying model. To build a powerful model, we propose to utilize Wikipedia articles and categories and adopt an entailment framework for zero-shot learning. The resulting **TE-Wiki** outperforms all existing zero-shot baselines in open-domain evaluations. Finally, we demonstrate the importance of choosing proper label names in open-domain topic classification through a crowdsourcing study.

Acknowledgements

This work was supported by Contracts FA8750-19-2-1004 and FA8750-19-2-0201 with the US Defense Advanced Research Projects Agency (DARPA). Approved for Public Release, Distribution Unlimited. The views expressed are those of the authors and do not reflect the official policy or position of the Department of Defense or the U.S. Government.

References

Ming-Wei Chang, Lev Ratinov, Dan Roth, and Vivek Srikumar. 2008. Importance of Semantic Representation: Dataless Classification. In *Proc. of the Conference on Artificial Intelligence (AAAI)*.

Zewei Chu, Karl Stratos, and Kevin Gimpel. 2021. NATCAT: Weakly supervised text classification with naturally annotated resources. In *3rd Conference on Automated Knowledge Base Construction*.

I. Dagan, O. Glickman, and B. Magnini. 2005. The pascal recognising textual entailment challenge. In *Proceedings of PASCAL first Workshop on Recognising Textual Entailment*.

Ido Dagan, Dan Roth, Mark Sammons, and Fabio Massimo Zanzoto. 2013. Recognizing Textual Entailment: Models and Applications.

Jacob Devlin, Ming-Wei Chang, Kenton Lee, and Kristina Toutanova. 2019. BERT: Pre-training of deep bidirectional transformers for language understanding. In *Proceedings of the 2019 Conference of the North American Chapter of the Association for Computational Linguistics: Human Language Technologies, Volume 1 (Long and Short Papers)*, pages 4171–4186, Minneapolis, Minnesota. Association for Computational Linguistics.

E. Gabrilovich and S. Markovitch. 2007. Computing semantic relatedness using wikipeida-based explicit semantic analysis. In *Proc. of the International Joint Conference on Artificial Intelligence (IJCAI)*.

Ken Lang. 1995. NewsWeeder: learning to filter netnews. In *Proc. of the International Conference on Machine Learning (ICML)*.

Jens Lehmann, Robert Isele, Max Jakob, Anja Jentzsch, Dimitris Kontokostas, Pablo N. Mendes, Sebastian Hellmann, Mohamed Morsey, Patrick van Kleef, Sören Auer, and Christian Bizer. 2015. Dbpedia - A large-scale, multilingual knowledge base extracted from wikipedia. *Semantic Web*, 6(2):167–195.

Han Liu, Xiaotong Zhang, Lu Fan, Xuandi Fu, Qimai Li, Xiao-Ming Wu, and Albert Y.S. Lam. 2019. Reconstructing capsule networks for zero-shot intent classification. In *Proceedings of the 2019 Conference on Empirical Methods in Natural Language Processing and the 9th International Joint Conference on Natural Language Processing (EMNLP-IJCNLP)*, pages 4799–4809, Hong Kong, China. Association for Computational Linguistics.

Ilya Loshchilov and Frank Hutter. 2019. Decoupled weight decay regularization. In *7th International Conference on Learning Representations, ICLR 2019, New Orleans, LA, USA, May 6-9, 2019*. OpenReview.net.

Stephen Mayhew, Tatiana Tsygankova, Francesca Marini, Zihan Wang, Jane Lee, Xiaodong Yu, Xingyu Fu, Weijia Shi, Zian Zhao, Wenpeng Yin, Karthikeyan K, Jamaal Hay, Michael Shur, Jennifer Sheffield, and Dan Roth. 2019. University of Pennsylvania LoReHLT 2019 Submission. Technical report.

Dheeraj Mekala and Jingbo Shang. 2020. Contextualized weak supervision for text classification. In *Proceedings of the 58th Annual Meeting of the Association for Computational Linguistics*, pages 323–333, Online. Association for Computational Linguistics.

Yu Meng, Yunyi Zhang, Jiaxin Huang, Chenyan Xiong, Heng Ji, Chao Zhang, and Jiawei Han. 2020. Text classification using label names only: A language model self-training approach. In *Proceedings of the 2020 Conference on Empirical Methods in Natural Language Processing (EMNLP)*, pages 9006–9017, Online. Association for Computational Linguistics.

Tomas Mikolov, Ilya Sutskever, Kai Chen, Gregory S. Corrado, and Jeffrey Dean. 2013. Distributed representations of words and phrases and their compositionality. In *Advances in Neural Information Processing Systems 26: 27th Annual Conference on Neural Information Processing Systems 2013. Proceedings of a meeting held December 5-8, 2013, Lake Tahoe, Nevada, United States.*

Jinseok Nam, Eneldo Loza Mencía, and Johannes Fürnkranz. 2016. All-in text: Learning document, label, and word representations jointly. In *Proceedings of the Thirtieth AAAI Conference on Artificial Intelligence, February 12-17, 2016, Phoenix, Arizona, USA*, pages 1948–1954. AAAI Press.

Pushpankar Kumar Pushp and Muktabh Mayank Srivastava. 2017. Train once, test anywhere: Zero-shot learning for text classification. *CoRR*, abs/1712.05972.

Anthony Rios and Ramakanth Kavuluru. 2018. Few-shot and zero-shot multi-label learning for structured label spaces. In *Proceedings of the 2018 Conference on Empirical Methods in Natural Language Processing*, pages 3132–3142, Brussels, Belgium. Association for Computational Linguistics.

Yangqiu Song and Dan Roth. 2014. On Dataless Hierarchical Text Classification. In *Proc. of the Conference on Artificial Intelligence (AAAI)*.

Yangqiu Song, Shyam Upadhyay, Haoruo Peng, and Dan Roth. 2016. Cross-lingual Dataless Classification for Many Languages. In *Proc. of the International Joint Conference on Artificial Intelligence (IJCAI)*.

Duyu Tang, Bing Qin, and Ting Liu. 2015. Document modeling with gated recurrent neural network for sentiment classification. In *Proceedings of the 2015 Conference on Empirical Methods in Natural Language Processing*, pages 1422–1432, Lisbon, Portugal. Association for Computational Linguistics.

James Thorne, Andreas Vlachos, Christos Christodoulopoulos, and Arpit Mittal. 2018. FEVER: a large-scale dataset for fact extraction and VERification. In *Proceedings of the 2018 Conference of the North American Chapter of the Association for Computational Linguistics: Human Language Technologies, Volume 1 (Long Papers)*, pages 809–819, New Orleans, Louisiana. Association for Computational Linguistics.

Alex Wang, Amanpreet Singh, Julian Michael, Felix Hill, Omer Levy, and Samuel R. Bowman. 2019. GLUE: A multi-task benchmark and analysis platform for natural language understanding. In *7th International Conference on Learning Representations, ICLR 2019, New Orleans, LA, USA, May 6-9, 2019*. OpenReview.net.

Sida Wang and Christopher Manning. 2012. Baselines and bigrams: Simple, good sentiment and topic classification. In *Proceedings of the 50th Annual Meeting of the Association for Computational Linguistics (Volume 2: Short Papers)*, pages 90–94, Jeju Island, Korea. Association for Computational Linguistics.

Adina Williams, Nikita Nangia, and Samuel Bowman. 2018. A broad-coverage challenge corpus for sentence understanding through inference. In *Proceedings of the 2018 Conference of the North American Chapter of the Association for Computational Linguistics: Human Language Technologies, Volume 1 (Long Papers)*, pages 1112–1122, New Orleans, Louisiana. Association for Computational Linguistics.

Congying Xia, Chenwei Zhang, Xiaohui Yan, Yi Chang, and Philip Yu. 2018. Zero-shot user intent detection via capsule neural networks. In *Proceedings of the 2018 Conference on Empirical Methods in Natural Language Processing*, pages 3090–3099, Brussels, Belgium. Association for Computational Linguistics.

Zichao Yang, Diyi Yang, Chris Dyer, Xiaodong He, Alex Smola, and Eduard Hovy. 2016. Hierarchical attention networks for document classification. In *Proceedings of the 2016 Conference of the North American Chapter of the Association for Computational Linguistics: Human Language Technologies*, pages 1480–1489, San Diego, California. Association for Computational Linguistics.

Wenpeng Yin, Jamaal Hay, and Dan Roth. 2019. Benchmarking Zero-shot Text Classification: Datasets, Evaluation, and Entailment Approach. In *Proc. of the Conference on Empirical Methods in Natural Language Processing (EMNLP)*.

Jingqing Zhang, Piyawat Lertvittayakumjorn, and Yike Guo. 2019. Integrating semantic knowledge to tackle zero-shot text classification. In *Proceedings of the 2019 Conference of the North American Chapter of the Association for Computational Linguistics: Human Language Technologies, Volume 1 (Long and Short Papers)*, pages 1031–1040, Minneapolis, Minnesota. Association for Computational Linguistics.

Xiang Zhang, Junbo Jake Zhao, and Yann LeCun. 2015. Character-level convolutional networks for text classification. In *Advances in Neural Information Processing Systems 28: Annual Conference on Neural Information Processing Systems 2015, December 7-12, 2015, Montreal, Quebec, Canada*, pages 649–657.

A Crowdsourcing Setup

We conduct crowdsourcing annotations for 1000 documents sampled from the *Yahoo! Answers* dataset and another 1000 from the *AG News* on Amazon Mechanical Turk (AMTurk). Both crowdsourcing subsets preserve the class-balance as in the original datasets. We avoid using long documents so that each document contains no more than 512 characters. The 1000 samples are split into 40 assignments, each containing 25 examples. We request 5 AMTurk workers for multiple-choice questions on each assignment. In order to ensure the response quality, we use anchor examples and gold annotations from the original datasets to filter out low-quality answers. Specifically, in each assignment we insert two anchor examples that we believe are easy enough for workers to choose the correct answer as long as they pay attention. We reject a submission if a worker's classification accuracy against gold annotations is below 30%, or both anchor examples are wrongly classified. With a small initial pilot, we estimate the average working time for labeling 25 examples to be 22 minutes, and we set the pay rate to be \$1.5 per assignment for each valid submission. The overall cost is \$300 for 200 valid submissions for each dataset.

SentSpace: Large-Scale Benchmarking and Evaluation of Text using Cognitively Motivated Lexical, Syntactic, and Semantic Features

Greta Tuckute* **Aalok Sathe*** **Mingye Wang**[◇] **Harley Yoder**[◇]
Cory Shain **Evelina Fedorenko**

{gretatu,asathe,mingyew,hyoder,cshain,evelina9} @ mit.edu

Dept. of Brain and Cognitive Sciences McGovern Institute for Brain Research
Massachusetts Institute of Technology, Cambridge, MA, USA

Abstract

SentSpace is a modular framework for streamlined evaluation of text. SentSpace characterizes textual input using diverse lexical, syntactic, and semantic features derived from corpora and psycholinguistic experiments. Core sentence features fall into three primary feature spaces: 1) *Lexical*, 2) *Contextual*, and 3) *Embeddings*. To aid in the analysis of computed features, SentSpace provides a web interface for interactive visualization and comparison with text from large corpora. The modular design of SentSpace allows researchers to easily integrate their own feature computation into the pipeline while benefiting from a common framework for evaluation and visualization. In this manuscript we will describe the design of SentSpace, its core feature spaces, and demonstrate an example use case by comparing human-written and machine-generated (GPT2-XL) sentences to each other. We find that while GPT2-XL-generated text appears fluent at the surface level, psycholinguistic norms and measures of syntactic processing reveal key differences between text produced by humans and machines. Thus, SentSpace provides a broad set of cognitively motivated linguistic features for evaluation of text within natural language processing, cognitive science, as well as the social sciences.

1 Introduction

Natural Language Processing (NLP) researchers and language scientists alike rely heavily on numeric representations of text in order to better understand how machines and humans process language. Consider the following text generated by a large pre-trained language model, GPT2:

> The scientist named the population, after their distinctive horn, Ovid's Unicorn. These four-horned, silver-white unicorns were previously unknown to science.

The passage demonstrates a remarkable facility with language, but also some potentially non-human aspects, both syntactic (e.g., an unnatural *forward shifting* of the phrase *"after their distinctive horn"*) and semantic (describing a four-horned animal as a unicorn). It is of growing interest to researchers to be able to characterize how any text compares to that from another source, be it generated by humans or artificial language models. For example, NLP practitioners are interested in understanding and improving language model output, and bringing it closer to human generated text e.g., Ettinger (2020); Hollenstein et al. (2021); Meister et al. (2022); similarly, language scientists are highly interested in using large-scale language models to develop and test hypotheses about language processing in the mind and brain, e.g., Schrimpf et al. (2021); Caucheteux and King (2022); Goldstein et al. (2022).

To support these shared goals, we developed SentSpace, an open source application for characterizing textual input using diverse lexical, syntactic, and semantic features. These features are derived from sources such as large, constructed corpora, behavioral psycholinguistic experiments, human judgment norms, and models based on theories of human sentence processing. We also developed functionality to compare textual inputs to one another and to large normative distributions based on natural language corpora. We envision the use cases of SentSpace to be diverse: **(i)** comparison of machine-generated text to human-generated text; **(ii)** comparison of text produced by different human populations (e.g., native and non-native speakers, neurotypical individuals and individuals with developmental or acquired communication disorders); **(iii)** comparison of different genres of text; **(iv)** evaluation of the normativity of stimuli/datasets to be used in psycholinguistic experiments or experiments with language models; and **(v)** investigation of sentences that present particular comprehension

*Equal contribution ◇Equal contribution

Proceedings of the 2022 Conference of the North American Chapter of the Association for Computational Linguistics: Human Language Technologies: System Demonstrations, pages 99 - 113
July 10-15, 2022 ©2022 Association for Computational Linguistics

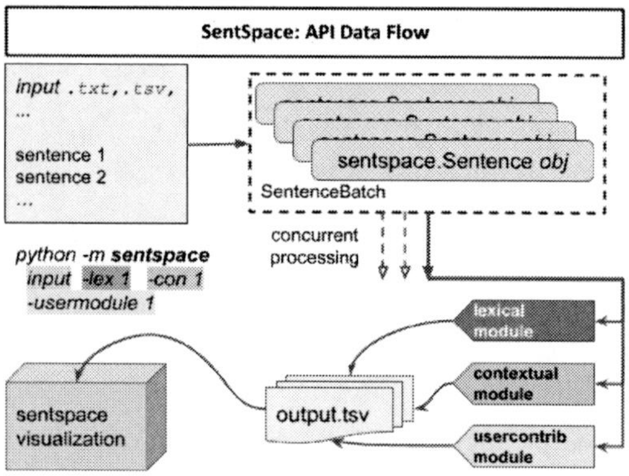

Figure 1: An overview of `SentSpace` data flow: users can supply text in a number of formats. The text is batch-processed in each selected module containing various features. The features computed from each module are then outputted in the specified output file format. These results can be readily plugged into the visualization module out of the box.

difficulties for humans and/or language models, e.g., eliciting a strong neural response in an electrophysiological or neuroimaging study, or producing non-typical or undesired behavior in the case of language models.

We make `SentSpace` publicly available via https://sentspace.github.io/sentspace in the following two forms: **(i)** an open source API implemented in Python (Figure 1), installable via the Python package index (PyPI) or as a self-contained Docker image; **(ii)** a hosted web interface for computing and visualizing features, thus making `SentSpace` accessible without running locally (Figures 2, 3, 4).

2 Structure and Design

At the core of `SentSpace` there are features associated with a sentence: $f : \texttt{sentence} \rightarrow \mathbb{R}^d$ where $\mathbb{R}^d$ can be any feature or representation space. The core features are organized into three core modules based on the nature of their characterization of a sentence. **(1)** The *Lexical* module acts at the individual lexical item (token) level. Sentence-level lexical features are computed by aggregating over the tokens of a sentence. **(2)** *Contextual* features are sentence-level features and are obtained as a result of some computation at the sentence level, such as, constructing and then processing a syntax parse tree. Finally, **(3)** *Embeddings* computes pooled vector representations from one of many popular embedding models, from GloVE (Pennington et al., 2014) to Transformer architectures (Radford et al., 2019; Devlin et al., 2019; Wolf et al., 2020). These three modules cover a wide range of features—derived from text corpora or behavioral experiments—that have some demonstrated relevance to language processing.

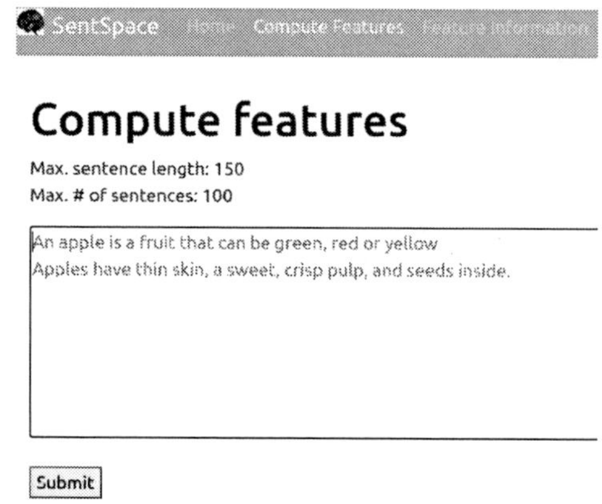

Figure 2: Public-facing hosted interface where users can input text and obtain features by downloading them from the same website. Each request gets a corresponding ID which is temporarily cached to enable repeated downloading and visualization of the same data.

The *Lexical* module consists of features that pertain to individual lexical items, words, regardless of the context in which they appear. These features include, for example, lexical frequency, concreteness, and valence. Because `SentSpace` is built to work with sentences, lexical-level features are aggregated across the sentence (cf. Gao et al. (2021)). As a default, `SentSpace` aggregates over all words with available norms in the sentence by computing the arithmetic mean across words.

The *Contextual* module consists of features that quantify contextual and combinatorial inter-word relations that are not captured by individual lexical items. This module encompasses features that relate to the syntactic structure of the sentence (*Contextual_syntax* features) and features that apply to the sentence context but are not (exclusively) related to syntactic structure (*Contextual_misc* features). *Contextual_syntax* include features related to syntactic complexity, instantiated as e.g., surprisal or integration cost, based on leading theoretical proposals (Gibson, 2000; Shain et al., 2016; Rasmussen and Schuler, 2018). Some syntactic features are computed for each word in the sentence and then subsequently aggregated; other features are computed for multi-word sequences or the entire sentence. *Contextual_misc* include features

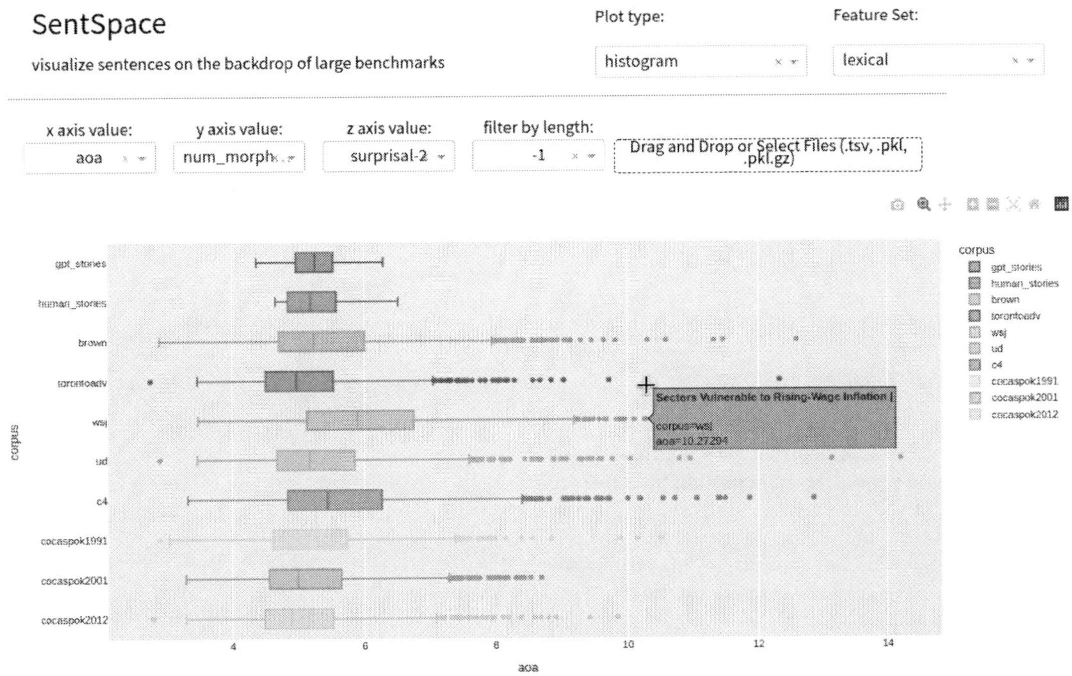

Figure 3: An example of multiple corpora visualized alongside each other for the feature "Age of Acquisition". Sentences from the Wall Street Journal and the Colossal Cleaned Common Crawl (C4) show a tendency of higher age of acquisition on average than other sources. Mouseover on dots enables users to see example sentences and their corresponding values. The 'x axis value' dropdown allows users to pick the feature to plot. The 'y' and 'z' axis values are used for a 3D scatter plot, which can be enabled using the 'Plot type' selector.

like lexical density or sentence sentiment.

The *Embedding* module consists of high-dimensional vectors derived from pre-trained language models.

`SentSpace` also provides functionality that allows users to contribute novel features and modules. A user may design their own features and plug-and-play into `SentSpace` to achieve a more streamlined analysis pipeline and integrated benchmarking and visualization (Figure 1). In order to contribute a module, users must adhere to the module call API, accepting a sentence batch and returning a dataframe whose columns consist of features. Users may make use of parallelism and other utils provided as a part of `SentSpace`. Users may also plug in their computed features in the visualization module and use the web interface.

2.1 Feature Modules

2.1.1 Lexical

Lexical features have been shown to affect language comprehension at the level of individual words. For instance, lexical features affect how people recognize and recall words, such as word frequency (e.g., Gorman (1961); Kinsbourne and George (1974)), concreteness/imageability (e.g., Gorman (1961); Rubin and Friendly (1986)), and valence/arousal (e.g., (Rubin and Friendly, 1986; Danion et al., 1995; Kensinger and Corkin, 2003). Moreover, lexical features have been shown to affect language processing when words are presented in context as measured by eye tracking and self-paced reading, such as surprisal (e.g., Levy (2015); Demberg and Keller (2008); Singh et al. (2016)), polysemy (e.g., Pickering and Frisson (2001)), ambiguity (e.g., Frazier and Rayner (1987); Rayner and Duffy (1986)), word frequency (e.g., Rayner and Duffy (1986)), and age of acquisition (e.g., Singh et al. (2016)). We implement these features using lookup tables for each token. In case the feature is unavailable for a token, we use a lemmatizer to obtain the feature corresponding to the word's lemma. We observe the various features are only moderately correlated with one another, thus each adding new information to the analysis (Figure 5). See Appendix A.1 for supported lexical features.

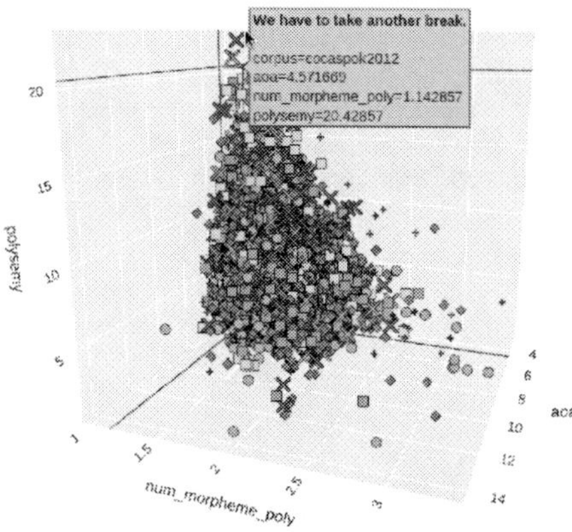

Figure 4: A zoomed-in view of a 3D scatterplot shows mouseover on a point in space revealing the sentence at that location and its features being plotted. A top bar (not displayed) allows the users to change the features to plot. A side bar (not displayed) enables selecting/deselecting corpora and files uploaded by the user to the visualization module. (Abbreviations are 'num_morpheme_poly': Number of Morphemes; 'aoa': Age of Acquisition.)

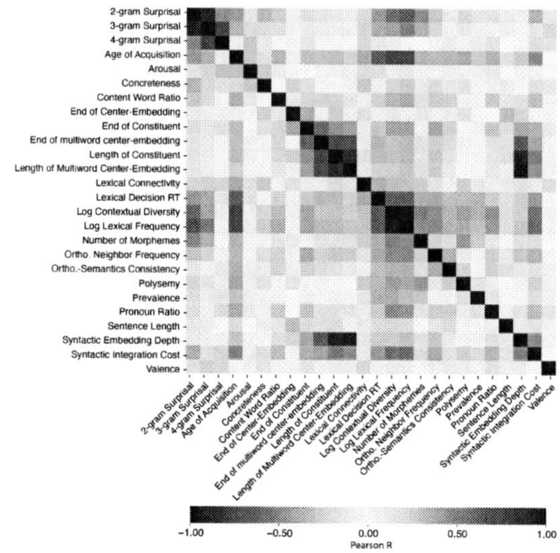

Figure 5: Pearson correlation among features from the *Lexical* and *Contextual* modules obtained from `SentSpace` for text written by humans and GPT2-XL (described in Section 4).

2.1.2 Contextual

Several properties of a sentence cannot be attributed to its individual lexical items (words). These features broadly fall into two categories: syntactic (denoted by *Contextual_syntax*) and miscellaneous (denoted by *Contextual_misc*). The syntactic features include measures of storage and integration cost as predicted by both the Dependency Locality Theory (DLT; Gibson (2000)) and left-corner theories of sentence processing (Rasmussen and Schuler, 2018). In brief, the Dependency Locality Theory is an influential theory of word-by-word comprehension difficulty during human language processing, with difficulty hypothesized to arise from working memory demand related to storing items in working memory (storage cost) and retrieving items from working memory (integration cost) as required by the dependency structure of the sentence. Memory costs derived from the DLT have been associated with self-paced reading (Grodner and Gibson, 2005), eye-tracking (Demberg and Keller, 2008), and fMRI (Shain et al., 2021b) measures of comprehension difficulty. Left-corner parsing models also posit storage and integration costs, but these costs are thought to derive not from dependency locality but from the number of unconnected fragments of phrase structure trees that must be maintained and combined in memory throughout parsing, word-by-word. Probabilistic left-corner parsers can also be used to define a probability distribution over the next word that conditions solely on hypotheses about the syntactic structure of the sentence, providing a critical tool for evaluating the degree to which syntax might influence both human and language model predictions of future words (Shain et al., 2020). See Appendix A.2.1 for supported contextual features.

2.1.3 Embeddings

Embeddings provide representations of words or sentences in high-dimensional, learned vector spaces. The information contained in these spaces depend on the objective function of the algorithm used to derive the vectors, but could be of semantic nature (e.g., Grand et al. (2022)). We provide a decontextualized embedding space (words have the same vector representation independent of context), GloVe (Pennington et al., 2014), as well as several commonly used contextualized embedding spaces (words have different vector representations based on the context in which they appear) from the HuggingFace framework (Wolf et al., 2020). See Appendix A.3 for supported embedding models.

3 Benchmarking Against Large Corpora

To understand where a sentence stands relative to other text, we facilitate comparison with sentences

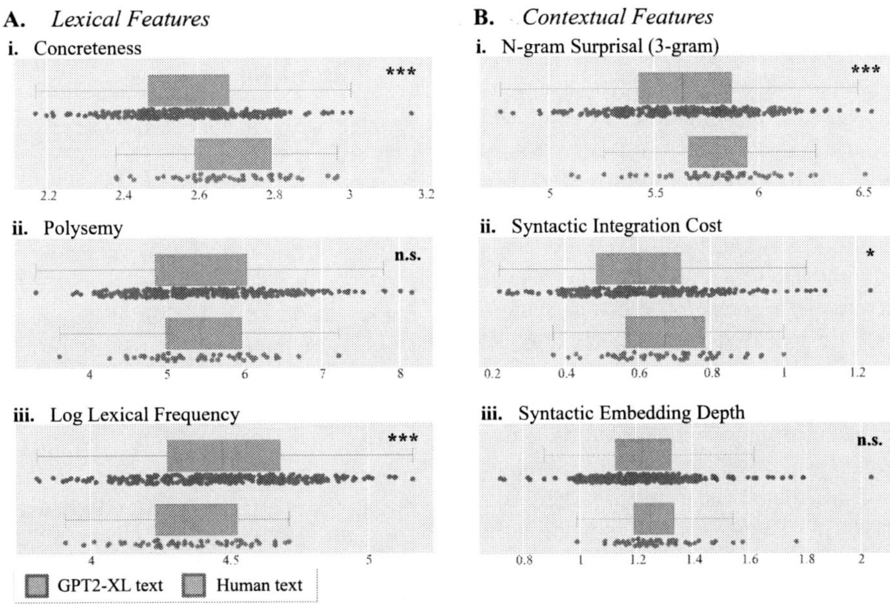

Figure 6: We use SentSpace to visualize sentences from two sources of interest. In one case, humans generated paragraphs, and in the other, a GPT2-XL language model did. We find several points of differences between the two sources, verified using statistical tests comparing the two distributions. p-values were obtained using two-tailed independent samples t-tests: Concreteness ($t = 4.24, p \ll 0.001$), Polysemy ($t = -0.27, p = n.s.$), Lexical Frequency ($t = -2.91, p < 0.005$), N-gram Surprisal (3-gram) ($t = 2.91, p < 0.005$), Syntactic Integration Cost ($t = 2.34, p < 0.05$), Syntactic Embedding Depth ($t = 1.81, p = n.s.$). $^*p < .05$, $^{**}p < .01$, $^{***}p < .005$.

from large corpora of human-generated text (both written and spoken). We allow this by subsampling from large corpora to include an approximately equal number (≈ 500) of sentences from each corpus. We pre-computed and cached SentSpace features for each of 8 corpora (≈ 4000 sentences in total), enabling quick and streamlined comparison with sentences from existing corpora. In the SentSpace[.vis] module, these corpora are loaded by default in addition to user-supplied input. Corpora benchmarking can be disabled to allow visualizing user input in isolation. We provide a list of corpora used in Appendix C.

4 System Demonstration and Results

In this section we provide an example of how SentSpace can be used to compare and visualize sets of sentences to one another using features from the *Lexical* ($n = 13$ features) and *Contextual* ($n = 13$ features) modules of SentSpace[1]. For this example demonstration, we compare two sets of materials: Human-generated text versus GPT2-XL-generated text. The texts consisted of 52 unique paragraphs written by multiple human writers. The first 10 words of each paragraph were used as a prompt to a pretrained GPT2-XL autoregressive language model (Radford et al., 2019; Wolf et al., 2020). Prompt completions were extracted across multiple random seeds using top-p sampling (Holtzman et al., 2020) with generation parameters $p = 0.9$ and $temperature = 1$. We selected 5 completions per prompt that most closely matched the human-generated prompt in word length (within ± 5 words) to control for any length-driven correlations. As a result, we had one human-generated and 5 GPT2-XL-generated paragraphs per prompt, yielding a total of $n = 52$ human-generated paragraphs and $n = 260$ GPT2-XL-generated paragraphs (for examples, see Appendix B). Features were averaged across sentences within each paragraph. For statistical tests, features for the $n = 5$ GPT2-XL-generated paragraphs for the same prompt were averaged to yield a matched sample of paragraphs with the human-generated paragraphs ($n = 52$). In Figure 6, we demonstrate that our feature measures can reveal subtle quantitative differences between machine-generated (blue) and human-generated (red) texts that may not be

[1]The code for analyses in this paper is available at http://github.com/sentspace/NAACL-HLT-2022

subjectively apparent.

Figure 6A demonstrates three features from the *Lexical* module: **i)** Concreteness (Brysbaert et al., 2014); a behavioral measure of the extent to which the concept denoted by the word refers to a perceptible entity, **ii)** Polysemy (Miller, 1992), and **iii)** Log lexical frequency from the SUBTLEX-us database (Brysbaert and New, 2009). As evident, GPT2-XL produces sentences that on average have less concrete words compared to human sentences ($p \ll .001$). Lexical frequency reflects how often a given word is used in language. Lexical frequency is known to affect language comprehension, for instance more frequent words are read faster (e.g., Rayner and Duffy (1986); Singh et al. (2016) and articulated faster (e.g., Jescheniak and Levelt (1994)). We can see this as being a trend towards GPT2-XL's use of more frequent wording compared to humans ($p \ll .001$).

Figure 6B demonstrates three *Contextual* features: **i)** N-gram surprisal (3-gram), **ii)** Average syntactic integration cost according to the Dependency Locality Theory (DLT, (Gibson, 2000); integration cost is roughly proportional to dependency length), and **iii)** Average syntactic center-embedding depth in a left-corner phrase-structure parser (van Schijndel et al., 2013). Although GPT2-XL usually generates sentences that are syntactically well-formed, their syntactic features differ on average from human-generated text. As shown, texts generated by GPT2-XL show lower 3-gram surprisal (t=2.91, $p \ll .001$), tend to be less syntactically complex on average than human-generated ones, with shorter syntactic dependencies (t=2.33, p=0.02) and numerically shallower center-embedded tree structures (t=1.8, p=0.09, n.s.). So, these findings might suggest GPT2-XL makes use of 'simpler' wording compared to humans.

The remaining `SentSpace` features obtained for the comparison between human- and GPT2-XL-generated text ($n = 26$ features in total) are summarized in the Appendix, Table 2. More features are in the progress of being added to the `SentSpace` framework (see Appendix A.1, A.2).

The comparison between human- and machine-generated text is a demonstration of one of the use cases of `SentSpace`: comparing and visualizing texts to one another. The `SentSpace` framework streamlines the process of obtaining corpora-backed features, parsing and syntactically analyzing texts, simplifying and accelerating such analyses for natural language generation.

5 Related work

Related work include Balota et al. (2007) who collected behavioral visual lexical decision and speeded naming reaction times and provided these along with a set of word-level, psycholinguistic features (The English Lexicon Project). Gao et al. (2021) provide a meta-base of word-level, psycholinguistic features. A different alley of related work includes visualization tools for high-dimensional embeddings obtained from pre-trained language models (e.g., van Aken et al. (2020); OpenAI).

A large body of work focuses on characterizing bias in text, particularly that either used in training language models, or that generated by language models (Sun et al., 2019). Related work also focuses on methods to mitigate bias in existing language models using debiasing methods. In the future we hope to include norms that characterize bias as one of the many features that will be added to `SentSpace`. We also hope that outputs from `SentSpace` will inform what data goes into training large language models to make them more human-like.

6 Conclusion

`SentSpace` is a system for obtaining numerical representations of sentences. Our core feature modules span lexical, semantic, and syntactic features from corpora and behavioral experiments. We provide an interface for comparing textual inputs to one another or to large normative distributions based on natural language corpora.

Within the last few years, contextualized embeddings obtained from large pre-trained language models have revolutionized and dominated the field of natural language processing. However, despite these embeddings being useful for diverse applications, it is unclear precisely which information is embedded in these high-dimensional feature representations. We view `SentSpace` as a complementary resource that can provide interpretability and grounding to these pre-trained high-dimensional embeddings.

A major limitation of `SentSpace` is that we currently only support English. Part of the limiting factor is the relative lack of behavioral and psycholinguistic experimental data for other languages, as well as mature linguistic features tailored to other languages.

We envision SentSpace as a dynamic platform with continuous collaboration across research labs for the addition of new features and we hope to make this framework valuable for a number of applications within natural language processing, cognitive science, psychology, linguistics, and social sciences.

Acknowledgements

We thank the authors of publicly available datasets that we have been able to use in SentSpace. We thank Adil Amirov, Alvincé Le Arnz Pongos, Benjamin Lipkin, and Josef Affourtit for their assistance towards developing the software for SentSpace. We thank Hannah Small and Matthew Siegelman for their assistance with the human- and GPT-generated texts.

References

David A. Balota, Melvin J. Yap, Keith A. Hutchison, Michael J. Cortese, Brett Kessler, Bjorn Loftis, James H. Neely, Douglas L. Nelson, Greg B. Simpson, and Rebecca Treiman. 2007. The English Lexicon Project. *Behavior Research Methods*, 39(3):445–459.

Thorsten Brants and Alexander Franz. 2009. Web 1t 5-gram, 10 european languages version 1. *Philadelphia, Pa.: Linguistic Data Consortium*, Computer file.

Marc Brysbaert, Paweł Mandera, Samantha F. McCormick, and Emmanuel Keuleers. 2019. Word prevalence norms for 62,000 English lemmas. *Behavior Research Methods*, 51(2):467–479.

Marc Brysbaert and Boris New. 2009. Moving beyond Kučera and Francis: A critical evaluation of current word frequency norms and the introduction of a new and improved word frequency measure for American English. *Behavior Research Methods*, 41(4):977–990.

Marc Brysbaert, Boris New, and Emmanuel Keuleers. 2012. Adding part-of-speech information to the SUBTLEX-US word frequencies. *Behavior Research Methods*, 44(4):991–997.

Marc Brysbaert, Amy Beth Warriner, and Victor Kuperman. 2014. Concreteness ratings for 40 thousand generally known English word lemmas. *Behavior Research Methods*, 46(3):904–911.

Charlotte Caucheteux and J. R. King. 2022. Brains and algorithms partially converge in natural language processing. *Communications Biology*, 5.

J.-M. Danion, Françoise Kauffmann-Muller, Daniel le Grange, M A Zimmermann, and Ph. Greth. 1995. Affective valence of words, explicit and implicit memory in clinical depression. *Journal of affective disorders*, 34 3:227–34.

Mark Davies. 2009. The 385+ million word corpus of contemporary american english (1990–2008+): Design, architecture, and linguistic insights. *International journal of corpus linguistics*, 14(2):159–190.

Simon De Deyne, Danielle J. Navarro, Amy Perfors, Marc Brysbaert, and Gert Storms. 2019. The "Small World of Words" English word association norms for over 12,000 cue words. *Behavior Research Methods*, 51(3):987–1006.

Vera Demberg and Frank Keller. 2008. Data from eye-tracking corpora as evidence for theories of syntactic processing complexity. *Cognition*, 109(2):193–210.

Jacob Devlin, Ming-Wei Chang, Kenton Lee, and Kristina Toutanova. 2019. Bert: Pre-training of deep bidirectional transformers for language understanding. *ArXiv*, abs/1810.04805.

Allyson Ettinger. 2020. What bert is not: Lessons from a new suite of psycholinguistic diagnostics for language models. *Transactions of the Association for Computational Linguistics*, 8:34–48.

W Nelson Francis and Henry Kucera. 1979. Brown corpus manual. *Letters to the Editor*, 5(2):7.

Lyn Frazier and Keith Rayner. 1987. Resolution of syntactic category ambiguities: Eye movements in parsing lexically ambiguous sentences. *Journal of Memory and Language*, 26(5):505–526.

Chuanji Gao, Svetlana V. Shinkareva, and Rutvik H. Desai. 2021. Scope: The south carolina psycholinguistic metabase.

Edward Gibson. 2000. The dependency locality theory: A distance-based theory of linguistic complexity. In *Image, Language, Brain*, pages 95–106. MIT Press.

Ariel Goldstein, Zaid Zada, Eliav Buchnik, Mariano Schain, Amy Rose Price, Bobbi Aubrey, Samuel A. Nastase, Amir Feder, Dotan Emanuel, Alon Cohen, Aren Jansen, Harshvardhan Gazula, Gina Choe, Aditi Rao, Catherine Kim, Colton Casto, Lora Fanda, Werner K. Doyle, Daniel Friedman, Patricia Dugan, Lucia Melloni, Roi Reichart, Sasha Devore, Adeen Flinker, Liat Hasenfratz, Omer Levy, Avinatan Hassidim, Michael Brenner, Y. Matias, Kenneth A. Norman, Orrin Devinsky, and Uri Hasson. 2022. Shared computational principles for language processing in humans and deep language models. *Nature Neuroscience*, 25:369 – 380.

Anna M. Gorman. 1961. Recognition memory for nouns as a function of abstractness and frequency. *Journal of experimental psychology*, 61:23–9.

Gabriel Grand, Idan Asher Blank, Francisco Pereira, and Evelina Fedorenko. 2022. Semantic projection recovers rich human knowledge of multiple object features from word embeddings. *Nature human behaviour.*

Daniel Grodner and Edward Gibson. 2005. Consequences of the serial nature of linguistic input for sentenial complexity. *Cognitive science*, 29 2:261–90.

Paul Hoffman, Matthew A. Lambon Ralph, and Timothy T. Rogers. 2013. Semantic diversity: A measure of semantic ambiguity based on variability in the contextual usage of words. *Behavior Research Methods*, 45(3):718–730.

Nora Hollenstein, Federico Pirovano, Ce Zhang, Lena A. Jäger, and Lisa Beinborn. 2021. Multilingual language models predict human reading behavior. In *NAACL.*

Ari Holtzman, Jan Buys, Maxwell Forbes, and Yejin Choi. 2020. The curious case of neural text degeneration. *ArXiv*, abs/1904.09751.

Jörg D. Jescheniak and Willem J. M. Levelt. 1994. Word frequency effects in speech production: Retrieval of syntactic information and of phonological form. *Journal of Experimental Psychology: Learning, Memory and Cognition*, 20:824–843.

Elizabeth A. Kensinger and Suzanne Corkin. 2003. Memory enhancement for emotional words: Are emotional words more vividly remembered than neutral words? *Memory & Cognition*, 31:1169–1180.

Marcel Kinsbourne and James W. George. 1974. The mechanism of the word-frequency effect on recognition memory. *Journal of Verbal Learning and Verbal Behavior*, 13:63–69.

Victor Kuperman, Hans Stadthagen-Gonzalez, and Marc Brysbaert. 2012. Age-of-acquisition ratings for 30 thousand English words. page 39.

Roger Levy. 2015. Memory and surprisal in human sentence comprehension. page 36.

Matthew H. C. Mak and Hope Twitchell. 2020. Evidence for preferential attachment: Words that are more well connected in semantic networks are better at acquiring new links in paired-associate learning. *Psychonomic Bulletin & Review*, 27(5):1059–1069.

Mitchell P. Marcus, Beatrice Santorini, and Mary Ann Marcinkiewicz. 1993. Building a large annotated corpus of english: The penn treebank. *Comput. Linguistics*, 19:313–330.

Marco Marelli and Simona Amenta. 2018. A database of orthography-semantics consistency (OSC) estimates for 15,017 English words. *Behavior Research Methods*, 50(4):1482–1495.

D.A. Medler and J.R. Binder. 2005. Mcword: An online orthographic database of the english language. volume http://www.neuro.mcw.edu/mcword/.

Clara Meister, Tiago Pimentel, Gian Wiher, and Ryan Cotterell. 2022. Typical decoding for natural language generation. *ArXiv*, abs/2202.00666.

George A. Miller. 1992. Wordnet: A lexical database for english. *Commun. ACM*, 38:39–41.

Saif Mohammad. 2018. Obtaining Reliable Human Ratings of Valence, Arousal, and Dominance for 20,000 English Words. In *Proceedings of the 56th Annual Meeting of the Association for Computational Linguistics (Volume 1: Long Papers)*, pages 174–184, Melbourne, Australia. Association for Computational Linguistics.

Luan Nguyen, Marten van Schijndel, and William Schuler. 2012. Accurate unbounded dependency recovery using generalized categorial grammars. In *COLING.*

OpenAI. Openai embeddings. `https://beta.openai.com/docs/guides/embeddings`. Accessed: 2022-02-11.

Douglas B Paul and Janet Baker. 1992. The design for the wall street journal-based csr corpus. In *Speech and Natural Language: Proceedings of a Workshop Held at Harriman, New York, February 23-26, 1992.*

Jeffrey Pennington, Richard Socher, and Christopher Manning. 2014. Glove: Global Vectors for Word Representation. In *Proceedings of the 2014 Conference on Empirical Methods in Natural Language Processing (EMNLP)*, pages 1532–1543, Doha, Qatar. Association for Computational Linguistics.

Penny M. Pexman, Emiko Muraki, David M. Sidhu, Paul D. Siakaluk, and Melvin J. Yap. 2019. Quantifying sensorimotor experience: Body–object interaction ratings for more than 9,000 English words. *Behavior Research Methods*, 51(2):453–466.

Steven T. Piantadosi, Harry Tily, and Edward Gibson. 2011. Word lengths are optimized for efficient communication. *Proceedings of the National Academy of Sciences*, 108(9):3526–3529.

Martin J. Pickering and Steven Frisson. 2001. Processing ambiguous verbs: Evidence from eye movements. *Journal of Experimental Psychology: Learning, Memory, and Cognition*, 27(2):556–573.

Alec Radford, Jeff Wu, Rewon Child, David Luan, Dario Amodei, and Ilya Sutskever. 2019. Language models are unsupervised multitask learners.

Colin Raffel, Noam Shazeer, Adam Roberts, Katherine Lee, Sharan Narang, Michael Matena, Yanqi Zhou, Wei Li, and Peter J. Liu. 2020. Exploring the limits of transfer learning with a unified text-to-text transformer. *Journal of Machine Learning Research*, 21(140):1–67.

Nathan Rasmussen and William Schuler. 2018. Left-corner parsing with distributed associative memory produces surprisal and locality effects. *Cognitive science*, 42 Suppl 4:1009–1042.

Keith Rayner and Susan A. Duffy. 1986. Lexical complexity and fixation times in reading: Effects of word frequency, verb complexity, and lexical ambiguity. *Memory & Cognition*, 14(3):191–201.

David C. Rubin and Michael Friendly. 1986. Predicting which words get recalled: Measures of free recall, availability, goodness, emotionality, and pronunciability for 925 nouns. *Memory & Cognition*, 14:79–94.

Martin Schrimpf, Idan Asher Blank, Greta Tuckute, Carina Kauf, Eghbal A. Hosseini, Nancy Kanwisher, Joshua B. Tenenbaum, and Evelina Fedorenko. 2021. The neural architecture of language: Integrative modeling converges on predictive processing. *Proceedings of the National Academy of Sciences*, 118(45):e2105646118.

Cory Shain, Idan A Blank, Evelina Fedorenko, Edward Gibson, and William Schuler. 2021a. Robust effects of working memory demand during naturalistic language comprehension in language-selective cortex. *bioRxiv*.

Cory Shain, Idan Asher Blank, Evelina Fedorenko, Edward Gibson, and William Schuler. 2021b. Robust effects of working memory demand during naturalistic language comprehension in language-selective cortex. *bioRxiv*.

Cory Shain, Idan Asher Blank, Marten van Schijndel, Evelina Fedorenko, and William Schuler. 2020. fmri reveals language-specific predictive coding during naturalistic sentence comprehension. *Neuropsychologia*, 138.

Cory Shain, Marten van Schijndel, Richard Futrell, Edward Gibson, and William Schuler. 2016. Memory access during incremental sentence processing causes reading time latency. In *CL4LC@COLING 2016*.

Abhinav Singh, Poojan Mehta, Samar Husain, and Rajkumar Rajakrishnan. 2016. Quantifying sentence complexity based on eye-tracking measures. In *CL4LC@COLING 2016*.

Tony Sun, Andrew Gaut, Shirlyn Tang, Yuxin Huang, Mai ElSherief, Jieyu Zhao, Diba Mirza, Elizabeth Belding, Kai-Wei Chang, and William Yang Wang. 2019. Mitigating gender bias in natural language processing: Literature review. In *Proceedings of the 57th Annual Meeting of the Association for Computational Linguistics*, pages 1630–1640, Florence, Italy. Association for Computational Linguistics.

Betty van Aken, Benjamin Winter, Alexander Löser, and Felix A. Gers. 2020. Visbert: Hidden-state visualizations for transformers. *Companion Proceedings of the Web Conference 2020*.

Walter J. B. van Heuven, Pawel Mandera, Emmanuel Keuleers, and Marc Brysbaert. 2014. Subtlex-UK: A New and Improved Word Frequency Database for British English. *Quarterly Journal of Experimental Psychology*, 67(6):1176–1190.

Marten van Schijndel, Andrew Exley, and William Schuler. 2013. A model of language processing as hierarchic sequential prediction. *Topics in cognitive science*, 5 3:522–40.

Sami Virpioja, Peter Smit, Stig-Arne Grönroos, and Mikko Kurimo. 2013. Morfessor 2.0: Python implementation and extensions for morfessor baseline.

WordNet Wikipedia. Wordnet. `https://en.wikipedia.org/wiki/WordNet`. Accessed: 2022-02-11.

Thomas Wolf, Lysandre Debut, Victor Sanh, Julien Chaumond, Clement Delangue, Anthony Moi, Pierric Cistac, Tim Rault, Rémi Louf, Morgan Funtowicz, Joe Davison, Sam Shleifer, Patrick von Platen, Clara Ma, Yacine Jernite, Julien Plu, Canwen Xu, Teven Le Scao, Sylvain Gugger, Mariama Drame, Quentin Lhoest, and Alexander M. Rush. 2020. Transformers: State-of-the-art natural language processing. In *Proceedings of the 2020 Conference on Empirical Methods in Natural Language Processing: System Demonstrations*, pages 38–45, Online. Association for Computational Linguistics.

Yukun Zhu, Ryan Kiros, Rich Zemel, Ruslan Salakhutdinov, Raquel Urtasun, Antonio Torralba, and Sanja Fidler. 2015. Aligning books and movies: Towards story-like visual explanations by watching movies and reading books. In *Proceedings of the IEEE international conference on computer vision*, pages 19–27.

A Feature Descriptions

A.1 Lexical Features

Lexical features are ordered alphabetically.

Age of Acquisition Age of acquisition is a metric that estimates when a person acquired (i.e., understood) a given word. Participants were asked for each word to enter the age at which they thought they had learned the word even if they could not use, read, or write it at the time. The norms were collected by (Kuperman et al., 2012).

Norms were available for 30,124 unique words.

Obtained from: `http://crr.ugent.be/archives/806`.

Arousal Arousal quantifies each word on a scale of active–passive. The norms were collected based on human ratings by (Mohammad, 2018) using Best-Worst scaling, where participants are presented with four words at a time and asked to select the word with the highest arousal. The two ends of the arousal dimension were: MOST arousal, activeness, stimulation, frenzy, jitteriness, alertness OR LEAST unarousal, passiveness, relaxation, calmness, sluggishness, dullness, sleepiness.

Norms were available for 20,007 unique words.

Obtained from: `https://saifmohammad.com/WebPages/nrc-vad.html`.

Concreteness Concreteness quantifies the extent to which the concept denoted by the word refers to a perceptible entity. Concrete words were defined as something that exists in reality and can be experienced directly through the five senses or actions. Conversely, abstract words refer to something one cannot experience directly through your senses or actions. The norms were collected based on human ratings by (Brysbaert et al., 2014).

Norms were available for 37,058 unique words.

Obtained from `http://crr.ugent.be/archives/1330`.

Log Contextual Diversity Contextual diversity (CD) is the number of contexts in which a word has been seen [cite Adelman 2005]. The metric available here was computed based on the SUBTLEXus database based on American subtitles (51 million words in total) (Brysbaert and New, 2009) and thus denotes the number of films in which the word appears. The CD metric is computed as log10(CDcount+1).

Norms were available for 74,286 unique words.

Obtained from the SUBTLEXus database: `https://www.ugent.be/pp/experimentele-psychologie/en/research/documents/subtlexus)`.

Log Lexical Frequency Lexical frequency denotes how frequent a word occurs in a given corpus/sets of corpora. The frequency metric available here was computed as log10(FREQcount+1) based on American subtitles (51 million words in total) from the SUBTLEXus database (Brysbaert and New, 2009).

Norms were available for 74,286 unique words.

Obtained from the SUBTLEXus database: `https://www.ugent.be/pp/experimentele-psychologie/en/research/documents/subtlexus)`.

Lexical Connectivity Lexical connectivity is a metric for how connected a given word is to other words based on association judgments. The metric views the mental lexicon as a semantic network where words are linked together by semantic relatedness. Lexical connectivity is computed as the total degree centrality of a given word node in the semantic graph. Norms were obtained from (Mak and Twitchell, 2020) who computed the total degree centrality based on free association norms collected by (De Deyne et al., 2019) (specifically, the first recalled word).

Norms were available for 12,215 unique words.

Obtained from: `https://osf.io/7942s/`.

Lexical Decision Reaction Time (RT) Lexical decision latency measures how quickly people classify strings as words or non-words. The lexical decision latency provides a proxy for how quickly a given word is extracted from the mental lexicon/semantic memory. The norms were collected by (Balota et al., 2007).

Norms were available for 40,482 unique words.

Obtained from the English Lexicon Project: `https://elexicon.wustl.edu/`.

Number of Morphemes A morpheme denotes the smallest meaningful lexical unit in a language. The number of morphemes quantifies how many morphemes a given word has. The primary morpheme counter available here is Morfessor (Virpioja et al., 2013) which uses machine learning to find morphological segmentations of words. If dependency issues arise with Morfessor, the morpheme count is obtained from the English Lexicon Project Database (Balota et al., 2007).

Orthographic Neighbor Frequency Orthographic neighbor frequency is a metric that quantifies the number of orthographic neighbors that a string has. The metric was computed by (Medler and Binder, 2005) and an orthographic neighbor was defined as a word of the same length that differs from the original string by only one letter. The frequency metric denotes the averaged frequency (per million) of orthographic neighbors.

Norms were available for 66,371 unique words.

Obtained from `http://www.neuro.mcw.edu/mcword/`.

Orthography-Semantics Consistency (OSC) Orthography–semantics consistency is a metric that quantifies the degree of semantic relatedness between a word and other words that are orthographically similar. The metric was computed by (Marelli and Amenta, 2018) as the frequency-weighted average semantic similarity between the meaning of a given word and the meanings of all the words containing that very same orthographic string.

Norms were available for 15,017 unique words.

Obtained from: `http://www.marcomarelli.net/resources/osc`.

Polysemy Polysemy provides a metric of how many distinct meanings a word has. Polysemy was measured by the number of definitions of a word in WordNet (Miller, 1992). Polysemy was implemented using NLTK's word_net library (synsets() function) which accepts a word and a part-of-speech tag as input and returns a list of synonyms. Parts-of-speech tags were taken from NLTK's pos_tag, then mapped to the four POS tags accepted by word_net. If a POS tag could not be mapped to one of word_net's ADJ, VERB, NOUN, or ADV then the tag given was an empty string. The number of synonyms for a given word were counted.

Norms were available for 155,327 words organized in 175,979 synsets for a total of 207,016 word-sense pairs (Wikipedia).

Obtained from the NLTK interface: `https://www.nltk.org/howto/wordnet.html`.

Prevalence Word prevalence is a metric that quantifies the number of people who know a given word. The norms were collected by (Brysbaert et al., 2019) based on human ratings of whether or not they knew the word.

Norms were available for 61,855 unique words.

Obtained from: `https://osf.io/g4xrt/`.

Valence Valence quantifies each word on a scale of positiveness–negativeness. The norms were collected based on human ratings by (Mohammad, 2018) using Best-Worst scaling, where participants are presented with four words at a time and asked to select the word with the highest valence. The two ends of the valence dimension were: MOST happiness, pleasure, positiveness, satisfaction, contentedness, hopefulness OR LEAST unhappiness, annoyance, negativeness, dissatisfaction, melancholy, despair.

Norms were available for 20,007 unique words.

Obtained from: `https://saifmohammad.com/WebPages/nrc-vad.html`.

The following features were not analyzed in the current work, but in the future we plan to add support for these features in the `SentSpace` framework:

Body-Object Interaction Body-object interaction quantifies the ease with which the human body can interact with what a word represents. The norms were collected using behavioral ratings on a scale from 1 to 7 with a value of 7 indicating a high body-object interaction rating by (Pexman et al., 2019).

The norms were available for 9,349 unique words.

Obtained from: `https://link.springer.com/article/10.3758%2Fs13428-018-1171-z#Sec9`.

Dominance Dominance quantifies each word on a scale of dominant–submissive. The norms were collected based on human ratings by (Mohammad, 2018) using Best-Worst scaling, where participants are presented with four words at a time and asked to select the word with the highest dominance. The two ends of the dominance dimension were: MOST dominant, in control of the situation, powerful, influential, important, autonomous OR LEAST submissive, controlled by outside factors, weak, influenced, cared-for, guided.

Norms were available for 20,007 unique words.

Obtained from: `https://saifmohammad.com/WebPages/nrc-vad.html`.

Part-of-Speech Ambiguity Parts-of-speech (POS) ambiguity is a metric to quantify how frequent the dominant POS of a given word is given all possible POS a word has. The value is a fraction between 0 and 1 where 1 denotes that the word always occurs in its most dominant POS form. POS values were obtained from the SUBTLEXus database (Brysbaert et al., 2012).

Norms were available for 74,286 unique words.

Obtained from the SUBTLEXus database: https://www.ugent.be/pp/experimentele-psychologie/en/research/documents/subtlexus).

Semantic Diversity Semantic diversity is a metric that quantifies semantic ambiguity based on variability in the contextual usage of words. The metric was computed by (Hoffman et al., 2013) and takes a step beyond simply summing the number of definitions that a word has. The underlying assumption is that words that appear in a wide range of contexts on diverse topics are more variable in meaning than those that appear in a restricted set of similar contexts. Hoffman et al. thus quantify the degree to which the different contexts associated with a given word vary in their meanings.

Norms were available for 31,739 English words.

Obtained from: https://link.springer.com/article/10.3758/s13428-012-0278-x#SecESM1.

Word Length Word length as measured by characters.

Zipf Lexical Frequency The Zipf lexical frequency is a metric of word frequency, but on a different scale than standard frequency. The Zipf scale was proposed by (van Heuven et al., 2014) as a scale that is easier to interpret than the usual frequency scales. Zipf values range from 1 to 7, with the values 1-3 indicating low-frequency words (with frequencies of 1 per million words and lower) and the values 4-7 indicating high-frequency words (with frequencies of 10 per million words and higher). Norms were based on American subtitles (51 million words in total) from the SUBTLEXus database (Brysbaert and New, 2009).

Norms were available for 74,286 unique words.

Obtained from the SUBTLEXus database: https://www.ugent.be/pp/experimentele-psychologie/en/research/documents/subtlexus).

A.2 Contextual Features

The contextual features broadly fall into two categories: syntactic (denoted by Contextual_syntax) and miscellaneous (denoted by Contextual_misc). Contextual features are ordered alphabetically.

A.2.1 Contextual Features — Syntax

Content Word Ratio — Misc Lexical density is the proportion of content words to function words in a sentence. It is a proxy for how much information a sentence contains. Content words were defined as nouns, verbs, adjectives, and adverbs and were defined using the NLTK part-of-speech tagger.

Dependency Locality Theory (DLT) Variants The Dependency Locality Theory (DLT) (Gibson, 2000) features are measures of storage and integration costs during sentence processing. The DLT is a theory of word-by-word comprehension difficulty during human language processing, with difficulty hypothesized to arise from working memory demand related to storing items in working memory (storage cost) and retrieving items from working memory (integration cost) as required by the dependency structure of the sentence. We include the traditional DLT metrics, as well as modifications as described in (Shain et al., 2016).

Left-Corner Features — Syntax The left-corner features are based on left-corner theories of sentence processing as described in (Rasmussen and Schuler, 2018). Similar to DLT, left-corner parsing models also posit storage and integration costs, but these costs are thought to derive not from dependency locality but from the number of unconnected fragments of phrase structure trees that must be maintained and combined in memory throughout parsing, word-by-word. See (Shain et al., 2021a) for detailed description of these features, but in brief they include: end of constituent, length of constituent (3 variants), end of center embedding, start of multi-word center-embedding, end of multi-word center embedding, length of multi-word center embedding (3 variants), and syntactic embedding depth. Features are derived from automatic parse trees generated by the van Schijndel et al. (2013) parser trained on a generalized categorial grammar reannotation (Nguyen et al., 2012) of the Penn Treebank corpus (Marcus et al., 1993).

N-gram Surprisal — Misc N-gram surprisal provides a metric of how surprising a word is given its context. The norms were computed by (Piantadosi et al., 2011) based on Google (Brants and Franz, 2009) using a standard probabilistic N-gram model which treats the context as consisting only of the local linguistic context containing the previous $N - 1$ words. The norms are available for $N = 2, 3, 4$, i.e. 2-grams, 3-grams and 4-grams.

Norms were available for 3,297,629 (2-grams), 2,133,709 (3-grams) and 1,600,987 (4-grams) unique words. Obtained from colala.berkeley.edu/data/PiantadosiTilyGibson2011/Google10L-1T.

Pronoun Ratio — Misc The pronoun ratio is

the proportion of pronoun words to all words in a sentence. It is a proxy for how much discourse is assumed in a sentence. Pronoun words were defined using the NLTK part-of-speech tagger.

The following features were not analyzed in the current work, but are in the process of being added to the `SentSpace` framework:

Language Model Surprisal Language model surprisal provides a metric for how surprising (i.e., likely) a given sentence is by using the probability distribution obtained from pre-trained state-of-the-art language models. The default probability is computed as the product of individual tokens' log probabilities.

The language models were obtained using the HuggingFace Transformers framework (Wolf et al., 2020).

Sentence-Level Sentiment — Misc Sentence-level sentiment provides a metric for how positive or negative a given sentence is. The feature was derived using a pre-trained transformer model fine-tuned to perform sentiment prediction from a large dataset of human-annotated sentiment norms. The code framework used to compute the feature was by HuggingFace (Wolf et al., 2020).

Syntactic Rule Frequency — Syntax The syntactic rule frequencies consist of counts of n-ary and binary syntactic rules. For both n-ary (n is an arbitrary number larger than two) and binary rules, the sentence is dependency parsed (CoNLL format). The n-ary version gets all heads, along with its part of speech and its dependency relations. So if there is a verb with a subject and object, an n-ary rule would be: nsubj-V-dobj. The binary version is similar, but takes each head/dependency relationship separately. So the rules would be nsubj-V, V-dobj, etc. Thus, the syntactic rule frequency features consists of the number of times each n-ary and binary rules occur. The code framework to compute the features was obtained from Kyle Mahowald (*preprint to appear*).

A.3 Embeddings

Embeddings provide representations of sentences in high-dimensional, learned vector spaces. We provide a context-independent embedding space (words have the same vector representation independent of context), GloVe (Pennington et al., 2014), as well as several commonly used contextualized embedding spaces (words have different vector representations based on the context in which they appear) from the HuggingFace framework (Wolf et al., 2020). These can be invoked using the corresponding model identifier from HuggingFace model hub as an argument to `SentSpace`.

B Materials Used in Demonstration

B.1 Example human-written paragraph

Montreal has a unique bagel tradition that dates back to at least 1919. The Montreal bagel is chewier, smaller, and less dense, but has a much bigger hole than its American cousin. Boiled in honey water and then baked in a wood-burning oven, it's a little sweet and has a harder exterior. It is hand-rolled in the shape of an oval hoop; you can wear one around your wrist like a bracelet.

B.2 Examples of GPT2-XL generated text

1 Montreal has a unique bagel tradition that dates back to the mid-nineteenth century. In the early days of the morning, tourists would arrive in Montreal in large numbers for a morning sandwich and coffee. You could be guaranteed to find several dozen different varieties in a pastry case. When the "Cappuccino" was introduced in 1894, the bagels came with it. You had to order your espresso and and your bagel separately.

2 Montreal has a unique bagel tradition that dates back to 1766, when an Englishman named J.D. Bagel opened the first of what would become five bakeries. Today, there are more than 70 Bagel East St. Laurent and 15 Bagel Central St. Laurent. It's not just the flavors of bagels that separate Montreal bagel restaurants from the rest of Canada. What also sets them apart are the quality ingredients.

3 Montreal has a unique bagel tradition that dates back to 1876, when the city hosted the Olympic Games. The tradition is still alive today. Because the bagel is such an American food, you won't find bagels being served in many Chinese restaurants, as French food in France is considered food that originated from the Americas. Desserts Although bagels have many tastes, you don't need to try every flavor to enjoy bagel ice cream or bagel sandwiches.

4 Montreal has a unique bagel tradition that dates back to 1917. In 2017, the Bagel Corner will open its doors again to celebrate Montreal's unique bagel heritage. This May, the Bagel Corner will offer a variety of bagels, bagel sandwiches and doughnuts, sold in Montreal and Montreal-area food trucks. With bags of fresh fruit, grapes, pickled veggies and other delicious bagels, this year's sale will be a great opportunity to indulge your taste buds.

5 Montreal has a unique bagel tradition that dates back to the early 1900's. The bagels that we now associate with Montreal are greatly influenced by the place that spawned them the Sea Route Bagel. This famous bagel began its long journey to Montreal with a group of Jewish immigrants arriving from Eastern Europe in the early 1900's. To say that they were fortunate would be an understatement.

C Corpora Benchmarks

As mentioned in the manuscript, we subsample a collection of corpora for use as benchmarks to compare against. We list these corpora in Table 1. These include: the Brown Corpus (Francis and Kucera, 1979), the Toronto Books Corpus Adventure genre (Zhu et al., 2015), Wall Street Journal corpus (Paul and Baker, 1992), Universal Dependencies `https://universaldependencies.org/#download`, Colossal Cleaned Common Crawl (C4) (Raffel et al., 2020), Corpus of Contemporary American English (Spoken) — 1991, 2001, 2012 (Davies, 2009).

Corpus name	Volume/Genre	No. of sentences	Duplicates	Sentence Length		
				Mean	Median	Std. deviation
(Total)		63,350,596	615,672			
Brown		26,954	3	12.681	13	4.462
Toronto Books	Adventure	1,040,936	0	14.519	13	7.632
UD		19,543	2	16.89	15	8.664
WSJ		541,790	960	22.351	21	8.734
COCA Spoken	1991	121,351	0	17.051	15	10.048
COCA Spoken	2001	113,330	3	15.734	13	9.269
COCA Spoken	2012	97,512	2	14.41	12	8.65
C4	10 random parts	49,772,404	614,602	17.481	16	8.905

Table 1: A list of Corpora used as Benchmarks

Feature	Mean		Standard Deviation	
	GPT2-XL	Human	GPT2-XL	Human
2-gram Surprisal***	7.86	8.13	0.46	0.40
3-gram Surprisal***	5.64	5.78	0.32	0.28
4-gram Surprisal	3.57	3.58	0.22	0.20
Age of Acquisition	5.28	5.26	0.53	0.46
Arousal	0.42	0.42	0.04	0.04
Concreteness***	2.58	2.69	0.16	0.15
Content Word Ratio*	0.50	0.53	0.11	0.08
End of Constituent*	0.23	0.24	0.03	0.03
End of Center-Embedding	0.65	0.64	0.04	0.04
End of Multi-Word Center-embedding	0.12	0.13	0.03	0.02
Length of Constituent*	1.33	1.38	0.18	0.12
Length of Multi-Word Center-Embedding	0.47	0.52	0.17	0.13
Lexical Connectivity	45.12	43.85	7.54	7.48
Lexical Decision RT	626.59	629.34	11.02	9.30
Log Contextual Diversity*	3.46	3.40	0.17	0.14
Log Lexical Frequency***	4.48	4.36	0.27	0.20
Number of Morphemes	1.52	1.54	0.09	0.08
Orthographic Neighbor Frequency	690.82	655.06	228.56	196.97
Orthography-Semantics Consistency	0.77	0.76	0.04	0.04
Polysemy	5.49	5.46	0.86	0.69
Prevalence	2.30	2.31	0.04	0.03
Pronoun Ratio	0.07	0.07	0.07	0.07
Sentence Length	104.59	102.63	12.50	9.59
Syntactic Integration Cost*	0.62	0.68	0.17	0.14
Syntactic Embedding Depth	1.23	1.27	0.17	0.14
Valence	0.62	0.62	0.05	0.04

Table 2: Mean values of `SentSpace` features for human- and GPT2-XL-generated text. Statistically significant differences (after a two-tailed t-test) are indicated by $*p < .05$, $**p < .01$, $***p < .005$.

PaddleSpeech: An Easy-to-Use All-in-One Speech Toolkit

Hui Zhang[1], **Tian Yuan**[1], **Junkun Chen**[3], **Xintong Li**[2], **Renjie Zheng**[2], **Yuxin Huang**[1], **Xiaojie Chen**[1], **Enlei Gong**[1], **Zeyu Chen**[1], **Xiaoguang Hu**[1], **Dianhai Yu**[1], **Yanjun Ma**[1], **Liang Huang**[2,3]

[1]Baidu Inc., Beijing, China
[2]Baidu Research, Sunnyvale, CA, USA
[3]Oregon State University, Corvallis, OR, USA

{zhanghui41, yuantian01, xintongli, renjiezheng, huangyuxin, chenxiaojie06, gongenlei, chenzeyu01}baidu.com

Abstract

PaddleSpeech is an open-source all-in-one speech toolkit. It aims at facilitating the development and research of speech processing technologies by providing an easy-to-use command-line interface and a simple code structure. This paper describes the design philosophy and core architecture of PaddleSpeech to support several essential speech-to-text and text-to-speech tasks. PaddleSpeech achieves competitive or state-of-the-art performance on various speech datasets and implements the most popular methods. It also provides recipes and pretrained models to quickly reproduce the experimental results in this paper. PaddleSpeech is publicly avaiable at `https://github.com/PaddlePaddle/PaddleSpeech`.[1]

1 Introduction

Speech processing technology enables humans to directly communicate with computers, which is an essential part of enormous applications such as smart home devices (Hoy, 2018), autonomous driving, and simultaneous translation (Zheng et al., 2020). Open-source toolkits boost the development of speech processing technology by lowering the barrier of application and research in this area (Young et al., 2002; Lee et al., 2001; Huggins-Daines et al., 2006; Rybach et al., 2011; Povey et al., 2011; Watanabe et al., 2018; Han et al., 2019; Wang et al., 2020; Ravanelli et al., 2021; Zhao et al., 2021).

However, the current prevailing speech processing toolkits presume that their users are experienced practitioners or researchers, so beginners might feel baffled when developing their exciting applications. For example, to prototype new speech applications with Kaldi (Povey et al., 2011), the users have to be comfortable reading and revising the provided recipes written in Bash, Perl, and Python scripts and be proficient at C++ to hack its implementation. The more recent toolkits, such as Fairseq S2T (Wang et al., 2020) and NeurST (Zhao et al., 2021), become more flexible by building on general-purpose deep learning libraries. But their complicated code styles also make it time-consuming to learn and hard to migrate from one to another. So, we have developed PaddleSpeech, providing a command-line interface and portable functions to make the development of speech-related applications accessible to everyone.

Notably, the Chinese community has many developers eager to contribute to the community. However, nearly all deep learning libraries, such as Pytorch (Paszke et al., 2019) and Tensorflow (Abadi et al., 2016), target the English community mainly, so it significantly increases the difficulty for Chinese developers. PaddlePaddle, as the only fully-functioning open-source deep learning platform targeting both the English and Chinese community, has accumulated more than 500k commits, 476k models, and is used by 157k enterprises. So, we expect PaddleSpeech, developed with PaddlePaddle can remove the barriers between the English and Chinese communities to boost the development of speech technologies and applications.

Developing speech applications for the industry is not the same scenario as conducting research in academia. The research papers mainly focus on developing novel models to perform better on specific datasets. However, a clean dataset usually does not exist when applying a speech product. So, PaddleSpeech provides on-the-fly preprocessing for the raw audios to make PaddleSpeech directly usable in product-oriented applications. Notably, some preprocessing methods are exclusive in PaddleSpeech, such as rule-based Chinese text-to-speech frontend, which can significantly benefit the performance of synthesized speech.

Performance is the cornerstone of all applica-

[1]Demo video: `https://paddlespeech.readthedocs.io/en/latest/demo_video.html`

Proceedings of the 2022 Conference of the North American Chapter of the Association for Computational Linguistics: Human Language Technologies: System Demonstrations, pages 114 - 123
July 10-15, 2022 ©2022 Association for Computational Linguistics

Task	**Description**	**Techniques**	**Datasets**
Sound Classification	*Label sound class*	Finetuned PANN (Kong et al., 2020b)	ESC-50 dataset (Piczak, 2015)
Speech Recognition	*Transcribe speech to text*	Deepspeech2 (Amodei et al., 2016) Conformer (Zhang et al., 2020) Transformer (Zhang et al., 2020)	Librispeech (Panayotov et al., 2015) AISHELL-1 (Bu et al., 2017)
Punctuation Restoration	*Post-add punctuation to transcribed text*	Finetuned ERNIE (Sun et al., 2019)	IWSLT2012-zh (Federico et al., 2012)
Speech Translation	*Translate speech to text*	Transformer (Vaswani et al., 2017)	MuST-C (Di Gangi et al., 2019)
Text To Speech	*Synthesis speech from text*	**Acoustic Model** Tacotron 2 (Shen et al., 2018) Transformer TTS (Li et al., 2019) SpeedySpeech (Vainer and Dušek, 2020) FastPitch (Łańcucki, 2021) FastSpeech 2 (Ren et al., 2020) **Vocoder** WaveFlow(Ping et al., 2020) Parallel WaveGAN (Yamamoto et al., 2020) MelGAN (Kumar et al., 2019) Style MelGAN (Mustafa et al., 2021) Multi Band MelGAN (Yang et al., 2021) HiFi GAN (Kong et al., 2020a)	CSMS (DataBaker) AISHELL-3 (Shi et al., 2020) LJSpeech (Ito and Johnson, 2017) VCTK (Yamagishi et al., 2019)

Table 1: List of speech tasks and corpora that are currently supported by PaddleSpeech.

tions. PaddleSpeech achieves state-of-the-art or competitive performers on various commonly used benchmarks, as shown in Table 1.

Our main contributions in this paper are two-folds.

- We introduce how we designed PaddleSpeech and what features it supports.
- We provide the implementation and reproducible experimental details that result in state-of-the-art or competitive performance on various tasks.

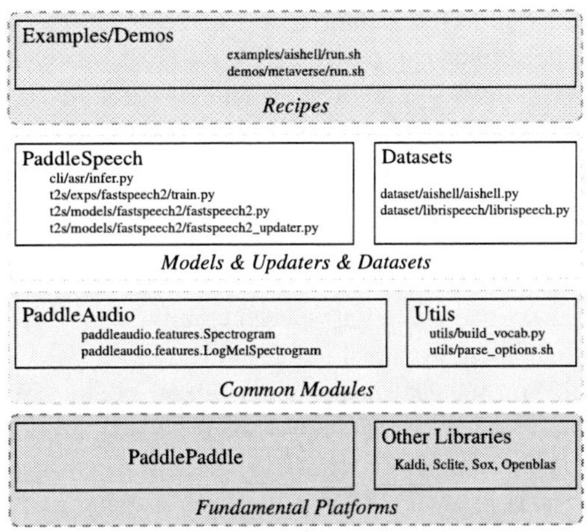

Figure 1: Software architecture of PaddleSpeech.

2 Design of PaddleSpeech

Figure 1 shows the software architecture of PaddleSpeech. As an easy-to-use speech processing toolkit, PaddleSpeech provides many complete recipes to perform various speech-related tasks and demo usage of the command line interface. Getting familiar with the top level should be enough for building speech-related applications.

The second level faces researchers in speech and language processing. The design philosophy of PaddleSpeech is model-centric to simplify the learning and development of speech processing methods. For a specific method, all computations of a specific model are included in two files under `PaddleSpeech/<task>/models/<model>`.[2]

PaddleSpeech has implemented most of the commonly used and well-performing models. A model architecture is implemented in a standalone file named by the method. Its corresponding training step and evaluation step are implemented in another `updater` file. Generally, reading or hacking these two files is enough to understand or design a model. More advanced hacking on more fine data processing or more compli-

[2] `<task>` includes `s2t` and `t2s` which stands for speech-to-text and text-to-speech respectively.

cated training/evaluation loop is also available at `PaddleSpeech/<task>/exps/<model>`. The original datasets can be obtained by scripts in corresponding `dataset/<dataset>/`. PaddleSpeech supports distributed multi-GPU training with good efficiency.

The standard modules, such as audio and text feature transformation and utility scripts, are implemented as libraries in the third level. The backend of PaddleSpeech is mainly PaddlePaddle with some functions from third-party libraries as shown in the fourth level. PaddleSpeech provides multiple ways to extract multiple types of speech features from raw audios using PaddleAudio and Kaldi, such as spectrogram and filterbanks, which can be varied according to the needs of the tasks.

3 Experiments

In this section, we compare the performance of models in PaddleSpeech with other popular implementations in five speech-related tasks, including sound classification, speech recognition, punctuation, speech translation, and speech synthesizing. The toolkit can reach SOTA on most tasks. All experiments in this section include details on data preparation, evaluation metrics, and implementation to enhance reproducibility.[3]

3.1 Sound Classification

Sound Classification is a task to recognize particular sounds, including speech commands (Warden, 2018), environment sounds (Piczak, 2015), identifying musical instruments (Engel et al., 2017), finding birdsongs (Stowell et al., 2018), emotion recognition (Xu et al., 2019) and speaker verification (Liu et al., 2018).

Datasets In this section, we analyze the performance of PaddleSpeech in Sound Classification on ESC-50 dataset (Piczak, 2015). The ESC-50 dataset is a labeled collection of 2000 environmental 5-second audio recordings consisting of 50 sound events, such as "Dog", "Cat", "Breathing" and "Fireworks", with 40 recordings per event.

Data Preprocessing First, we resample all audio recordings to 32 kHz, and convert them to monophonic to be consistent with the PANNs trained on AudioSet (Kong et al., 2020b). And then, we transform the recordings into log mel spectrograms by applying short-time Fourier transform on the waveforms with a Hamming window of size 1024 and a hop size of 320 samples. This configuration leads to 100 frames per second. Following Kong et al. (2019), we apply 64 mel filter banks to calculate the log mel spectrogram.

Model	Accuracy
AST-P (Gong et al., 2021)	95.6 ± 0.4
PANNs-CNN14	95.00
PANNs-CNN10	89.75
PANNs-CNN6	88.25

Table 2: 5-fold cross validation accuracy of ESC-50.

Implementation PANNs (Kong et al., 2020b) is one of the pre-trained CNN models for audio-related tasks, which is characterized in terms of being trained with the AudioSet (Gemmeke et al., 2017). PANNs are helpful for tasks where only a limited number of training clips are provided. In this case, we fine-tune all parameters of a PANN for the environment sounds classification task. All parameters are initialized from the PANN, except the final fully-connected layer which is randomly initialized. Specifically, we implement CNNs with 6, 10 and 14 layers, respectively (Kong et al., 2020b).

Results We report 5-fold cross validation accuracy values on ESC-50 dataset. As shown in Table 2, PANNs-CNN14 achieves 0.9500 5-fold cross validation accuracy that is comparable to the current state-of-the-art method (Gong et al., 2021).

3.2 Automatic Speech Recognition

Automatic Speech Recognition (ASR) is a task to transcribe the audio content to text in the same language.

Datasets We conduct the ASR experiments on two major datasets including Librispeech[4] (Panayotov et al., 2015) and Aishell-1[5] (Bu et al., 2017). Librispeech contains 1000 hours speech data. The whole dataset is divided into 3 training sets (100h clean, 360h clean, 500h other), 2 validation sets (clean, other), and 2 test sets (clean, other). Aishell contains 178 hours speech data. 400 speakers from different accent areas in China participate in the recording. The dataset is divided into the training

[3] https://github.com/PaddlePaddle/PaddleSpeech/tree/develop/examples

[4] http://www.openslr.org/12/

[5] http://www.aishelltech.com/kysjcp

Data	Model	Streaming	Test Data	Language Model	CER	WER
Aishell	WeNet Conformer†* (Yao et al., 2021)	✓			5.45	-
	WeNet Conformer† (Yao et al., 2021)				4.61	-
	WeNet Transformer† (Yao et al., 2021)				5.30	-
	ESPnet Conformer† (Inaguma et al., 2020)				5.10	-
	ESPnet Transformer† (Inaguma et al., 2020)				6.70	-
	SpeechBrain Transformer† (Ravanelli et al., 2021)				5.58	-
	Deepspeech 2	✓		char 5-gram	6.66	-
	Deepspeech 2			char 5-gram	6.40	-
	Transformer				5.23	-
	Conformer*	✓			5.44	-
	Conformer				4.64	-
Librispeech	WeNet Conformer† (Yao et al., 2021)		test-clean		-	2.85
	SpeechBrain Transformer† (Ravanelli et al., 2021)		test-clean	TransformerLM	-	2.46
	ESPnet Transformer† (Inaguma et al., 2020)		test-clean	TransformerLM	-	2.60
	Deepspeech 2		test-clean	word 5-gram	-	7.25
	Conformer		test-clean		-	3.37
	Transformer		test-clean	TransformerLM	-	2.40

† denotes the results are reported in their public repositories.
* denotes the results are streaming with chunk size 16.

Table 3: WER/CER on Aishell, Librispeech for ASR Tasks.

set (340 speakers), validation set, (40 speakers) and test set (20 speakers).

Data Preprocessing Deepspeech 2 takes character-level vocabularies for both English and Mandarin tasks. For other models, we use character-level vocabulary for Mandarin. And English text is preprocessed with SentencePiece (Kudo and Richardson, 2018). Both two kinds of datasets are added four additional characters, which are `<' >`, `<space>`, `<blank>` and `<eos>`. For cepstral mean and variance normalization (CMVN), a subset of or full of the training set is selected and be used to compute the feature mean and standard error. For feature extraction, we have several methods implemented, such as linear spectrogram, filterbank, and mfcc. Currently, the Deepspeech 2 model uses linear spectrogram or filterbank, but Transformer and Conformer models use filterbank. For a fair comparison, we take additional 3 dimensional pitch features into Transformer to be consistent with ESPnet.

Implementation We implement both streaming and non-streaming Deepspeech 2 (Amodei et al., 2016). The non-streaming model has 2 convolution layers and 3 LSTM layers. The streaming model has 2 convolution layers and 5 LSTM layers. The Conformer and Transformer models are implemented following Zhang et al. (2020) with 12 encoder layers and 6 decoder layers.

Results We report word error rate (WER) and character error rate (CER) for Librispeech (English) and Aishell (Mandarin) speech recognition, respectively. As shown in Table 3, Conformer and Transformer are better than Deepspeech 2. Our best models achieve comparable performance on both datasets compared with related works.

3.3 Punctuation Restoration

Punctuation restoration is a post-processing problem for ASR systems. It is crucial to improve the readability of the transcribed text for the human reader and facilitate down-streaming NLP tasks.

Datasets We conduct experiments on IWSLT2012-zh[6] dataset, which contains 150k Chinese sentences with punctuation. We select comma, period, and question marks as restore targets in this task, so we replace other punctuation with these three marks before training a model. We split the data into training, validation and testing sets with 147k, 2k, and 1k samples, respectively.

Implementation We formulate the problem of punctuation restoration as a sequence labeling task with four target classes including `EMPTY`, `COMMA`, `PERIOD`, and `QUESTION` (Nagy et al., 2021b). ERNIE (Sun et al., 2019), as a pretrained language model, achieves new state-of-the-art results on five Chinese natural language processing tasks, including natural language inference, semantic similarity,

[6] `https://hltc.cs.ust.hk/iwslt/`

Frameworks	De	Es	Fr	It	Nl	Pt	Ro	Ru
ESPnet-ST (Inaguma et al., 2020)	22.9	**28.0**	32.8	**23.8**	**27.4**	28.0	21.9	**15.8**
fairseq-ST (Wang et al., 2020)	22.7	27.2	32.9	22.7	27.3	28.1	21.9	15.3
NeurST (Zhao et al., 2021)	22.8	27.4	**33.3**	22.9	27.2	28.7	**22.2**	15.1
PaddleSpeech	**23.0**	27.4	32.9	22.9	26.7	**28.8**	**22.2**	15.4

Table 4: Case-sensitive detokenized BLEU scores on MuST-C *tst-COMMON*.

model	COMMA	PERIOD	QUESTION	Overall
BERTLinear†	0.4646	0.4227	0.7400	0.5424
BERTBiLSTM†	0.5190	0.5707	0.8095	0.6330
ERNIELinear	0.5142	0.5447	0.8406	0.6331

† denotes the results come from our reproduced models.

Table 5: F1-score values on IWSLT2012-zh dataset.

named entity recognition, sentiment analysis, and question answering. So, we finetune an ERNIE model for this task. More specifically, all parameters are initialized from the ERNIE pretrained model, except the final shared fully-connected layer, which is randomly initialized.

Results We report F1-score values on IWSLT2012-zh dataset. As shown in Table 5, our ERNIELinear model achieves 0.6331 overall F1-score, which is comparable with the previous work (Nagy et al., 2021a).

3.4 Speech Translation

Speech translation, where translating speech in a source language to text in another language, is beneficial in human communications.

Datasets In this section, we analyze the performance of speech-to-text translation with PaddleSpeech on MuST-C dataset (Di Gangi et al., 2019) with 8 different language translation pairs, which take the English speech as the source input.

Implementation We process the raw audios with Kaldi (Povey et al., 2011) and extract 80-dimensional log-mel filterbanks stacked with 3-dimensional pitch feature using a 25ms window size and a 10ms step size. Text is firstly tokenized with Moses tokenizer[7] and then processed by SentencePiece (Kudo and Richardson, 2018) with a joint vocabulary whose size is 8K for each language pair. We employ Transformer (Vaswani et al., 2017) as the base architecture for the speech translation experiments. In detail, the Transformer model has 12 encoder layers that follow 2 layers of 2D convolution with kernel size of 3 and stride size of 2, and 6 decoder layers. Each layer contains 4 attention heads with a size of 256. The encoder is initialized from a pretrained ASR model.

Results We report detokenized case-sensitive BLEU[8]. As shown in Table 4, PaddleSpeech can achieve competitive results compared with other frameworks.

3.5 Text-To-Speech

A Text-To-Speech (TTS) system converts given language text into speech. PaddleSpeech's TTS pipeline includes three steps. We first convert the original text into the characters/phonemes through the text frontend module. Then, through an Acoustic model, we convert the characters or phonemes into acoustic features, such as mel spectrogram, Finally, we generate waveform from the acoustic features through a Vocoder. In PaddleSpeech, the text frontend is a rule-based model inspired by expert knowledge. The Acoustic models and Vocoders are trainable.

Datasets In PaddleSpeech, we mainly focus on Mandarin and English speech synthesis. We have benchmarks on CSMSC[9], AISHELL-3[10], LJSpeech[11], VCTK[12]. Due to the limit of space, we only list the experimental results on CSMSC, which includes 12 hours speech audio corresponding to 10k sentences.

Text Frontend A text frontend module is used to extract linguistic features, characters and phonemes from given text. It mainly includes: Text Segmentation, Text Normalization (TN), Word Segmentation (WS), Part-of-Speech Tagging, Prosody Prediction and Grapheme-to-Phoneme (G2P) (see Table 6).

[7] https://github.com/moses-smt/mosesdecoder

[8] https://github.com/mjpost/sacrebleu

[9] https://www.data-baker.com/open_source.html

[10] http://www.aishelltech.com/aishell_3

[11] https://keithito.com/LJ-Speech-Dataset/

[12] https://datashare.ed.ac.uk/handle/10283/3443

	Module	Result								
PaddleSpeech	*Text*	*jīn tiān* 今天 today	shì 是 is	2020/10/29	,	zuì dī 最低 lowest	wēn dù 温度 temperature	shì 是 is	-3°C	。
	TN	今天	是	*èr líng èr líng nian shí yùe èr shí jǐu rì* 二零二零年十月二十九日 2 0 0 2 year 10 month 29 day	,	最低	温度	是	*líng xià sān dù* 零下 三 度 *negative three degree*	。
	WS	今天 /	是 /	二零二零年 / 十月 / 二十九日	,	/ 最低	温度 /	是 /	零下 / 三度	。
	G2P	jin1 tian1	shi4	er4 ling2 er4 ling2 nian2 shi4 yue4 er4 shi2 jiu3 ri4		zui4 di1	wen1 du4	shi4	ling2 xia4 san1 du4	
ESPnet		jin1 tian1 shi4		2020/10/29		zui4 di1	wen1 du4	shi4	-3°C	

Table 6: An example of the text preprocessing pipeline for Mandarin TTS of PaddleSpeech and ESPnet. **TN** stands for the text normalization module, **WS** stands for the word segmentation module, **G2P** stands for the grapheme-to-phoneme module. The text normalization module for mandarin of ESPnet is not able to correctly handle dates (2020/10/29) and temperatures (-3°C).

For Mandarin, our G2P system consists of a polyphone module, which uses pypinyin and g2pM, and a tone sandhi module which uses rules based on chinese word segmentations. To the best of our knowledge, our Mandarin text frontend system is the most complete one compared with other publicly released works.

Data Preprocessing PaddleSpeech TTS uses the following modules for data preprocessing[13]: First, we use Montreal-Forced-Aligner to get the duration for corresponding phonemes. Second, we extract mel spectrograms as the features (additional pitch and energy features for Fastspeech 2). Last, we conduct the statistical normalization for each feature.

Acoustic Model Acoustic models can be mainly classified into autoregressive and non-autoregressive models. The decoding of the autoregressive model relies on previous predictions at each step, which leads to longer inference time but relatively better quality. While the non-autoregressive model generates the outputs in parallel, so the inference speed is faster, but the quality of generated result is relatively poor.

As shown in Table 1, PaddleSpeech has implemented the following commonly used autoregressive acoustic models: Tacotron 2 and Transformer TTS, and non-autoregressive acoustic models: SpeedySpeech, FastPitch and FastSpeech 2.

Vocoder As shown in Table 1, PaddleSpeech has implemented the following vocoders: WaveFlow, Parallel WaveGAN, MelGAN, Style MelGAN, Multi Band MelGAN, and HiFi GAN.

	Acoustic Model	Vocoder	MOS ↑
ESPnet	Fastspeech 2	PWGAN	2.55 ± 0.19
PaddleSpeech	Tacotron 2	PWGAN	3.69 ± 0.11
	Speedyspeech	PWGAN	3.79 ± 0.09
	Fastspeech 2	PWGAN	4.25 ± 0.09
	Fastspeech 2	Style MelGAN	4.32 ± 0.10
	Fastspeech 2	MB MelGAN	4.43 ± 0.09
	Fastspeech 2	HiFi GAN	4.72 ± 0.08

Table 7: The MOS evaluation with 95% confidence intervals for TTS models trained using CSMSC dataset. PWGAN stands for Parallel WaveGan, MB MelGAN stands for Multi-Band MelGAN.

Implementation The PadddleSpeech TTS implementation of FastSpeech 2 adopts some improvement from FastPitch and uses MFA to obtain the forced alignment (the original FastSpeech paper uses Tacotron 2). Notably, the speech feature parameters of the acoustic model and the vocoder of one TTS pipeline should be the same. Detailed settings can be found in the sample config file[14] on CSMSC dataset.

Results We report the mean opinion score (MOS) for naturalness evaluation in Table 7. We use the crowdMOS toolkit (Ribeiro et al., 2011), where 14 Mandarin samples (see Appendix A) from these 7 different models were presented to 14 workers on Mechanical Turk. As shown in Table 7, PaddleSpeech can largely outperform ESPnet on Mandarin TTS. The main reason is that PaddleSpeech TTS has a better text frontend as shown in Table 6. Compared with other models, Fastspeech 2 with

[13] https://github.com/PaddlePaddle/PaddleSpeech/blob/develop/examples/csmsc/tts3/local/preprocess.sh

[14] https://github.com/PaddlePaddle/PaddleSpeech/blob/develop/examples/csmsc/tts2/conf/default.yaml

HiFi GAN can achieve the best results.

4 Conclusion

This paper introduces PaddleSpeech, an open-source, easy-to-use, all-in-one speech processing toolkit. We illustrated the main design philosophy behind this toolkit to conduct development and research on various speech-related tasks accessible. A number of reproducible experiments and comparisons show that PaddleSpeech achieves state-of-the-art or competitive performance with the most popular models on standard benchmarks.

5 Acknowledgment

We sincerely thank the anonymous reviewers for their valuable comments and suggestions. This work was supported by the National Key Research and Development Project of China (2020AAA0103503).

References

Martín Abadi, Paul Barham, Jianmin Chen, Zhifeng Chen, Andy Davis, Jeffrey Dean, Matthieu Devin, Sanjay Ghemawat, Geoffrey Irving, Michael Isard, et al. 2016. Tensorflow: A system for large-scale machine learning. In *12th {USENIX} symposium on operating systems design and implementation ({OSDI} 16)*, pages 265–283.

Dario Amodei, Sundaram Ananthanarayanan, Rishita Anubhai, Jingliang Bai, Eric Battenberg, Carl Case, Jared Casper, Bryan Catanzaro, Qiang Cheng, Guoliang Chen, et al. 2016. Deep speech 2: End-to-end speech recognition in english and mandarin. In *International conference on machine learning*, pages 173–182. PMLR.

Hui Bu, Jiayu Du, Xingyu Na, Bengu Wu, and Hao Zheng. 2017. Aishell-1: An open-source mandarin speech corpus and a speech recognition baseline. In *2017 20th Conference of the Oriental Chapter of the International Coordinating Committee on Speech Databases and Speech I/O Systems and Assessment (O-COCOSDA)*, pages 1–5. IEEE.

Mattia A Di Gangi, Roldano Cattoni, Luisa Bentivogli, Matteo Negri, and Marco Turchi. 2019. Must-c: a multilingual speech translation corpus. In *2019 Conference of the North American Chapter of the Association for Computational Linguistics: Human Language Technologies*, pages 2012–2017. Association for Computational Linguistics.

Jesse Engel, Cinjon Resnick, Adam Roberts, Sander Dieleman, Mohammad Norouzi, Douglas Eck, and Karen Simonyan. 2017. Neural audio synthesis of musical notes with wavenet autoencoders. In *ICML*.

Marcello Federico, Mauro Cettolo, Luisa Bentivogli, Paul Michael, and Stüker Sebastian. 2012. Overview of the iwslt 2012 evaluation campaign. In *IWSLT-International Workshop on Spoken Language Translation*, pages 12–33.

Jort F. Gemmeke, Daniel P. W. Ellis, Dylan Freedman, Aren Jansen, Wade Lawrence, R. Channing Moore, Manoj Plakal, and Marvin Ritter. 2017. Audio set: An ontology and human-labeled dataset for audio events. *2017 IEEE International Conference on Acoustics, Speech and Signal Processing (ICASSP)*, pages 776–780.

Yuan Gong, Yu-An Chung, and James R. Glass. 2021. Ast: Audio spectrogram transformer. *ArXiv*, abs/2104.01778.

Kun Han, Junwen Chen, Hui Zhang, Haiyang Xu, Yiping Peng, Yun Wang, Ning Ding, Hui Deng, Yonghu Gao, Tingwei Guo, Yi Zhang, Yahao He, Baochang Ma, Yulong Zhou, Kangli Zhang, Chao Liu, Ying Lyu, Chenxi Wang, Cheng Gong, Yunbo Wang, Wei Zou, Hui Song, and Xiangang Li. 2019. DELTA: A DEep learning based Language Technology plAtform. *arXiv e-prints*.

Matthew B Hoy. 2018. Alexa, siri, cortana, and more: an introduction to voice assistants. *Medical reference services quarterly*, 37(1):81–88.

David Huggins-Daines, Mohit Kumar, Arthur Chan, Alan W Black, Mosur Ravishankar, and Alexander I Rudnicky. 2006. Pocketsphinx: A free, real-time continuous speech recognition system for hand-held devices. In *2006 IEEE International Conference on Acoustics Speech and Signal Processing Proceedings*, volume 1, pages I–I. IEEE.

Hirofumi Inaguma, Shun Kiyono, Kevin Duh, Shigeki Karita, Nelson Yalta, Tomoki Hayashi, and Shinji Watanabe. 2020. Espnet-st: All-in-one speech translation toolkit. In *Proceedings of the 58th Annual Meeting of the Association for Computational Linguistics: System Demonstrations*, pages 302–311.

Keith Ito and Linda Johnson. 2017. The lj speech dataset. `https://keithito.com/LJ-Speech-Dataset/`.

Jungil Kong, Jaehyeon Kim, and Jaekyoung Bae. 2020a. Hifi-gan: Generative adversarial networks for efficient and high fidelity speech synthesis. *arXiv preprint arXiv:2010.05646*.

Qiuqiang Kong, Yin Cao, Turab Iqbal, Yuxuan Wang, Wenwu Wang, and Mark D. Plumbley. 2020b. Panns: Large-scale pretrained audio neural networks for audio pattern recognition. *IEEE/ACM Transactions on Audio, Speech, and Language Processing*, 28:2880–2894.

Qiuqiang Kong, Yin Cao, Turab Iqbal, Yong Xu, Wenwu Wang, and Mark D. Plumbley. 2019. Cross-task learning for audio tagging, sound event detection and spatial localization: Dcase 2019 baseline systems. *ArXiv*, abs/1904.05635.

Taku Kudo and John Richardson. 2018. Sentencepiece: A simple and language independent subword tokenizer and detokenizer for neural text processing. In *Proceedings of the 2018 Conference on Empirical Methods in Natural Language Processing: System Demonstrations*, pages 66–71.

Kundan Kumar, Rithesh Kumar, Thibault de Boissiere, Lucas Gestin, Wei Zhen Teoh, Jose Sotelo, Alexandre de Brébisson, Yoshua Bengio, and Aaron Courville. 2019. Melgan: Generative adversarial networks for conditional waveform synthesis. *arXiv preprint arXiv:1910.06711*.

Adrian Łańcucki. 2021. Fastpitch: Parallel text-to-speech with pitch prediction. In *ICASSP 2021-2021 IEEE International Conference on Acoustics, Speech and Signal Processing (ICASSP)*, pages 6588–6592. IEEE.

Akinobu Lee, Tatsuya Kawahara, and Kiyohiro Shikano. 2001. Julius—an open source real-time large vocabulary recognition engine. *EUROSPEECH2001: the 7th European Conference on Speech Communication and Technology*.

Naihan Li, Shujie Liu, Yanqing Liu, Sheng Zhao, and Ming Liu. 2019. Neural speech synthesis with transformer network. In *Proceedings of the AAAI Conference on Artificial Intelligence*, volume 33, pages 6706–6713.

Bin Liu, Shuai Nie, Yaping Zhang, Shan Liang, and Wenju Liu. 2018. Deep segment attentive embedding for duration robust speaker verification.

Ahmed Mustafa, Nicola Pia, and Guillaume Fuchs. 2021. Stylemelgan: An efficient high-fidelity adversarial vocoder with temporal adaptive normalization. In *ICASSP 2021-2021 IEEE International Conference on Acoustics, Speech and Signal Processing (ICASSP)*, pages 6034–6038. IEEE.

Attila Nagy, Bence Bial, and Judit Ács. 2021a. Automatic punctuation restoration with bert models. *arXiv preprint arXiv:2101.07343*.

Attila Matyas Nagy, Bence Bial, and Judit Ács. 2021b. Automatic punctuation restoration with bert models. *ArXiv*, abs/2101.07343.

Vassil Panayotov, Guoguo Chen, Daniel Povey, and Sanjeev Khudanpur. 2015. Librispeech: an asr corpus based on public domain audio books. In *2015 IEEE international conference on acoustics, speech and signal processing (ICASSP)*, pages 5206–5210. IEEE.

Adam Paszke, Sam Gross, Francisco Massa, Adam Lerer, James Bradbury, Gregory Chanan, Trevor Killeen, Zeming Lin, Natalia Gimelshein, Luca Antiga, et al. 2019. Pytorch: An imperative style, high-performance deep learning library. *Advances in neural information processing systems*, 32:8026–8037.

Karol J. Piczak. 2015. Esc: Dataset for environmental sound classification. *Proceedings of the 23rd ACM international conference on Multimedia*.

Wei Ping, Kainan Peng, Kexin Zhao, and Zhao Song. 2020. Waveflow: A compact flow-based model for raw audio. In *International Conference on Machine Learning*, pages 7706–7716. PMLR.

Daniel Povey, Arnab Ghoshal, Gilles Boulianne, Lukas Burget, Ondrej Glembek, Nagendra Goel, Mirko Hannemann, Petr Motlicek, Yanmin Qian, Petr Schwarz, et al. 2011. The kaldi speech recognition toolkit. In *IEEE 2011 workshop on automatic speech recognition and understanding*, CONF. IEEE Signal Processing Society.

Mirco Ravanelli, Titouan Parcollet, Peter Plantinga, Aku Rouhe, Samuele Cornell, Loren Lugosch, Cem Subakan, Nauman Dawalatabad, Abdelwahab Heba, Jianyuan Zhong, et al. 2021. Speechbrain: A general-purpose speech toolkit. *arXiv preprint arXiv:2106.04624*.

Yi Ren, Chenxu Hu, Xu Tan, Tao Qin, Sheng Zhao, Zhou Zhao, and Tie-Yan Liu. 2020. Fastspeech 2: Fast and high-quality end-to-end text to speech. *arXiv preprint arXiv:2006.04558*.

Flávio Ribeiro, Dinei Florêncio, Cha Zhang, and Michael Seltzer. 2011. Crowdmos: An approach for crowdsourcing mean opinion score studies. In *2011 IEEE international conference on acoustics, speech and signal processing (ICASSP)*, pages 2416–2419. IEEE.

David Rybach, Stefan Hahn, Patrick Lehnen, David Nolden, Martin Sundermeyer, Zoltan Tüske, Simon Wiesler, Ralf Schlüter, and Hermann Ney. 2011. Rasr-the rwth aachen university open source speech recognition toolkit. In *Proc. ieee automatic speech recognition and understanding workshop*.

Jonathan Shen, Ruoming Pang, Ron J Weiss, Mike Schuster, Navdeep Jaitly, Zongheng Yang, Zhifeng Chen, Yu Zhang, Yuxuan Wang, Rj Skerrv-Ryan, et al. 2018. Natural tts synthesis by conditioning wavenet on mel spectrogram predictions. In *2018 IEEE International Conference on Acoustics, Speech and Signal Processing (ICASSP)*, pages 4779–4783. IEEE.

Yao Shi, Hui Bu, Xin Xu, Shaoji Zhang, and Ming Li. 2020. Aishell-3: A multi-speaker mandarin tts corpus and the baselines. *arXiv preprint arXiv:2010.11567*.

Dan Stowell, Yannis Stylianou, Mike Wood, Hanna Pamula, and Hervé Glotin. 2018. Automatic acoustic detection of birds through deep learning: the first bird audio detection challenge. *ArXiv*, abs/1807.05812.

Yu Sun, Shuohuan Wang, Yukun Li, Shikun Feng, Xuyi Chen, Han Zhang, Xin Tian, Danxiang Zhu, Hao Tian, and Hua Wu. 2019. Ernie: Enhanced representation through knowledge integration. *ArXiv*, abs/1904.09223.

Jan Vainer and Ondřej Dušek. 2020. Speedyspeech: Efficient neural speech synthesis. *arXiv preprint arXiv:2008.03802*.

Ashish Vaswani, Noam Shazeer, Niki Parmar, Jakob Uszkoreit, Llion Jones, Aidan N Gomez, Łukasz Kaiser, and Illia Polosukhin. 2017. Attention is all you need. In *Advances in neural information processing systems*, pages 5998–6008.

Changhan Wang, Yun Tang, Xutai Ma, Anne Wu, Dmytro Okhonko, and Juan Pino. 2020. Fairseq S2T: Fast speech-to-text modeling with fairseq. In *Proceedings of the 1st Conference of the Asia-Pacific Chapter of the Association for Computational Linguistics and the 10th International Joint Conference on Natural Language Processing: System Demonstrations*, pages 33–39, Suzhou, China. Association for Computational Linguistics.

Pete Warden. 2018. Speech commands: A dataset for limited-vocabulary speech recognition. *ArXiv*, abs/1804.03209.

Shinji Watanabe, Takaaki Hori, Shigeki Karita, Tomoki Hayashi, Jiro Nishitoba, Yuya Unno, Nelson Enrique Yalta Soplin, Jahn Heymann, Matthew Wiesner, Nanxin Chen, et al. 2018. Espnet: End-to-end speech processing toolkit. *arXiv preprint arXiv:1804.00015*.

Haiyang Xu, Hui Zhang, Kun Han, Yun Wang, Yiping Peng, and Xiangang Li. 2019. Learning alignment for multimodal emotion recognition from speech. *CoRR*, abs/1909.05645.

Junichi Yamagishi, Christophe Veaux, Kirsten MacDonald, et al. 2019. Cstr vctk corpus: English multi-speaker corpus for cstr voice cloning toolkit (version 0.92). *University of Edinburgh. The Centre for Speech Technology Research (CSTR)*.

Ryuichi Yamamoto, Eunwoo Song, and Jae-Min Kim. 2020. Parallel wavegan: A fast waveform generation model based on generative adversarial networks with multi-resolution spectrogram. In *ICASSP 2020-2020 IEEE International Conference on Acoustics, Speech and Signal Processing (ICASSP)*, pages 6199–6203. IEEE.

Geng Yang, Shan Yang, Kai Liu, Peng Fang, Wei Chen, and Lei Xie. 2021. Multi-band melgan: Faster waveform generation for high-quality text-to-speech. In *2021 IEEE Spoken Language Technology Workshop (SLT)*, pages 492–498. IEEE.

Zhuoyuan Yao, Di Wu, Xiong Wang, Binbin Zhang, Fan Yu, Chao Yang, Zhendong Peng, Xiaoyu Chen, Lei Xie, and Xin Lei. 2021. Wenet: Production oriented streaming and non-streaming end-to-end speech recognition toolkit. *arXiv preprint arXiv:2102.01547*.

Steve Young, Gunnar Evermann, Mark Gales, Thomas Hain, Dan Kershaw, Xunying Liu, Gareth Moore, Julian Odell, Dave Ollason, Dan Povey, et al. 2002. The htk book. *Cambridge university engineering department*, 3(175):12.

Binbin Zhang, Di Wu, Zhuoyuan Yao, Xiong Wang, Fan Yu, Chao Yang, Liyong Guo, Yaguang Hu, Lei Xie, and Xin Lei. 2020. Unified streaming and non-streaming two-pass end-to-end model for speech recognition. *arXiv preprint arXiv:2012.05481*.

Chengqi Zhao, Mingxuan Wang, Qianqian Dong, Rong Ye, and Lei Li. 2021. NeurST: Neural speech translation toolkit. In *Proceedings of the 59th Annual Meeting of the Association for Computational Linguistics and the 11th International Joint Conference on Natural Language Processing: System Demonstrations*, pages 55–62, Online. Association for Computational Linguistics.

Renjie Zheng, Mingbo Ma, Baigong Zheng, Kaibo Liu, Jiahong Yuan, Kenneth Church, and Liang Huang. 2020. Fluent and low-latency simultaneous speech-to-speech translation with self-adaptive training. In *Findings of the Association for Computational Linguistics: EMNLP 2020*, pages 3928–3937.

A TTS Examples

We use the following sentences as the MOS evaluation test set in Table 7.

- 早上好，今天是2020/10/29，最低温度是-3°C。
- 你好，我的编号是37249，很高兴为您服务。
- 我们公司有37249个人。
- 我出生于2005年10月8日。
- 我们习惯在12:30吃中午饭。
- 只要有超过3/4的人投票同意，你就会成为我们的新班长。
- 我要买一只价值999.9元的手表。
- 我的手机号是18544139121，欢迎来电。
- 明天有62%的概率降雨。
- 手表厂有五种好产品。
- 跑马场有五百匹很勇敢的千里马。
- 有一天，我看到了一栋楼，我顿感不妙，因为我看不清里面有没有人。
- 史小姐拿着小雨伞去找她的老保姆了。
- 不要相信这个老奶奶说的话，她一点儿也不好。

DadmaTools: a Natural Language Processing Toolkit for the Persian Language

Romina Etezadi, Mohammad Karrabi, Najmeh Zare Maduyieh,
Mohammad Bagher Sajadi, and **Mohammad Taher Pilehvar**
Dadmatech, Tehran, Iran
{roetezadi,karrabi,n_zare,sajadi}@dadmatech.ir

Abstract

We introduce DadmaTools, an open-source Python Natural Language Processing toolkit for the Persian language. The toolkit is a neural pipeline based on spaCy for several text processing tasks, including normalization, tokenization, lemmatization, part-of-speech, dependency parsing, constituency parsing, chunking, and *ezafe* detecting. DadmaTools relies on fine-tuning of ParsBERT using the PerDT dataset for most of the tasks. Dataset module and embedding module are included in DadmaTools that support different Persian datasets, embeddings, and commonly used functions for them. Our evaluations show that DadmaTools can attain state-of-the-art performance on multiple NLP tasks. The source code is freely available at `https://github.com/Dadmatech/DadmaTools`.

1 Introduction

With the increased accessibility of open-source natural language processing toolkits, users are now able to more easily develop tools that perform sophisticated linguistic tasks. There are several Persian NLP toolkits, such as Stanza (Qi et al., 2020), Hazm[1], Parsivar[2], and jPTDP (Nguyen and Verspoor, 2018). However, they suffer from several limitations. First, most Persian toolkits are based on conventional non-neural models which prevents them from taking full advantage of the recent developments in the filed. Examples include Parsivar (Mohtaj et al., 2018), STeP1 (Shamsfard et al., 2010), Virastar[3], Virastyar[4], and ParsiAnalyzer[5]. Second, most Persian toolkits either do not cover all the basic processing tools (e.g., Perstem[6] and farsiNLPTools) or are not open-source (e.g., FarsiYar[7]). Third, there is no single toolkit that provides state-of-the-art results across different basic tasks. Table 1 lists the toolkits available for Persian NLP along with their task coverage.

We introduce DadmaTools, an open-source Python Natural Language Processing toolkit for Persian. DadmaTools provides the following advantages compared to existing toolkits:

- Using the DadmaTools framework, users can easily download various standard Persian **datasets** and perform a variety of operations on them.
- Several pre-trained static **word embeddings** exits for the Persian language. Many of these embeddings are integrated in the DadmaTools toolkit.
- We evaluated DadmaTools on different Persian datasets, reporting **state-of-the-art** or competitive performance at each step of the pipeline.

Moreover, DadmaTools is based on the spaCy framework which allows users to integrate our toolkit with other piplelines implemented in spaCy. We note that Stanza is a widely used Persian toolkit. Hence, we mainly compare DadmaTools to Stanza. Many of the standard tasks, such as constituency parsing, chunking, and *ezafe* detection[8], are not supported by Stanza for Persian. In addition to covering these tasks, our toolkit also provides support for datasets and word embeddings. DadmaTools is

[1] `https://github.com/sobhe/hazm`
[2] `https://github.com/ICTRC/Parsivar`
[3] `https://github.com/aziz/virastar`
[4] `https://github.com/alishakiba/virastyar`
[5] `https://github.com/NarimanN2/ParsiAnalyzer`
[6] `https://github.com/jonsafari/perstem`
[7] `https://www.text-mining.ir/`
[8] Ezafe is a grammatical particle in Pesrsian language that links two words together

Proceedings of the 2022 Conference of the North American Chapter of the Association for Computational Linguistics: Human Language Technologies: System Demonstrations, pages 124 - 130
July 10-15, 2022

Toolkit	Normalizer	Lemma	POS	dependency	Constintuency	Chunker	Ezafe
Stanza	✗	✓	✓	✓	✗	✗	✗
spaCy	✗	✓	✓	✓	✗	✗	✗
Hazm	✓	✓	✓	✓	✗	✓	✗
farsiNLPTools (Feely et al., 2014)	✗	✗	✓	✓	✗	✗	✗
Perstem	✗	✗	✓	✗	✗	✗	✗
persianp Toolbox	✗	✗	✓	✗	✗	✗	✗
UM-wtlab pos tagger	✗	✗	✓	✗	✗	✗	✗
RDRPOSTagger	✗	✗	✓	✗	✗	✗	✗
jPTDP	✗	✗	✓	✓	✗	✗	✗
Parsivar	✓	✗	✓	✓	✗	✓	✗
text_mining	✓	✓	✓	✗	✗	✗	✗
DadmaTools	✓	✓	✓	✓	✓	✓	✓

Table 1: Persian NLP toolkits and the corresponding tasks they support.

fully open-source. We hope it can facilitate NLP research and application for the Persian language.

2 System Design

DadmaTools is a neural NLP pipeline, but it also includes modules for embeddings and datasets. In this section, we first describe these modules, followed by the main pipeline.

2.1 Dataset Module

Popular text processing libraries such as Transformers[9], NLTK (Bird and Loper, 2004), and PyTorchtext have poor support for low-resource language datasets such as Persian. The dataset module of DadmaTools provides a convenient solution for automatic downloading and utilizing of some popular Persian NLP datasets. Each available dataset can be called by a function of the same name and loaded as a generator object. For instance, the Arman (Poostchi et al., 2018) dataset can be loaded with the following lines of code:

```
import dadmatools

# load dataset
arman = dadmatools.datasets.ARMAN()

# working with dataset
len_train = len(arman.train)
test_sample = next(arman.test)
```

DadmaTools allows users to load different sets (e.g., train, test, or dev), if there are any, by using the `<DATASET>.<SET>` format (e.g., `arman.train`). Moreover, the details of the selected dataset can be viewed by using `<DATASET>.info`. DadmaTools comes with a set containing the most commonly used Persian datasets for various tasks, such as text summarization, named entity recognition (NER), spell checking, textual entailment, text classification, sentiment classification, text translation, and universal dependency. There is also a search operation in DadmaTools for finding datasets that belong to specific tasks by using `get_all_datasets_info(tasks=['<task1>', '<task2>',...])`. The list of datasets that are currently included in DadmaTools is shown in Table 2. We will keep integrating new datasets to the toolkit.

2.2 Embedding Module

One of the challenges in developing NLP tools for the Persian language is the lack of a library to support different pre-trained embedding models. In order to overcome this challenge, we have developed an embedding module in DadmaTools which provides a variety of public Persian embeddings. For any given embedding space, an object is created which provides a wide range of functions.

```
# download and load embedding
em_name = 'glove-wiki'
embedding = get_embedding(em_name)

# word embedding
vec = embedding(<your_word>)

# sentence embedding
text = <your_text>
t_vec = embedding.embedding_text(text)

# embedding functions
w1 = <word_1>
w2 = <word_2>
similarity_rateembedding.similarity(w1,w2)
top = embedding.top_nearest(10, w1)
```

[9] https://github.com/huggingface/transformers

Dataset	Task
PersianNER[8]	NER
ARMAN (Poostchi et al., 2018)	NER
PEYMA (Shahshahani et al., 2018)	NER
FarsTail (Amirkhani et al., 2020)	Textual Entailment
FaSpell[9]	Spell Checking
PersianNews (Farahani et al., 2020)	Text Classification
PerDT	Universal Dependency
PnSummary (Farahani et al., 2021)	Text Summarization
SnappfoodSentiment (Farahani et al., 2020)	Sentiment Classification
TEP (Pilevar et al., 2011)	Text Translation(eng-fa)
WikipediaCorpus	Corpus
PersianTweets (Khojasteh et al., 2020)	Corpus

Table 2: Persian Datasets that are currently integrated in the DadmaTools toolkit.

The details of the corresponding embeddings can be shown with `get_embedding_info(<EMBEDDING>)`. Several functions are present in DadmaTools that can be used for word embeddings, such as finding top nearest neighbours, finding similarity scores between two given words, or getting sentence embedding of a text. Word embeddings that are currently included in DadmaTools are listed in Table 3. Similarly to the datasets module, we will keep updating the list when new embedding models are available.

2.3 NLP Pipeline

The pipeline consists of models that range from tokenizing raw text to performing syntactic parsing and high-level task such as NER. The artchitecture of models employed in DadmaTools is mostly based on Stanza (Qi et al., 2020) and ACE (Wang et al., 2021).

Normalization. Each sentence can be passed to a normalizer so that different optional procedures can be applied to it, such as whitespace correction, character unification, stopwords/punctuations removal, and email/number/URL replacement. As different settings can be used, this task can be used independently of the pipeline. However, the pipeline uses a default normalizer, which only corrects whitespace and unifies the character.

Tokenization, Sentence Splitting, and MWT. As for tokenization and sentence splitting, DadmaTools uses a similar seq2seq architecture to that of Stanza trained on the PerDT dataset.

The tokenizer also identifies whether or not a token is a multi-word token (MWT). Once a word is detected as an MWT, the word is expanded into the underlying syntactic subwords using the MWT Expander.

Lemmatization. Lemmatization is the task of converting the input word to its canonical form. For this purpose, we also utilize the seq2seq model presented in the Stanza for lemmatization. However, we manually validate the training dataset and remove wrong or empty instances which results in a better performance (cf. Table 5).

Part of Speech Tagging. For each word in a given input text DadmaTools assign a POS tag. To predict the POS tag, we used the ACE model based on ParsBERT pre-trained model (Mehrdad Farahani, 2021) fine-tunned on the PerDT dataset for the sequence labeling task.

Dependency Parsing. Similarly to POS tagging, our dependency parsing module is based on the ACE model. In this case, we fine-tuned ParsBERT for dependency parsing on the PerDT dataset.

Constituency Parsing. A constituency parse tree breaks a text into sub-phrases. Non-terminals in

[8]https://github.com/Text-Mining/Persian-NER

[9]https://lindat.mff.cuni.cz/repository/xmlui/handle/11372/LRT-1547

[10]https://github.com/Text-Mining/Persian-Wikipedia-Corpus/tree/master/models/glove

[11]https://fasttext.cc/docs/en/crawl-vectors.html

[12]http://vectors.nlpl.eu/repository/

[13]https://commoncrawl.org/

Embedding	Model	Training corpus
glove-wiki[10]	GloVe	Wikipedia
fasttext-commoncrawl-bin[11]	FastText	CommonCrawl[12]
fasttext-commoncrawl-vec[11]	FastText	CommonCrawl
word2vec-conll[13]	word2vec	Persian CoNLL17 corpus

Table 3: Persian word embeddings currently supported by DadmaTools.

Dataset	# of Instances	Lemma	POS Tags	Dependency Tags	Constituency parses
Seraji	6,000	✓	✓	✓	✗
PerDT (Rasooli et al., 2020)	29,107	✓	✓	✓	✗
Bijankhan	83,991	✗	✓	✗	✗
Dorsa Treebank (Dehghan et al., 2018)	30,000	✗	✗	✗	✓

Table 4: Persian datasets that are currently included in the toolkit.

the tree are types of phrases, the terminals are the words in the sentence, and the edges are unlabeled. To construct the constituency parser, we used the Supar library CRFConstituencyParser[14] using the constituency dataset provided by Dorsa Treebank (Dehghan et al., 2018). It is worth mentioning that the output parse tree tags are different from the tags produced by the POS tagger.

Chunking. Chunking is the process of separating and segmenting a sentence into its sub constituents, such as nouns, verbs, etc. We implemented a rule-based chunker. The rules have been written based on words, POS tags, and Dependency tags. The chunking module functions based on around sixty rules.

Ezafe Detecting. Ezafe is a grammatical particle in Pesrsian language that links two words together. Ezafe carries valuable information about the grammatical structure of sentences. However, it is not explicitly written in Persian scripts. To create a model to detect ezafe we used the Bijankhan corpus, as it includes ezafe as one of its POS tags. Therefore, we trained the sequence labeling model, ParsBERT, on reprocessed Bijankhan corpus for detecting the ezafe.

3 System Usage

It is possible to use the Normalizer directly without triggering the pipeline using the `normalizer` class. The DadmaTools pipline can be also initialized with `pipline` class. By default, only the tokenizer with sentence splitting and MWT are loaded. However, it is possible to load custom processors by adding their names as arguments. The `pipeline` will generate a `Doc` instance, which contains all the raw text's properties regarding the processes that have been called, in the form of the spaCy `Doc`. The following code snippet shows a minimal usage example of DadmaTools.

```
import datamatools.pipeline as pipe

# pipes gets the models e.g.
# pips = 'lem' will only contain
# lemmatizer in pupeline
pips = 'lem,pos,dep,cons'
nlp = pipe.language.Pipeline(pips)

# you can see the pipeline
# with this code
info = nlp.analyze_pipes(pretty=True)
print(info)
# doc is an SpaCy pbject
doc = nlp(<your_text>)
```

DadmaTools is designed to run on different types of hardware (CUDA and CPU). Priority is given to CUDA devices, if available.

4 Training Datasets

There are multiple Persian datasets that provide training data for various NLP tasks. Table 4 provides details about some of these dataset. We experimented with these datasets, both in isolation and when combined. Taking these results as our basis, we chose the best models as default for Dadma-Tools. The merging of different datasets for POS tags and dependencies was carefully evaluated by linguists.

- **Seraji**. This dataset has 6K instances. Our manual validation revealed noisy lemmas in

[14]https://parser.yzhang.site/en/latest/parsers/const.html

Toolkit	Seraji			PerDT			PerDT + Seraji		
	Dependency	POS	Lemm.	Dependency	POS	Lemm.	Dependency	POS	Lemm.
Stanza	87.20 / 83.89	97.43	–	93.34 / 91.05	97.35	98.97	84.95 / 80.55	88.53	96.92
jPTDP	– / 84.07	96.66	–	–	–	–			
Hazm	–	–	86.93	–	–	89.01	–	–	87.95
DadmaTools	**92.5 / 89.23**	**97.83**	–	**95.36 / 92.54**	**97.52**	**99.14**	**92.3 / 88.79**	**96.15**	**97.86**

Table 5: F1 score percentage for various models on different Persian datasets. For dependency we report two scores, for UAS (Unlabeled Attachment Score) and LAS (Labeled Attachment Score), as UAS/LAS.

the dataset which might be due to its automatic construction procedure.

- **PerDT**. This dataset has almost 30K instances. Thanks to its manual curation by linguists, the dataset is relatively free of annotation errors and mistakes.
- **PerDT + Seraji**. Combining these two datasets was challenging in the case of dependency parsing and POS tagging. We tried to unify tags based on some rules. However, the dataset was not fully unified. Therefore, we did not train the final DadmaTools model based on this combination.
- **Bijankhan**. This dataset has almost 80K instances. The tokenized sentences in this dataset is completely different from the previous ones. However, it has the ezafe tage in its tagset which we used for training the ezafe detection.
- **Dorsa Treebank**. This dataset is a Persian constituency treebank. The treebank was developed by using a bootstrapping approach which converts a dependency structure tree to a phrase structure tree. The annotations are then manually verified. The treebank consists of approximately 30,000 sentences.

5 Experiments

Models presented in Table 5 are separately trained on Seraji, PerDT, and combination of both. The evaluations are carried out on corresponding test sets of each dataset. We carried out a set of experiments to compare DadmaTools with other popular toolkits. We opted for Stanza as our main competitor, given that it is the most widely used toolkit for the Persian language. We were limited to compare our toolkit only with those models that were trained on the same datasets (or had public source codes allowing us to train and test on specific datasets). It is worth mentioning that the final models (lemmatizer, POS tagger, and dependacny parser) presented in DadmaTools is based on the PerDT dataset only.

Lemmatizer. We compare DadmaTools against Stanza and hazm on the lemmatization task. As shown in Table 5, DadmaTools outperforms the other two tools.

POS Tagger. For this experiment, we compared DadmaTools against Stanza given that both models use the same dataset for their training. As shown in Table 5, DadmaTools achieved a better result in predicting the universal tags.

Dependency Parser. Similarly to the previous setting, Stanza is our main baseline for dependency parsing, given their training on the same dataset. As shown in Table 5, DadmaTools outperforms Stanza (+1.5% for LAS and +2% in UAS) in predicting the universal tags.

Constituency Parser. To train the constituency parser model we used the Dorsa Treebank. One fifth of the treebank was split for testing and the F-score percentage on the test dataset was 82.88. There is no other similar constituency parser model to compare the results with.

Chunker. Our chunker is rule-based model that employs nearly eighty rules. There is no gold dataset in the Persian language that would allow us to evaluate the chunking module.

5.1 Speed

In order to test the speed of DadmaTools, we combined PerDT and Seraji (PerDT + Seraji) to have a large dataset which would allow us to draw reliable conclusions. Table 6 shows the average run time of models on PerDT + Seraji, computed based on running the models on GPU. Hazm is faster for POS tagging and lemmatizing due to its rule-based nature (as opposed to our neural model).

Toolkit	Dependency parser	POS tagger	Lemmatizer
Stanza	0.065	0.051	0.032
Hazm	2.404	0.001	0.000
DadmaTools	0.027	0.029	0.038

Table 6: Average run time (in seconds) per instance in the PerDT test set, using an Nvidia GeForce RTX 3090 GPU
.

6 Conclusion and Future Work

We introduced DadmaTools, an open-source Python Natural Language Processing toolkit for the Persian language. DadmaTools supports different NLP tasks. Moreover, it is based on the spaCy framework which allows users to integrate the toolkit with other processors in a pipeline. As future work, we intend to extend the supported tasks by adding high-level NLP tasks, such as sentiment analysis, entailment, and summarization. We also plan to provide users with the ability to add new datasets and models to the toolkit. We hope that the toolkit can pave the way for research and development for the Persian language.

References

Hossein Amirkhani, Mohammad AzariJafari, Zohreh Pourjafari, Soroush Faridan-Jahromi, Zeinab Kouhkan, and Azadeh Amirak. 2020. FarsTail: A Persian Natural Language Inference Dataset. *arXiv preprint arXiv:2009.08820*.

Steven Bird and Edward Loper. 2004. NLTK: The natural language toolkit. In *Proceedings of the ACL Interactive Poster and Demonstration Sessions*, pages 214–217, Barcelona, Spain. Association for Computational Linguistics.

Mohammad Hossein Dehghan, Mohammad Molla-Abbasi, and Heshaam Faili. 2018. Toward a multi-representation persian treebank. In *2018 9th International Symposium on Telecommunications (IST)*, pages 581–586. IEEE.

Mehrdad Farahani, Mohammad Gharachorloo, Marzieh Farahani, and Mohammad Manthouri. 2020. ParsBERT: Transformer-based model for persian language understanding. *ArXiv*, abs/2005.12515.

Mehrdad Farahani, Mohammad Gharachorloo, and M. Manthouri. 2021. Leveraging ParsBERT and pretrained mT5 for persian abstractive text summarization. *2021 26th International Computer Conference, Computer Society of Iran (CSICC)*, pages 1–6.

Weston Feely, Mehdi Manshadi, Robert Frederking, and Lori Levin. 2014. The cmu metal farsi nlp approach. In *Proceedings of the Ninth International Conference on Language Resources and Evaluation (LREC'14)*, pages 4052–4055.

Hadi Abdi Khojasteh, Ebrahim Ansari, and Mahdi Bohlouli. 2020. LSCP: Enhanced large scale colloquial persian language understanding. *arXiv preprint arXiv:2003.06499*.

Marzieh Farahani Mohammad Manthouri Mehrdad Farahani, Mohammad Gharachorloo. 2021. Parsbert: Transformer-based model for persian language understanding. *Neural Processing Letters*.

Salar Mohtaj, Behnam Roshanfekr, Atefeh Zafarian, and Habibollah Asghari. 2018. Parsivar: A language processing toolkit for persian. In *Proceedings of the Eleventh International Conference on Language Resources and Evaluation (LREC 2018)*.

Dat Quoc Nguyen and Karin Verspoor. 2018. An improved neural network model for joint POS tagging and dependency parsing. In *Proceedings of the CoNLL 2018 Shared Task: Multilingual Parsing from Raw Text to Universal Dependencies*, pages 81–91, Brussels, Belgium. Association for Computational Linguistics.

Mohammad Taher Pilevar, Heshaam Faili, and Abdol Hamid Pilevar. 2011. Tep: Tehran english-persian parallel corpus. In *International Conference on Intelligent Text Processing and Computational Linguistics*, pages 68–79. Springer.

Hanieh Poostchi, Ehsan Zare Borzeshi, and Massimo Piccardi. 2018. BiLSTM-CRF for persian named-entity recognition ArmanPersoNERCorpus: the first entity-annotated persian dataset. In *LREC*.

Peng Qi, Yuhao Zhang, Yuhui Zhang, Jason Bolton, and Christopher D. Manning. 2020. Stanza: A Python natural language processing toolkit for many human languages. In *Proceedings of the 58th Annual Meeting of the Association for Computational Linguistics: System Demonstrations*.

Mohammad Sadegh Rasooli, Pegah Safari, Amirsaeid Moloodi, and Alireza Nourian. 2020. The persian dependency treebank made universal. *arXiv preprint arXiv:2009.10205*.

Mahsa Sadat Shahshahani, Mahdi Mohseni, Azadeh Shakery, and Heshaam Faili. 2018. PEYMA: A tagged corpus for persian named entities. *arXiv preprint arXiv:1801.09936*.

Mehrnoush Shamsfard, Hoda Sadat Jafari, and Mahdi Ilbeygi. 2010. STeP-1: A set of fundamental tools for persian text processing. In *LREC*.

Xinyu Wang, Yong Jiang, Nguyen Bach, Tao Wang, Zhongqiang Huang, Fei Huang, and Kewei Tu. 2021. Automated Concatenation of Embeddings for Structured Prediction. In *the Joint Conference of the 59th Annual Meeting of the Association for Computational Linguistics and the 11th International Joint Conference on Natural Language Processing (**ACL-IJCNLP 2021**)*. Association for Computational Linguistics.

FAMIE: A Fast Active Learning Framework for Multilingual Information Extraction

Minh Van Nguyen[1], **Nghia Trung Ngo**[1], **Bonan Min**[2], **and Thien Huu Nguyen**[1]
[1] Dept. of Computer and Information Science, University of Oregon, Eugene, OR, USA
[2] Raytheon BBN Technologies, USA
{minhnv@cs,nghian@,thien@cs}.uoregon.edu,
bonan.min@raytheon.com

Abstract

This paper presents FAMIE, a comprehensive and efficient active learning (AL) toolkit for multilingual information extraction. FAMIE is designed to address a fundamental problem in existing AL frameworks where annotators need to wait for a long time between annotation batches due to the time-consuming nature of model training and data selection at each AL iteration. This hinders the engagement, productivity, and efficiency of annotators. Based on the idea of using a small proxy network for fast data selection, we introduce a novel knowledge distillation mechanism to synchronize the proxy network with the main large model (i.e., BERT-based) to ensure the appropriateness of the selected annotation examples for the main model. Our AL framework can support multiple languages. The experiments demonstrate the advantages of FAMIE in terms of competitive performance and time efficiency for sequence labeling with AL. We publicly release our code (https://github.com/nlp-uoregon/famie) and demo website (http://nlp.uoregon.edu:9000/). A demo video for FAMIE is provided at: https://youtu.be/I2i8n_jAyrY.

1 Introduction

Information Extraction (IE) systems provide important tools to extract structured information from text (Li et al., 2014; Nguyen and Nguyen, 2019; Lai et al., 2021; Veyseh et al., 2021; Nguyen et al., 2021a). At the core of IE involves sequence labeling tasks that aim to recognize word spans and semantic types for some objects of interest (e.g., entities and events) in text. For example, two typical sequence labeling tasks in IE feature Named Entity Recognition (NER) to find names of entities of interest, and Event Detection (ED) to identify triggers of specified event types (Walker et al., 2006). Despite extensive research effort for sequence labeling (Lafferty et al., 2001; Ma and Hovy, 2016; Pouran Ben Veyseh et al., 2021b), a major bottleneck of existing IE methods involves the requirement for large-scale human-annotated data to build high-quality models. As annotating data is often expensive and time-consuming, large-scale labeled data is not practical for various domains and languages.

To address the annotation cost for IE, previous work has resorted to active learning (AL) approaches (Settles and Craven, 2008; Settles, 2009) where only a selective set of examples are annotated to minimize the annotation effort while maximizing the performance. Starting with a set of unlabeled data, AL methods train and improve a sequence labeling model via multiple human-model collaboration iterations. At each iteration, three major steps are performed in order: (i) training the model on the current labeled data, (ii) using the trained model to select the most informative examples in the current unlabeled set for annotation, and (iii) presenting the selected examples to human annotators to obtain labels. In AL, the number of annotated samples or annotation time might be limited by a budget to make it realistic.

Unfortunately, despite much potentials, existing AL methods and frameworks are still not applied widely in practice due to their main focus on devising the most effective example selection algorithm for human annotation, e.g., based on the diversity of the examples (Shen et al., 2017; Yuan et al., 2020) and/or the uncertainty of the models (Roth and Small, 2006; Wang and Shang, 2014; Shelmanov et al., 2021). Training and selection time in the first and second steps of each AL interaction is thus not considered in prior work for sequence labeling. This is a critical issue that limits the application of AL: annotators might need to wait for a long period between annotation batches due to the long training and selection time of the models at each AL iteration. Given the widespread trend of using large-scale pre-trained language models

Proceedings of the 2022 Conference of the North American Chapter of the Association for Computational Linguistics: Human Language Technologies: System Demonstrations, pages 131 - 139

(e.g., BERT), this problem of long waiting or training/selection time in AL can only become worse. On the one hand, the long idle time of annotators reduces the number of annotated examples given an annotation budget. Further, the engagement of annotators in the annotation process can drop significantly due to the long interruptions between annotation rounds, potentially affecting the quality of their produced annotation. In all, current AL frameworks are unable to optimize the available time of annotators to maximize the annotation quantity and quality for satisfactory performance.

To this end, we demonstrate a novel AL framework (called FAMIE) that leverages large-scale pretrained language models for sequence labeling to achieve optimal modeling capacity while significantly reducing the waiting time between annotation rounds to optimize annotator time. Instead of training the full/main large-scale model for data selection at each AL iteration, our key idea is to train only a small proxy model on the current labeled data to recommend new examples for annotation in the next round. In this way, the training and data selection time can be reduced significantly to enhance annotation engagement and quality. An important issue in this idea is to ensure that the examples selected by the proxy model are also optimal for the main large model. To this end, we introduce a novel knowledge distillation mechanism for AL that encourages the synchronization between the proxy and main models, and promotes the fitness of selected examples for the main model. To update the main model with new annotated data for effective distillation, we propose to train the main large model on current labeled data during the annotation time, thus not adding to the waiting time of annotators between annotation rounds. This is in contrast to previous AL frameworks that leave the computing resources unused during annotation time. Our approach can thus efficiently exploit both human and computer time for AL.

To evaluate the proposed AL framework FAMIE, we conduct experiments for multilingual sequence labeling problems, covering two important IE tasks (i.e., NER and ED) in three languages (i.e., English, Spanish, and Chinese). The experiments demonstrate the efficiency and effectiveness of FAMIE that can achieve strong performance with significantly less human-computer collaboration time. Compared to existing AL systems such as ActiveAnno (Wiechmann et al., 2021) and Paladin (Nghiem et al., 2021), our system FAMIE features important advantages. First, FAMIE introduces a novel approach to reduce model training and data selection time for AL via a small proxy model and knowledge distillation while still benefiting from the advances in large-scale language models. Second, while previous AL systems only focus on some specific task in English, FAMIE can support different sequence labeling tasks in multiple languages due to the integration of our prior multilingual toolkit Trankit (Nguyen et al., 2021b) to perform fundamental NLP tasks in 56 languages. Third, in contrast to previous AL systems that only implement one data selection algorithm, FAMIE covers a diverse set of AL algorithms. Finally, FAMIE is the first complete AL system that allows users to define their sequence labeling problems, work with the models to annotate data, and eventually obtain a ready-to-use model for deployment.

2 System Description

In AL, we are given two initial datasets, a small seed set of labeled examples $D_0 = \{(\mathbf{w}, \mathbf{y})\}$ and an unlabeled example set $U_0 = \{\mathbf{w}\}$ (the seed set D_0 is optional and our system can work directly with only U_0). For sequence labeling, models consume a sequence of K words $\mathbf{w} = [w_1, w_2, \ldots, w_K]$ (i.e., a sentence/example) to output a tag sequence $\mathbf{y} = [y_1, y_2, \ldots, y_K]$ (y_i is the label tag for w_i). The tag sequence is represented in the BIO scheme to capture spans and types of objects of interest.

A typical AL process contains multiple rounds/iterations of model training, data selection, and human annotation in a sequential manner. Let D and U be the overall labeled and unlabeled set of examples at the beginning of the current t-th iteration (initialized with D_0 and U_0). At the current iteration, a sequence labeling model is first trained on the current labeled set D. A sample selection algorithm then employs the trained model to suggest the most informative subset of examples U^t in U (i.e., $U^t \subset U$) for annotation. Afterwards, a human annotator will provide labels for the sentences in the selected set U^t, leading to the labeled examples D^t for U^t. The labeled and unlabeled sets can then be updated via: $D \leftarrow D \cup D^t$ and $U \leftarrow U \setminus U^t$.

2.1 Model

We employ the typical Transformer-CRF architecture for sequence labeling (Nguyen et al., 2021b). In particular, given the input sentence

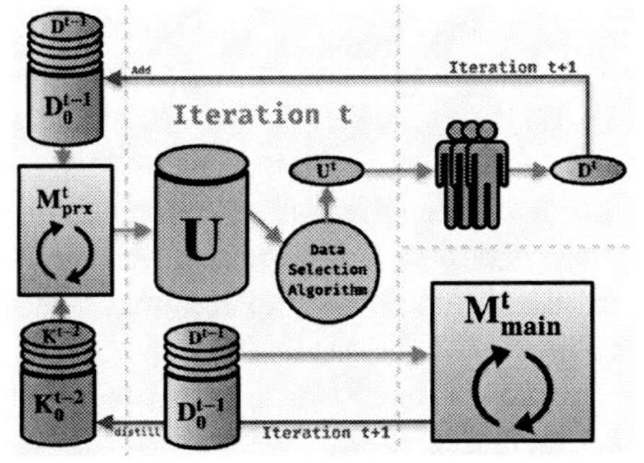

Figure 1: The overall Proxy Active Learning process.

$\mathbf{w} = [w_1, w_2, \ldots, w_K]$, the state-of-the-art multilingual language model XLM-Roberta (Conneau et al., 2020) is used to obtain contextualized embeddings for the words: $\mathbf{X} = \mathbf{x}_1, \ldots, \mathbf{x}_K =$ XLMR$(w_1, \ldots, w_K)$ (i.e., to support multiple languages). Afterwards, the word embeddings are sent to a feed-forward network with softmax in the end to obtain the score vectors: $\mathbf{z}_i = \text{softmax}(\mathbf{h}_i)$ where $\mathbf{h}_i = \text{FFN}(\mathbf{x}_i)$. Here, each value in $\mathbf{z}_i$ represents a score for a tag in the tag set V. The score vectors are then fed into a Conditional Random Field (CRF) layer to compute a distribution for possible tag sequences for $\mathbf{w}$: $P(\hat{\mathbf{y}}|\mathbf{w}) = \frac{\exp(s(\hat{\mathbf{y}},\mathbf{w}))}{\sum_{\hat{\mathbf{y}}' \in Y(\mathbf{w})} \exp(s(\hat{\mathbf{y}}',\mathbf{w}))}$ where $Y(\mathbf{w})$ is the set of all possible tag sequences for $\mathbf{w}$. Also, $s(\hat{\mathbf{y}}, \mathbf{w})$ is the score for a tag sequence $\hat{\mathbf{y}} = [\hat{y}_1, \ldots, \hat{y}_K]$: $s(\hat{\mathbf{y}}, \mathbf{w}) = \sum_i \mathbf{z}_i[\hat{y}_i] + \sum_i \pi_{\hat{y}_i \rightarrow \hat{y}_{i+1}}$. Here, $\pi_{\hat{y}_i \rightarrow \hat{y}_{i+1}}$ is the transition score from the tag $\hat{y}_i$ to the tag $\hat{y}_{i+1}$. The model is trained by minimizing the negative log likelihood: $L_{task} = -\log P(\mathbf{y}|\mathbf{w})$. For inference, the Viterbi algorithm is used for decoding: $\hat{\mathbf{y}^*} = \max_{\hat{\mathbf{y}}'} P(\hat{\mathbf{y}}'|\mathbf{w})$.

Adapter-based Finetuning To further improve the memory and time efficiency, we incorporate light-weight adapter networks (Houlsby et al., 2019; Peters et al., 2019) into our model. In form of small feed-forward networks, adapters are injected in between the transformer layers of XLM-Roberta. For training, we only update the adapters while the parameters of XLM-Roberta are fixed. This significantly reduces the amount of learning parameters while sacrificing minimal extraction loss, or in case of low-resource learning even surpassing performance of fully fine-tuned models.

2.2 Data Selection Strategies

To improve the flexibility to accommodate different problems, our AL framework supports a wide range of data selection strategies for choosing the best batch of examples to label at each iteration for sequence labeling. These algorithms are categorized into three groups, i.e., uncertainty-based, diversity-based, and hybrid. For each group, we explore its most popular methods as follows.

Uncertainty-based. These methods select examples for annotation according to the main model's confidence over the predicted tag sequences for unlabeled examples. Early methods sort the unlabeled examples by the uncertainty of the main model. To avoid the preference over longer examples, the method Maximum Normalized Log-Probability (**MNLP**) (Shen et al., 2017) proposes to normalize the likelihood over example lengths. In particular, MNLP selects examples with the highest MNLP scores: $MNLP(\mathbf{w}) = -\max_{\hat{\mathbf{y}}'} \frac{1}{K} \log P(\hat{\mathbf{y}}'|\mathbf{w})$.

Diversity-based. Algorithms in this category assume that a representative set of examples can act as a good surrogate for the whole dataset. **BERT-KM** (Yuan et al., 2020) uses K-Means to cluster the examples in unlabeled data based on the contextualized embeddings of the sentences (i.e., the representations for the [CLS] tokens in the trained BERT-based models). The nearest neighbors to the K cluster centers are then chosen for labeling.

Hybrid. Recently, several works have proposed data selection strategies for BERT-based AL to balance between uncertainty and diversity. The **BADGE** method (Ash et al., 2019; Kim, 2020) chooses examples from clusters of gradient embeddings, which are formed with the token representations $\mathbf{h}_i$ from the penultimate layer of the main model and the gradients of the cross-entropy loss with respect to such token representations. The gradient embeddings are then sent to the K-Means++ to find the initial K cluster centers that are distant from each other, serving as the selected examples (Kim, 2020).

In addition, we implement the AL framework **ALPS** (Yuan et al., 2020) that does not require training the main model for data section. ALPS employs the surprisal embedding of **w**, which is obtained from the likelihoods of masked tokens from pre-trained language models (i.e., XLM-Roberta). The surprisal embeddings are also clustered to select annotation examples as in BERT-KM.

2.3 Proxy Active Learning

As discussed in the introduction, model training and data selection at each iteration of traditional AL methods might consume significant time (especially with the current trend of large-scale language models), thus introducing a long idle time for annotators that might reduce annotation quality and quantity. To this end, (Shelmanov et al., 2021) have explored approaches to accelerate training and data selection steps for AL by leveraging smaller and approximate models during the AL iterations. To make it more efficient, the main large model is only trained once in the end over all the annotated examples in AL. Unfortunately, this approach suffers from the mismatch between the approximate and main models as they are separately trained in AL, thus limiting the effectiveness of the selected examples for the main model (Lowell et al., 2019).

To overcome these issues, our AL framework FAMIE trains a small proxy network at each iteration to suggest new unlabeled samples. Dealing with the mismatch between the proxy-selected examples and the main model, FAMIE proposes to involve the main model in the training and data selection for the proxy model. In particular, at each AL iteration, the main model will still be trained over the latest labeled data. However, to avoid the interference of the main large model with the waiting time of annotators, we propose to train the main model during the annotation time of the annotators (i.e., main model training and data annotation are done in parallel). Given the main model trained at previous iteration, knowledge distillation will be employed to synchronize the knowledge between the main and proxy models at the current iteration.

The complete framework for FAMIE is presented in Figure 1. At iteration t, a proxy acquisition model is trained on the current labeled data set $D_0^{t-1} = D^0 \cup D^1 \ldots \cup D^{t-1}$. The trained proxy model at the current step is called M_{prx}^t. Also, we use knowledge distillation signals K_0^{t-2} that is computed from the main model M_{main}^{t-1} trained at the previous iteration $t-1$ to synchronize the proxy model M_{prx}^t and the main model M_{main}^{t-1} (M_{prx}^1 is trained only on D^0). Afterwards, a data selection algorithm is used to select a batch of examples U^t from the current unlabeled set U for annotation, leveraging the feedback from M_{prx}^t. Next, a human annotator will label U^t to produce the labeled data batch D^t for the next iteration $t+1$. During this annotation time, the main model will also be trained again over the current labeled data D_0^{t-1} to produce the current version M_{main}^t of the model. The distillation signal K_0^{t-1} for the next step will also be computed after the training of M_{main}^t. This process is repeated over multiple iterations and the last version of M_{main} will be returned for users.

To improve the fitness of the proxy-based selected examples for M_{main}, we leverage the distilled version miniLM of XLM-Roberta (Wang et al., 2021) that employs similar stacks of transformer layers for the proxy model M_{prx}. Note that M_{prx} also includes a CRF layer on top of miniLM.

2.4 Uncertainty Distillation

Although the proxy and main model M_{prx} and M_{main} are trained on similar data, they might still exhibit large mismatch, e.g., regarding decision boundaries. This prompts a demand for regularizing the proxy model's predictions to be consistent with those of a trained main model to improve the fitness of the selected examples for M_{main}. Ideally, we expect the tag sequence distribution $P_{prx}(\mathbf{y}|\mathbf{w})$ learned by the proxy model to mimic the tag sequence distribution $P_{main}(\mathbf{y}|\mathbf{w})$ learned by the main model. To this end, we propose to minimize the difference between the intermediate outcomes (i.e., the unary and transition scores) of the two distributions. In particular, we introduce the following distillation objective for each sentence $\mathbf{w}$ at one AL iteration: $L_{dist} = -\sum_i \sum_v p_i^{main}[v] \log p_i^{prx}[v] + \sum_i (\pi_{y_i \to y_{i+1}}^{main} - \pi_{y_i \to y_{i+1}}^{prx})^2$ where p_i^{main} and p_i^{prx} are the tag distributions computed by the main and proxy models respectively for the word $w_i \in \mathbf{w}$ (i.e., the scores $\mathbf{z}_i$). Note that p_i^{main} and $\pi_{y_i \to y_{i+1}}^{main}$ serve as the knowledge distillation signal that is obtained once the main model finishes its training at each iteration. Here, we will use the newly selected examples for the current annotation to compute the distillation signals. The overall objective to train M_{prx} at each AL iteration is thus: $L = L_{task} + L_{dist}$.

3 Usage

Detailed documentation for FaMIE is provided at: `https://famie.readthedocs.io/`. The codebase is written in Python and Javascript, which can be easily installed through PyPI at : `https://pypi.org/project/famie/`.

Initialization. To initialize a project, users first choose a data selection strategy and upload a label set to define a sequence labeling problem. Next,

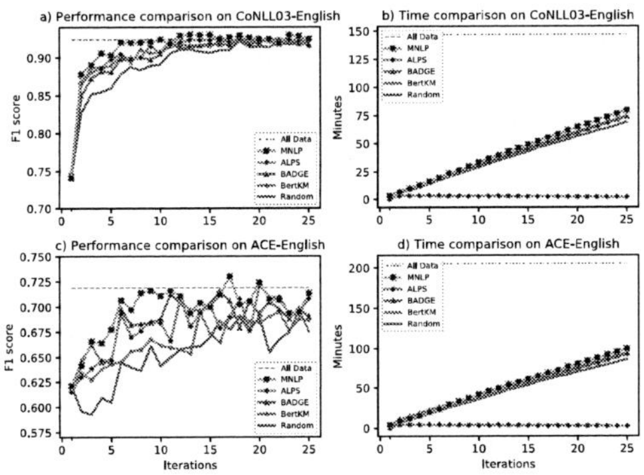

Figure 2: Comparison among data selection strategies.

the dataset U with unlabeled sentences should be submitted. FAMIE then allows users to interact with the models and annotate data over multiple rounds with a web interface. Also, FAMIE can detect languages automatically for further processing.

Annotating procedure. Given one annotation batch in an iteration, annotators label one sentence at a time as illustrated in Figure 3. In particular, the annotators annotate the word spans for each label by first choosing the label and then highlighting the appropriate spans. Also, FAMIE designs the size of the annotation batches to allow enough time to finish the training of the main model during the annotation time at each iteration.

Output. Unlike previous AL toolkits which focus only on their web interfaces to produce labeled data, FAMIE provides a simple and intuitive code interface for interacting with the resulting labeled dataset and trained main models after the AL processes. The code snippet in Figure 4 presents a minimal usage of our **famie** Python package to use the trained main model for inference over new data. This allows users to immediately evaluate their models and annotation efforts on data of interest.

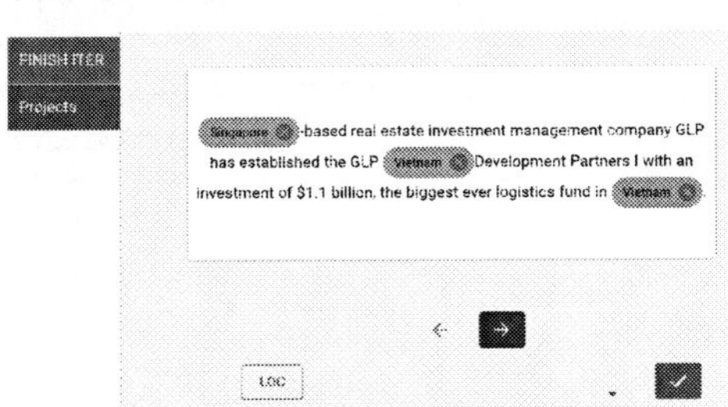

Figure 3: Annotation interface in FAMIE.

4 Evaluation

Datasets and Hyper-parameters. To comprehensively evaluate our AL framework FAMIE,

```
import famie
# access a project via its name
p = famie.get_project('NewProject')
# access the project's labeled data
data = p.get_labeled_data()

# access the project's trained target model
model = p.get_trained_model()
# make predictions with the trained model
doc = '''Nick is happy.'''
output = model.predict(doc)
print(output)
# [('Nick', 'B-Person'), ('is', 'O'), ('happy', 'O'), ('.', 'O')]
```

Figure 4: Accessing the labeled dataset and the trained main model returned by an AL project.

we conduct experiments on two IE tasks (i.e., NER and ED) for three languages using four datasets: CoNLL03-English (Tjong Kim Sang and De Meulder, 2003) and CoNLL02-Spanish (Tjong Kim Sang, 2002) for NER, and ACE-English and ACE-Chinese for ED (i.e., using the multilingual ACE-05 dataset (Walker et al., 2006; Nguyen and Grishman, 2015, 2018)). The CoNLL datasets cover 4 entity types while 33 event types are annotated in ACE-05 datasets. We follow the standard data splits for train/dev/test portions for each dataset (Li et al., 2013; Lai et al., 2020; Pouran Ben Veyseh et al., 2021a).

For the main target model M_{main}, the full-scale XLM-Roberta$_{large}$ model is used as the encoder. Our framework for AL thus inherits the ability of XLM-Roberta to support more than 100 languages. Also, we employ the compact miniLM architecture (distilled from the pre-trained XLM-Roberta) for the proxy model M_{prx}. In all experiments, the main model is trained for 40 epochs while the proxy model is trained for 20 epochs at each iteration. We use the Adam optimizer with batch size of 16 and learning rate of $1e$-5 to train the models.

We follow the AL settings in previous work to achieve consistent evaluation (Kim, 2020; Shelmanov et al., 2021; Liu et al., 2022). Specifically, the unlabeled pool is created by discarding labels from the original training data of each dataset; 2% of which ($\sim$ 242 sentences) is selected for labeling at each iteration for a total of 25 iterations (examples of the first iteration are randomly sampled to serve as the seed D_0). The annotation is simulated by recovering the ground-truth labels of the corresponding instances. The model performance is measured on the test datasets by taking average over 3 runs with different random seeds.

Comparing Data Selection Strategies. In this experiment, we aim to determine the best data selection strategy for our AL framework. To this end, we perform the standard AL process (i.e., training the full transformer-CRF model with no adapters,

	Idle	CoNLL03-English						CoNLL02-Spanish						ACE-English						ACE-Chinese					
	mins/iter	10%	20%	30%	40%	50%	100%	10%	20%	30%	40%	50%	100%	10%	20%	30%	40%	50%	100%	10%	20%	30%	40%	50%	100%
Full Data	✗	✗	✗	✗	✗	✗	92.4	✗	✗	✗	✗	✗	89.6	✗	✗	✗	✗	✗	71.9	✗	✗	✗	✗	✗	69.1
Large	41.6	**90.3**	**92.4**	**93.0**	**92.4**	92.4	✗	86.9	**88.6**	**89.4**	**89.3**	89.0	✗	**67.8**	**71.1**	**70.0**	**72.4**	**71.3**	✗	**64.8**	67.6	**71.3**	68.7	**71.5**	✗
FaMIE	**3.4**	90.1	91.7	91.8	91.7	**92.7**	✗	86.5	88.2	88.5	88.1	**89.4**	✗	67.0	69.3	69.5	68.9	70.6	✗	61.3	**67.9**	68.5	**69.8**	69.6	✗
FaMIE-A	5.7	89.7	90.8	91.3	91.9	91.7	✗	**87.4**	87.2	89.0	87.7	89.1	✗	67.2	68.0	69.5	68.9	70.6	✗	62.8	66.5	67.9	66.3	69.4	✗
FaMIE-AD	5.6	87.0	90.1	90.5	90.7	90.5	✗	85.5	86.9	87.7	88.8	88.6	✗	64.9	65.4	67.7	66.8	69.1	✗	58.1	65.4	66.5	64.8	70.3	✗
Random	✗	86.0	89.1	90.6	91.4	91.9	✗	80.8	85.3	88.1	88.7	88.6	✗	60.4	64.1	66.9	69.0	67.5	✗	48.4	58.2	65.1	65.4	66.6	✗

Table 1: Main model's performance on multilingual NER and ED tasks. "Idle" indicate average waiting time of annotators.

selecting data, and annotating data at each iteration) for different data selection strategies to measure performance and time. We focus on English datasets in this experiment. Figure 2 reports the performance across AL iterations of the model for different data selection methods. As can be seen, "*MNLP*" is the overall best method for data selection in AL. We will thus leverage MNLP as the data section strategy for the evaluation of FAMIE.

Also, Figure 2 shows the annotators' idle time (the combined time for model training and data selection) across iterations for each selection strategy. The major difference comes from ALPS that has significantly less waiting time than other methods as it does not require model training. However, ALPS's performance is considerably worse than MNLP as a result, especially in early iterations. This demonstrates the importance of training and including the main model during the AL iterations for data section. Importantly, we find that the waiting time of annotators at each iteration is very high in current AL methods (e.g., more than 30 minutes after the first 8 iterations with the MNLP strategy), thus affecting the annotators' productivity.

Performance and Time Efficiency. To evaluate the performance and time efficiency of FAMIE, Table 1 compares our full proposed framework FAMIE (with proxy model, knowledge distillation, and adapters) with the following baselines: (i) "**Large**": the best AL baseline from the previous experiment employing the full-scale transformer encoder and MNLP for data selection; (ii) "**Random**": this is the same as "**Large**", but replaces MNLP with random selection; (iii) "**FAMIE-A**": this is the proposed framework FAMIE without adapter-based tuning (all parameters from the main model are fine-tuned); and (iv) "**FAMIE-AD**": we further remove the knowledge distillation loss from "**FAMIE-A**" in this method. The experiments are done for all four datasets of NER and ED.

The first observation is that FAMIE's performance is only marginally below that of Large despite only using the small proxy network for data selection. Importantly, annotators only have to wait for about 3.4 minutes per AL iteration before they can annotate the next data batch in FAMIE. This is over 10 times faster compared to the standard AL approaches (e.g., in Large). Second, the adapters in FAMIE not only boost the overall performance for AL but also reduce the waiting time for annotators. Also, we note that using adapters, the training time of M_{main} only takes 32 minutes at each iteration (on average). This is reasonable to fit into the time that an annotator needs to spend to label an annotation batch at each AL iteration, thus accommodating our proposal for training the main model during annotation time. Finally, FAMIE-AD performs worst (i.e., similar or even worse than Random) in most cases, which confirms the necessity of our distillation component in FAMIE.

5 Related Work

Despite the potential of AL in reducing annotation cost for a target task, most previous AL work focuses on developing data selection strategies to maximize the model performance (Wang and Shang, 2014; Sener and Savarese, 2017; Ash et al., 2019; Kim, 2020; Liu et al., 2022; Margatina et al., 2021). As such, previous AL methods and frameworks tend to ignore the necessary time to train models and perform data selection at each AL iteration that can be significantly long and hinder annotators' productivity and model performance. To make AL frameworks practical, few recent works have attempted to minimize the model training and data selection time by leveraging simple and non state-of-the-art architectures as the main model, e.g., ActiveAnno (Wiechmann et al., 2021) and Paladin (Nghiem et al., 2021). However, an issue with these approaches is the inability to exploit recent advances in large-scale language models to achieve optimal performance. In addition, some recent works have also explored large-scale language models for AL (Shelmanov et al., 2021; Yuan et al., 2020); however, to reduce waiting time for annotators, such methods need to exclude the training of the large models in the AL iterations or employ small models for data selection, thus suffering from a harmful mismatch between the annotated examples and the main models (Lowell et al., 2019).

6 Conclusion

We introduce FAMIE, a comprehensive AL framework that supports model creation and data annotation for sequence labeling in multiple languages. FAMIE optimizes the annotators' time by leveraging a small proxy network for data selection and a novel knowledge distillation to synchronize the proxy and main target models for AL. As FAMIE is task-agnostic, we plan to extend FAMIE to cover other NLP tasks in future work.

Acknowledgement

This research has been supported by the Army Research Office (ARO) grant W911NF-21-1-0112 and the NSF grant CNS-1747798 to the IUCRC Center for Big Learning. This research is also based upon work supported by the Office of the Director of National Intelligence (ODNI), Intelligence Advanced Research Projects Activity (IARPA), via IARPA Contract No. 2019-19051600006 under the Better Extraction from Text Towards Enhanced Retrieval (BETTER) Program. The views and conclusions contained herein are those of the authors and should not be interpreted as necessarily representing the official policies, either expressed or implied, of ARO, ODNI, IARPA, the Department of Defense, or the U.S. Government. The U.S. Government is authorized to reproduce and distribute reprints for governmental purposes notwithstanding any copyright annotation therein. This document does not contain technology or technical data controlled under either the U.S. International Traffic in Arms Regulations or the U.S. Export Administration Regulations.

References

Jordan T Ash, Chicheng Zhang, Akshay Krishnamurthy, John Langford, and Alekh Agarwal. 2019. Deep batch active learning by diverse, uncertain gradient lower bounds. *arXiv preprint arXiv:1906.03671*.

Alexis Conneau, Kartikay Khandelwal, Naman Goyal, Vishrav Chaudhary, Guillaume Wenzek, Francisco Guzmán, Edouard Grave, Myle Ott, Luke Zettlemoyer, and Veselin Stoyanov. 2020. Unsupervised cross-lingual representation learning at scale. In *Proceedings of the 58th Annual Meeting of the Association for Computational Linguistics*, pages 8440–8451, Online. Association for Computational Linguistics.

Neil Houlsby, Andrei Giurgiu, Stanislaw Jastrzebski, Bruna Morrone, Quentin De Laroussilhe, Andrea Gesmundo, Mona Attariyan, and Sylvain Gelly. 2019. Parameter-efficient transfer learning for nlp. In *Proceedings of the International Conference on Machine Learning*.

Yekyung Kim. 2020. Deep active learning for sequence labeling based on diversity and uncertainty in gradient. In *Proceedings of the 2nd Workshop on Life-long Learning for Spoken Language Systems*, pages 1–8, Suzhou, China. Association for Computational Linguistics.

John Lafferty, Andrew McCallum, and Fernando CN Pereira. 2001. Conditional random fields: Probabilistic models for segmenting and labeling sequence data.

Viet Dac Lai, Minh Van Nguyen, Thien Huu Nguyen, and Franck Dernoncourt. 2021. Graph learning regularization and transfer learning for few-shot event detection. In *Proceedings of the 44th International ACM SIGIR Conference on Research and Development in Information Retrieval*, pages 2172–2176.

Viet Dac Lai, Tuan Ngo Nguyen, and Thien Huu Nguyen. 2020. Event detection: Gate diversity and syntactic importance scores for graph convolution neural networks. In *Proceedings of the 2020 Conference on Empirical Methods in Natural Language Processing (EMNLP)*.

Qi Li, Heng Ji, Yu Hong, and Sujian Li. 2014. Constructing information networks using one single model. In *Proceedings of the 2014 Conference on Empirical Methods in Natural Language Processing*.

Qi Li, Heng Ji, and Liang Huang. 2013. Joint event extraction via structured prediction with global features. In *Proceedings of the 51th Annual Meeting of the Association for Computational Linguistics*.

Mingyi Liu, Zhiying Tu, Tong Zhang, Tonghua Su, Xiaofei Xu, and Zhongjie Wang. 2022. Ltp: A new active learning strategy for crf-based named entity recognition. *Neural Processing Letters*, pages 1–22.

David Lowell, Zachary C. Lipton, and Byron C. Wallace. 2019. Practical obstacles to deploying active learning. In *Proceedings of the 2019 Conference on Empirical Methods in Natural Language Processing and the 9th International Joint Conference on Natural Language Processing (EMNLP-IJCNLP)*, pages 21–30, Hong Kong, China. Association for Computational Linguistics.

Xuezhe Ma and Eduard Hovy. 2016. End-to-end sequence labeling via bi-directional lstm-cnns-crf. In *Proceedings of the 54th Annual Meeting of the Association for Computational Linguistics*.

Katerina Margatina, Giorgos Vernikos, Loïc Barrault, and Nikolaos Aletras. 2021. Active learning by acquiring contrastive examples. *arXiv preprint arXiv:2109.03764*.

Minh-Quoc Nghiem, Paul Baylis, and Sophia Ananiadou. 2021. Paladin: an annotation tool based on active and proactive learning. In *Proceedings of the 16th Conference of the European Chapter of the Association for Computational Linguistics: System Demonstrations*, pages 238–243, Online. Association for Computational Linguistics.

Minh Van Nguyen, Viet Lai, and Thien Huu Nguyen. 2021a. Cross-task instance representation interactions and label dependencies for joint information extraction with graph convolutional networks. In *Proceedings of the 2021 Conference of the North American Chapter of the Association for Computational Linguistics: Human Language Technologies*, pages 27–38, Online. Association for Computational Linguistics.

Minh Van Nguyen, Viet Dac Lai, Amir Pouran Ben Veyseh, and Thien Huu Nguyen. 2021b. Trankit: A light-weight transformer-based toolkit for multilingual natural language processing. In *Proceedings of the 16th Conference of the European Chapter of the Association for Computational Linguistics: System Demonstrations*.

Thien Huu Nguyen and Ralph Grishman. 2015. Event detection and domain adaptation with convolutional neural networks. In *The 53rd Annual Meeting of the Association for Computational Linguistics and the 7th International Joint Conference on Natural Language Processing*.

Thien Huu Nguyen and Ralph Grishman. 2018. Graph convolutional networks with argument-aware pooling for event detection. In *Proceedings of the AAAI Conference on Artificial Intelligence*.

Trung Minh Nguyen and Thien Huu Nguyen. 2019. One for all: Neural joint modeling of entities and events. In *Proceedings of the AAAI Conference on Artificial Intelligence*.

Matthew E Peters, Sebastian Ruder, and Noah A Smith. 2019. To tune or not to tune? adapting pretrained representations to diverse tasks. In *RepL4NLP@ACL*.

Amir Pouran Ben Veyseh, Viet Lai, Franck Dernoncourt, and Thien Huu Nguyen. 2021a. Unleash GPT-2 power for event detection. In *Proceedings of the 59th Annual Meeting of the Association for Computational Linguistics and the 11th International Joint Conference on Natural Language Processing (Volume 1: Long Papers)*.

Amir Pouran Ben Veyseh, Minh Van Nguyen, Nghia Ngo Trung, Bonan Min, and Thien Huu Nguyen. 2021b. Modeling document-level context for event detection via important context selection. In *Proceedings of the 2021 Conference on Empirical Methods in Natural Language Processing*.

Dan Roth and Kevin Small. 2006. Margin-based active learning for structured output spaces. In *European Conference on Machine Learning*, pages 413–424. Springer.

Ozan Sener and Silvio Savarese. 2017. Active learning for convolutional neural networks: A core-set approach. *arXiv preprint arXiv:1708.00489*.

Burr Settles. 2009. Active learning literature survey.

Burr Settles and Mark Craven. 2008. An analysis of active learning strategies for sequence labeling tasks. In *Proceedings of the 2008 Conference on Empirical Methods in Natural Language Processing*, pages 1070–1079, Honolulu, Hawaii. Association for Computational Linguistics.

Artem Shelmanov, Dmitri Puzyrev, Lyubov Kupriyanova, Denis Belyakov, Daniil Larionov, Nikita Khromov, Olga Kozlova, Ekaterina Artemova, Dmitry V. Dylov, and Alexander Panchenko. 2021. Active learning for sequence tagging with deep pre-trained models and Bayesian uncertainty estimates. In *Proceedings of the 16th Conference of the European Chapter of the Association for Computational Linguistics: Main Volume*, pages 1698–1712, Online. Association for Computational Linguistics.

Yanyao Shen, Hyokun Yun, Zachary C Lipton, Yakov Kronrod, and Animashree Anandkumar. 2017. Deep active learning for named entity recognition. *arXiv preprint arXiv:1707.05928*.

Erik F. Tjong Kim Sang. 2002. Introduction to the CoNLL-2002 shared task: Language-independent named entity recognition. In *COLING-02: The 6th Conference on Natural Language Learning 2002 (CoNLL-2002)*.

Erik F. Tjong Kim Sang and Fien De Meulder. 2003. Introduction to the CoNLL-2003 shared task: Language-independent named entity recognition. In *Proceedings of the Seventh Conference on Natural Language Learning at HLT-NAACL 2003*, pages 142–147.

Amir Pouran Ben Veyseh, Minh Van Nguyen, Bonan Min, and Thien Huu Nguyen. 2021. Augmenting open-domain event detection with synthetic data from gpt-2. In *Joint European Conference on Machine Learning and Knowledge Discovery in Databases*, pages 644–660. Springer.

Christopher Walker, Stephanie Strassel, Julie Medero, and Kazuaki Maeda. 2006. Ace 2005 multilingual training corpus. In *Technical report, Linguistic Data Consortium*.

Dan Wang and Yi Shang. 2014. A new active labeling method for deep learning. In *2014 International joint conference on neural networks (IJCNN)*, pages 112–119. IEEE.

Wenhui Wang, Hangbo Bao, Shaohan Huang, Li Dong, and Furu Wei. 2021. MiniLMv2: Multi-head self-attention relation distillation for compressing pre-trained transformers. In *Findings of the Association for Computational Linguistics: ACL-IJCNLP 2021*, pages 2140–2151, Online. Association for Computational Linguistics.

Max Wiechmann, Seid Muhie Yimam, and Chris Biemann. 2021. ActiveAnno: General-purpose document-level annotation tool with active learning integration. In *Proceedings of the 2021 Conference of the North American Chapter of the Association for Computational Linguistics: Human Language Technologies: Demonstrations*, pages 99–105, Online. Association for Computational Linguistics.

Michelle Yuan, Hsuan-Tien Lin, and Jordan Boyd-Graber. 2020. Cold-start active learning through self-supervised language modeling. In *Proceedings of the 2020 Conference on Empirical Methods in Natural Language Processing (EMNLP)*, pages 7935–7948, Online. Association for Computational Linguistics.

Author Index

Association for Computational Linguistics
209 N. Eighth Street
Stroudsburg, Pennsylvania 18360

CURRAN ASSOCIATES INC.
proceedings.com

ISBN 978-1-7138-5620-7